CHRONICA BOTANICA

AN INTERNATIONAL BIOLOGICAL AND AGRICULTURAL SERIES

Consulting Editor, Frans Verdoorn

No. 21

MAKERS OF

NORTH AMERICAN

BOTANY

HARRY BAKER HUMPHREY

LATE PRINCIPAL PATHOLOGIST
DIVISION OF CEREAL CROPS AND DISEASES
BUREAU OF PLANT INDUSTRY
U. S. DEPARTMENT OF AGRICULTURE

THE RONALD PRESS COMPANY · NEW YORK

Library of Congress Catalog Card Number: 61–18435

PRINTED IN THE UNITED STATES OF AMERICA

Foreword

I never knew my father to be idle. This industry and desire always to be constructively active resulted, during his retirement years, in the biographies here assembled. After his retirement at seventy from the U.S. Department of Agriculture, his time was, if anything, more fully occupied than before. One of his activities, initiated in a room made available to him at the Library of Congress, was the writing of this series of lives of North American botanists.

There is, or should be, a *raison d'être* for the various activities of men. In the preparation of this book the primary motivation was a desire to make available to scientists and others the lives of botanists whose activities and contributions were becoming ever more obscure with the passage of time. Instrumental also was my father's lifelong urge to use his time constructively. And, incidentally, he enjoyed writing and, as he used to phrase it, "making correct use of the King's English."

In 1950 my father and mother moved to Palo Alto, California, near the Stanford Campus they both had known and loved during the early years of their married life. It was here that my father had received his Ph.D. degree in botany fifty-four years before. Both had cherished a hope through the years that some day they might return to the rolling California hills that they had known so well in their youth. When this hope materialized, the facilities of the Stanford University Library were made available, and the research and writing continued.

Living botanists were not considered eligible for inclusion in the biographies. During these last few years my father used jokingly to say that he would never run out of material since new candidates were continually becoming eligible. He never did run out of material, only time.

Contacts with botanists, first at the University of Minnesota, later at Stanford and Washington State College, and finally at Washington, D.C. and at experiment stations throughout the United States and Canada, gave my father a personal acquaintance with many of his contemporaries. Several of these ultimately found a place in his series of biographies. Among these were such botanists of note as J. Arthur Harris, Douglas Houghton Campbell, Frederic E. Clements, and Frederick V. Colville.

Botanists are cast in many molds, as morphologists, taxonomists, physiologists, pathologists, and a number of others. Most are lovers of plants and nature and all that these suggest. Although in his official capacity with the Department of Agriculture my father was a pathologist, unofficially he was more nearly an ecologist. He always liked to get out in the woods, whether in Minnesota, California, the Pacific Northwest, Quebec, Maryland, or wherever he happened to be. Camping out, for the most part at a time when camping was not accompanied by the luxuries that make it easy today, and long strenuous hikes were often a means to the end of maintaining his acquaintance with nature. This interest extended to and included a study of those men throughout the world who have had a hand in developing the field of botany. His restriction of the present work to North America was necessitated by limitations of time and facilities, rather than by any wish to place undue emphasis on the botanists of this continent.

These same limitations prevented the inclusion of many North American botanists whose contributions may have been noteworthy. For the most part my father selected those botanists who in his opinion had made outstanding contributions to the field. In a few instances he also probably included individuals whose overall contributions may not have been particularly outstanding but to whom his attention had been directed as having pioneered in some phase of botany.

The lapse of time, even though short, since my father's passing has made many other names available for inclusion in the work. In addition to the 115 biographies that he prepared, I have added those of Liberty Hyde Bailey, Albert Francis Blakeslee, Benjamin Minge Duggar, Merritt Lyndon Fernald, Daniel Trembly Mac-Dougal, and Elmer Drew Merrill.

The value of a work of this sort is extended beyond the covers of the book by its bibliographic references. Although my father was indebted to many of whom we now have no record, no one contributed so much to the research of piecing together his bibliographic source material as my mother. It fell to her lot to assemble much of this material after his death. In other less tangible ways also, my mother contributed to this work. It is, therefore, an expression of cooperative effort.

ROBERT R. HUMPHREY

Tucson, Arizona
    October, 1961

Contents

MAKERS OF
NORTH AMERICAN
BOTANY

Timothy Field Allen
1837–1902

Timothy Field Allen, physician and botanist, was born **April 24,** 1837. He was the son of Dr. David and Eliza (Graves) Allen. A native of Westminster, Vermont, he was reared in the Connecticut Valley, where he acquired the love of nature which was an important factor in shaping his life obectives and his ultimate career as a botanist. Although he was a born naturalist, he, like so many of our early botanists, turned to the study and pursuit of medicine for a livelihood.

Having completed his college preparatory work at East Winsor, Connecticut, Timothy entered Amherst College, where he received his A.B. degree in 1858. On leaving Amherst, he entered the medical department of the then University of the City of New York, where he received the M.D. degree in 1861. On June 3, 1861, he married Julia Bissell of Litchfield, Connecticut. He then moved to Brooklyn, New York, where he practiced medicine. Thereafter he served as assistant surgeon in the U.S. Army, at Point Lookout, Maryland. On his release from this assignment, he returned to the practice of medicine in Brooklyn. In 1863, he moved to New York City, where he remained the rest of his life.

It was after his establishment as a physician in New York City that Dr. Allen became actively interested in botany. He became acquainted with the noted botanist, John Torrey, an incident which marked the advent of his major interest in botany. He was one of the founders of the Torrey Botanical Club in 1871 and served as its vice president for several years. During the interval of 1870–1876 the Torrey Botanical Club published a flora of New York City, to which Allen was an important contributor. His growing interest in the stoneworts (Characeae), his scholarly papers on this interesting group of aquatic plants and his world-wide col-

3

lection of its species, resulted in his recognition as an authority on the Characeae. Dr. Allen died December 5, 1902.

ANON. 1903. Dr. Timothy Field Allen. *Botan. Gaz.* 35: 79–80.

BRITTON, N. S. 1903. *Bull. Torrey Club* 30: 173–177, with portrait and botanical bibliography.

BRITTON, N. S. 1902. Death of Dr. Timothy F. Allen, *J. N.Y. Botan. Gard.* 3: 232.

Joseph Charles Arthur
1850–1942

Joseph Charles Arthur, only son of Charles and Ann (Allen) Arthur, was born on January 11, 1850, in Lowville, New York. While but a child of six years his family moved first to a home near Stirling, Illinois, thence to Charles City, Iowa, and finally to Spirit Lake in that state.

Arthur's elementary schooling began in the country schools of Floyd County, Iowa, and his preparation for college was in the Charles City High School. He very early showed an unusual interest in botany, and it was his good fortune during his sophomore year at Iowa State College to have as his teacher of botany Prof. Charles E. Bessey, a man of eminence in his profession. A warm and enduring friendship developed between young Arthur and his teacher. It was then that the aspiring student decided upon botany as his major interest. He completed his undergraduate work in 1872, at a time when botany was being offered by but few colleges and universities in America, and when opportunities for trained botanists to obtain employment as such were indeed few. The demand for specialists in botanical research did not develop until some years later.

Arthur, bent on becoming a botanist, taught country school several winters and, in 1877, was granted a Master's degree by his alma mater. In 1879, he became an instructor in botany at the University of Wisconsin. This was his first appointment to a botanical position but before the year had passed he received from Johns Hopkins University a complimentary fellowship, carrying a stipend of one hundred dollars. This offered him the privilege of three months of study. While at Johns Hopkins, Arthur attended a series of botanical lectures delivered by William Gilson Farlow. During the summer months, he continued his studies under Dr. Farlow at Harvard University, where he became acquainted with Prof. George Lincoln Goodale and Dr. Asa Gray. There it was that John Merle Coulter and Charles R. Barnes entered the charmed circle of his botanical associates and friends. These three—Arthur, Barnes, and Coulter—a few years later issued the "Handbook of Plant Dissection."

In 1884, Arthur was offered the position of botanist in the newly organized Geneva (New York) Agricultural Experiment Station. Thus it was possible for him to continue his research and to complete the requirements for the Doctor of Science degree, which was conferred upon him by Cornell University in 1886. In 1887, he accepted a professorship in botany at Purdue University. The next year his professional status was raised from professor of botany to professor of vegetable physiology and pathology and botanist to the Indiana Agricultural Experiment Station, positions he held until his retirement in 1915.

From 1915 to 1942, he was emeritus professor of botany at Purdue, where he devoted himself to an extended study of the Uredinales. His first paper on the plant rusts appeared in 1882. In 1899, Arthur set out upon the ambitious project of publishing a special series of rust-culture studies. These he continued for nineteen years and determined the life histories and host relationships of approximately one hundred species. These determinations involved the use of some 2,400 collections and the making of approximately 3,750 greenhouse cultures.

In 1905, Dr. Arthur issued a new classification of the Uredinales, and, in 1907, undertook a complete taxonomic presentation of North American rusts for publication by the New York Botanical Garden. The completion of this undertaking consumed twenty years and the parts totaled 765 pages. In addition to this, he was the senior author of a biological treatise on the rusts entitled "The Plant Rusts" published in 1929. In 1934 appeared his "Manual of the Rusts of the United States and Canada," an extensive taxonomic treatise. In addition to these more ambitious works on the Uredinales, Arthur was the author of many papers dealing with the varied aspects of the plant rusts.

Although he did not travel widely, Dr. Arthur made good use of various collecting trips. He identified and reported the rusts of many important collections from Central and South America, the Philippines, Puerto Rico, and Cuba. He visited certain European herbaria, studied type specimens, and conferred with Old World authorities, some of whom had devoted their lives to a study of the problem of uredinology.

Dr. Arthur was a delegate to several botanical congresses of international importance, notably those of Vienna (1905), Brussels (1910), and Cambridge (1930). He participated in their deliberations and established helpful contacts with mycologists confronted with problems of classification and nomenclature.

In 1901, Dr. Arthur married Emily Stiles Potter of Lafayette, Indiana whom he survived by approximately seven years. He enjoyed membership in many scientific societies and was active in their support. He died on the 30th of April, 1942 at the age of 92.

EDINGTON, W. E. 1943. Joseph Charles Arthur. *Proc. Ind. Acad. Sci.* 52: 1–3.
KERN, F. D. 1942. Joseph Charles Arthur. *Phytopath.* 32: 833–844, with portrait and bibliography prepared by Dr. Geo. B. Cummins.
KERN, F. D. 1942. *Science* n.s. 95: 617–619.
MAINS, E. B. 1942. *Mycologia* 34: 601–605, with portrait.

George Francis Atkinson
1854–1918

George Francis Atkinson, botanist and educator, was born in Raisinville, Monroe County, Michigan, January 26, 1854. He was the son of Joseph and Josephine (Fish) Atkinson and a direct descendant of William Atkinson who came from England to settle in New Jersey in the early years of the seventeenth century. Atkinson received his preparatory schooling at Olivet College (Michigan), but in January, 1884 entered Cornell University as a junior and was graduated the following year.

In 1885, Atkinson was awarded a fellowship, but resigned to accept an assistant professorship in entomology and general zoology at the University of North Carolina. In his new position he at once busied himself with research, devoting no little time to the study of certain trap-door spiders whose nest-building and feeding habits were not clearly understood. The results of this investigation were published in the "American Naturalist" of August, 1886. That year he was promoted to an associate professorship and was active in research on problems in economic entomology. The results were published in several American journals.

In 1888 Atkinson was appointed professor of botany and zoology at the University of South Carolina, and the following year he was offered the newly-created position of professor of biology and botany at the Alabama Polytechnic Institute. While at the latter he published, as a bulletin of the Agricultural Experiment Station, the results of his studies on the root-gall nematode *Heterodera radicicola*. At this time he also became more and more engrossed in botanical research and in plant pathology in particular.

In 1892 Atkinson received a call from Cornell University to return to that institution as assistant professor of botany, a position left vacant when William R. Dudley accepted a professorship at Stanford University. So we next find Atkinson at Cornell, where, in 1893, he was promoted to associate professor. The then head of the department of botany and horticulture, Professor Prentiss, died in 1896 and was succeeded by Professor Atkinson who remained as head of his department until his death on November 15, 1918.

Until 1906, Atkinson had charge of the botanical research conducted by the Cornell University Agricultural Experiment Station. As a member of the Committee of Nine of the New York Science Teachers' Association, he had an active part in developing the outline of courses in natural history proposed for secondary schools. His extensive knowledge of plant science led to an invitation to deliver some lectures at Woods Hole (Massachusetts), where, in 1899, he offered a short course and gave a series of lectures of special interest to workers in laboratory technique and field botany. During the summers of 1898–1901, he was in charge of botanical instruction in the Cornell summer school.

Professor Atkinson's enthusiasm and versatility caused him to delve into many botanical fields, such as morphology, plant physiology, mycology, plant pathology, and cytology. The fleshy fungi were of particular interest to him, and his contributions to knowledge of the development and life history of these and other fungi are notable. A number of semi-popular botanical texts are to be credited to him; for example: "The Biology of the Ferns," "Lessons in Botany," "First Lessons in Plant Life," "Mushrooms—Edible, Poisonous," etc.

Among the more important of his technical contributions are his "Monograph of the *Lemaneaceae* of the United States"; "Contributions to the Life History of a Root-gall Nematode, *Heterodera radicicola*"; "On the Evolution of the Vegetative Phase of the Sporophyte"; "Reducing Division of the Chromosomes of *Arisaema triphyllum* by Ring and Tetrad Formation During Sporogenesis"; "Some Tendencies and Problems in the Evolution of Parasitic Fungi"; and "The *Erysipheae* of Alabama and Carolina."

In addition to his contributions as a research botanist, Atkinson was a distinguished teacher and editor. He served in the latter capacity for the *Botanical Gazette*, the *Botanisches Centralblatt*, the *Centralblatt für Bacteriologie und Parasitenkunde*, and *The New Systematic Botany of North America*. He was a fellow of the American Association for the Advancement of Science, a member of the Botanical Society of America, the Society for Plant Physiology and Morphology; the Society for the Promotion of Agriculture, the Elisha Mitchell Scientific Society, a corresponding member of the Torrey Botanical Club, and a member of the New York State Teachers' Association.

FARLOW, W. G., R. THAXTER, and L. H. BAILEY. 1919. George Francis Atkinson. *Am. J. Botany* 6: 301–302. Publications of George Francis Atkinson, 303–308, compiled by Henry M. Fitzpatrick.
FITZPATRICK, H. M. 1919. *Science* n.s. 49: 371–372.
THOM, C. 1956. George Francis Atkinson. *Nat. Acad. Sci. Biog. Mem.* 29: 17–44, with portrait and bibliography as given in *Am. J. Botany*.
WHETZEL, H. H. 1919. *The Guide to Nature* 12: 70–72.
WHETZEL, H. H. 1919. *Botan. Gaz.* 67: 366–368.

Jacob Whitman Bailey
1811–1857

Jacob Whitman Bailey, botanist, chemist, and geologist, the son of Rev. Isaac and Jane (Whitman) Bailey, was born in Ward (now Auburn), Massachusetts, on April 29, 1811. He was a descendant of John Bailey who came to America in 1635 and settled in Newbury, Massachusetts. Even as a boy he showed a marked interest in natural history and particularly so in botany, as did his great-grandfather, the Rev. Ralph Emerson, and his great-grandmother Whitman. Because of limited financial resources, the boy Jacob, then but twelve years old, was obliged to discontinue his formal schooling and seek employment. He found an opportunity to work in a circulating library and bookstore in Providence, Rhode Island. While there, his studious habits were observed by John Kingsbury, then Secretary of Brown University, who invited the boy to his home that he might study Latin and French. At this time Bailey made an impressive collection of shells and insects.

At seventeen he was appointed a cadet at West Point where, in 1832, he was graduated fifth in his class. In 1833, he was stationed at Bellona Arsenal, near Richmond, Virginia, where he served as commissary quartermaster. In 1834, he was appointed assistant professor of chemistry, geology, and mineralogy at West Point and was advanced in July, 1838, to a full professorship, a position he occupied until his death in February, 1857.

Although faithful to his responsibilities as a teacher, Bailey's reputation as a scientist rests chiefly on his research in microscopy and his studies of the Diatomaceae. He made examinations of deep-sea soundings obtained during United States government surveys. He corresponded extensively with several European microscopists and was a member of many scientific societies. He was a charter member of the American Association for the Advancement of Science and was elected its president while on his deathbed.

Bailey was the first in the United States to observe and record diatoms in fossil formation. He is also to be credited as the first American botanist to observe and note the occurrence of crystals in plant tissues and to detect the presence of plant structures in the ash of anthracite coal. These facts bore testimony to his originality and scientific ability.

Professor Bailey was married on January 23, 1835 to Maria Slaughter of West View, Virginia, whose tragic death by fire occurred on the occasion of the destruction of the steamer, Henry Clay, in July 1852. He died on February 26, 1857.

ANON. 1857. Prof. James W. Bailey. *Am. J. Sci.* 2nd Ser. 23: 447–448.
COULTER, S. 1888. *Botan. Gaz.* 13: 118–124.
GOULD, A. A. 1857–1858. *Am. Ass'n. Adv. Sci.* Aug. 17, 1857: 1–8.

Liberty Hyde Bailey
1858–1954

Botanists, like other scientists, often become specialists to the point where they may be aware of little that goes on in areas outside their own field. Or, not infrequently, they may be familiar with only a small segment of the field of botany. Liberty Hyde Bailey was not one of these. He was an international authority in his field and a specialist of the first order, but he had a breadth of interests and abilities granted to few. His reputation among horticulturists was founded primarily on his work in systematic horticulture and on the practical application of his botanical knowledge. His wide range of interests and inexhaustible energy made him chiefly renowned in the field of botany, but he was also known to many as an explorer, an educator, an administrator, or as a writer, lecturer, and editor. To still others he was principally a poet and philosopher. Underlying everything he did was a neverceasing interest in his fellow man and a desire to improve rural living conditions by modifying the biotic environment.

Liberty Hyde Bailey was born March 15, 1858, on a fruit farm in Van Buren County, Michigan. He died ninety-six years later on December 25, 1954. Most of Michigan was a frontier wilderness when young Liberty was born. Indian children were his frequent playmates and the forests his playground. The love of the earth and of growing things that served as a constant stimulus for his productive life was cultivated in these early years. He was endowed not only with an insatiable curiosity but also with more of the energy, mental ability, and long life to find answers than falls to the lot of most men.

Always an ardent field naturalist and collector, even in his later years, when most men are pretty well content to let others take over the more active phases of their profession, he was still roaming out-of-the-way places of the earth. Thus, at seventy-three, he was collecting palms in the tropical Mohinya swamp of Panama. At eighty, while collecting in the Bahamas, he was cast adrift in a yawl during a storm and helped subdue a sailor gone berserk. Even after his ninetieth year his youthful enthusiasm and energy did not desert him. At ninety-one, while planning an expedition to Africa, he was knocked down and fractured a leg in a street accident in New York. Although he never fully recovered, he continued to plan and apparently fully expected to make the projected journey. The story is told that, when advised to have a young man accompany him to Africa, he opposed the idea because of the possibility of his companion having an accident and thus interfering with the collecting.

Although he never attended high school, Bailey was admitted to Michigan State Agricultural College in the fall of 1877 and graduated five years later. Illness kept him out of school during the 1880–1881 school year. Three years after graduation, following a few months as a newspaper reporter and two years as a botanist at Harvard University assisting Asa Gray, Bailey returned to Michigan State College as professor of horticulture and landscape gardening. Here he remained for six years, establishing a sound reputation as a teacher and leader of students. Research facilities at the Michigan school were limited, however, and a variety of college responsibilities came to occupy so great a share of his time that, when he received an offer of a position at Cornell University as professor of botany and horticulture, he accepted. Although an increase in salary was one factor that influenced him in making the move, he was motivated principally by the opportunity for more and broader research. This opportunity included European travels that enabled him to visit leading experiment stations and talk over problems and solutions with foreign scientists.

Bailey remained at Cornell until 1903, when he became dean of the newly established New York State College of Agriculture at Cornell, and director of the Experiment Station. He had worked for ten years toward the founding of the College and the Experiment Station and was a logical choice for these administrative posts. In 1913, at fifty-five, he became professor emeritus but used the time made available by his release from administrative and other duties to build the "hortorium." This planned program was in conformity with the three periods into which Bailey felt life should be divided: first, preparation for a vocation; second, practical application of that preparation; and third, doing what one most wants to do. He had completed the first two; he was now ready to embark on the final stage, a study of horticulture and botany.

Bailey was an ardent believer in placing the results of research in the hands of those who needed and could apply them. This conviction was expressed in his continual efforts through the years to promote and develop extension programs and the research on which they are, of necessity, based. In 1908, he wrote, "Most of us must be experiment-teachers and spreaders of propaganda. The former has been the more needed in the past few years; they always will be of equal importance with the investigators, and they represent an equally high type of effort."

Bailey's life was an unusual blend of religion in its deepest sense and a poetic appreciation of the beauty of the world about him, combined with the pragmatist's wish to devote his knowledge to improving the well-being of his fellow man. His poems and other writings, as indeed almost everything that he did, indicate these facets of his character. His work consisted essentially of a communion with nature in an effort to learn and use for the benefit of mankind hitherto unknown facts.

It was natural that one with so great a love of nature and of his fellow man should try to bring the two together. Development of the nature study movement was the result. Although the initial objective of this movement was to interest and educate children, Bailey's simple, direct approach stimulated the imagination of adults as well. Using the outdoors as his classroom and living materials and earth and water as his classroom materials, it was inevitable that this approach should find a wide and ready audience and should take hold as it did. On the other hand, there was much objection to this unorthodox method of teaching and to the breaking away from the old tried, and frequently dry, presentation of scientific subject matter. Bailey was not one to be discouraged, however, and the soundness of his approach is indicated by the wide application of his teaching methods in the years that have elapsed since he initiated them.

The Bailey Hortorium was a unique institution founded in 1935 as a gift from Professor and Mrs. Bailey to Cornell University. It had as its objective "the identification of all cultivated plants as such, with facilities for investigation, covering both herbaceous and woody subjects, and relating the knowledge to the needs of the cultivator and the investigator." The hortorium consisted initially of his private herbarium of 125,000 plant specimens and his library of 3,000 volumes dealing with the herbarium. Although graduate students and others had had access to these materials for many years, they became even more accessible as the Hortorium. At that time Bailey estimated that there were some 25,000 plant species in cultivation and that in North America alone about 1,000 names were being added annually to the list. It was his desire to establish a degree of order in the somewhat chaotic information pertaining to the taxonomy of this large and important group. This, added to a realization of his own increasing age (he was seventy-seven) and inability adequately to maintain his herbarium and library, was in large part responsible for the decision to present them as a gift to Cornell University.

Although Bailey carried on extensive studies in a large number of plant genera, he is known for his publications on *Carex*, *Rubus* and the palms. Some of his earliest taxonomic work, on the American carices, included 18 papers published from 1883 to 1900. Some of these were monographic in nature. The period 1923–1949 was particularly productive and saw the publication of more than a hundred additional papers on the taxonomy of the palms, *Rubus, Vitis, Brassica,* and others. During this period, he was extremely active in the collection and classification of palms and was recognized as a world authority on this large group of plants.

Bailey's industry and constant desire to contribute to the good of mankind were responsible for an enormous literary output. In addition to over 700 technical and many philosophical papers and poems, he wrote 38 different books in the fields of horticulture and agriculture. These included such major works as the four-volume "Cyclopedia of American Agriculture," the four-volume "Cyclopedia of American Horticulture," and "The Standard Cyclopedia of Horticulture" (6 volumes). In their revised form these were combined into three volumes as "The Standard Cyclopedia" and "Hortus," a one-volume handbook. "The Holy Earth," first published in 1915 but subsequently three times reprinted, was the book that he felt best expressed the message he wished to leave the world. This message is simply expressed in his words of a later time, "It is a marvelous planet on which we ride. It is a great privilege to live thereon, to partake of the journey and to experience its goodness. . . . We should try to find the meaning rather than be satisfied with the spectacle. . . . My life has been a continuous fulfillment of dreams."

Many honors came to Liberty Hyde Bailey during his long life. He was awarded honorary degrees from several universities and medals from horticultural societies the world over. During 1925, he served simultaneously as president of the American Association for the Advancement of Science and the Botanical Society of America. Later he was re-elected to these offices, though the terms in these instances did not run concurrently. In 1926, the International Congress of Plant Sciences elected him president and presiding chairman of the meetings being held at Ithaca, New York. Several times he served as president of the American Society of Horticultural Science. He was also honored with the presidencies of the American Pomological Society and the American Nature Study Society. The American Academy of Arts and Sciences elected him a fellow; The National Academy of Sciences and the American Philosophical Society to membership. He gave of himself freely with improvement of the lot of mankind as his goal. Much was given him in return.

ANON. 1955. Dr. L. H. Bailey. *The New York Times,* Jan. 11, p. 10.
ARONOVICI, CAROL. 1951. Liberty H. Bailey. *The Survey* 87: 123–127.
KNUDSON, LEWIS. 1955. Liberty Hyde Bailey. *Science* n.s. 121: 322–323.
LAWRENCE, G. H. M. 1955. Prof. L. H. Bailey. *Nature* 175: 451–452.
LAWRENCE, G. H. M. 1955. Liberty Hyde Bailey, 1858–1954. *Baileya* 3: 26–40.
RODGERS, ANDREW DENNY, III. 1949. *Liberty Hyde Bailey—A Story of American Plant Sciences.* Princeton University Press, Princeton, N.J.
RODGERS, ANDREW DENNY, III. 1951. Portrait—Liberty Hyde Bailey. *The American Scholar* 20: 336–340.

William Baldwin

1779–1819

William Baldwin, botanist and physician, was born in Newlin, Pennsylvania, March 29, 1779. He was the son of Thomas Baldwin, an approved minister of the Society of Friends, and Elizabeth (Garretson) Baldwin. At twenty-three he entered the University of Pennsylvania, where he attended a term of medical lectures. It was here that he became acquainted with the eminent botanist, Dr. William Darlington. This chance acquaintance developed into a lifelong friendship, one that influenced Baldwin's interest in natural history. Later still he made the acquaintance of another botanist, Dr. Moses Marshall, from whom he acquired further interest in plant life. Poor health, however, prevented him from continuing his botanical study under Dr. Marshall.

In 1805, Baldwin enlisted as a ship's surgeon on a merchant ship sailing from Philadelphia to Canton, China. On returning to Philadelphia, he resumed his medical studies at the University of Pennsylvania, where he was graduated a Doctor of Medicine in April, 1807. He next moved to Wilmington, Delaware and began the practice of medicine. About the same time he married Hannah M. Webster of Wilmington. His growing interest in botany was further stimulated by Dr. Benamin Smith Barton. At this time he made a collection of the local flora and corresponded with the Rev. Harry Mühlenberg of Lancaster, Pennsylvania, until Mühlenberg's death in 1815.

Baldwin's worsening health compelled him to seek a milder climate. He moved to Georgia and spent several months among the Creek Indians in the western part of the state. In 1812, he was appointed a naval surgeon with headquarters at St. Mary's, Georgia, where he remained for several years. In addition to his duties as surgeon, he continued his interest in the plants of the locality.

Although his botanical observations failed for the most part to be published, most of them will be found in Baldwin's letters to Dr. Darlington, to the Rev. Henry Mühlenberg, and others. His botanical contributions are mostly to be found in books written by others, chief among which are Darlington's "Reliquiae Baldwinianae"; Stephen Elliott's "A Sketch of Botany of South Carolina and Georgia"; Asa Gray's "A Monograph of the North American Species of Rhynchospora" in "Annals of the Lyceum of Natural History of New York 1828–1836," III, 191–220; and John Torrey's, "Monograph of North American Cyperaceae," *Ibid.*, III, 239–448. Baldwin's herbarium is at present at the Philadelphia Academy of Sciences.

In 1819, Dr. Baldwin obtained permission to join Major Stephen H. Long's Rocky Mountain Expedition. By July 13, the Expedition had arrived at Franklin, Missouri, where he withdrew and on August 31, 1819, passed away.

DARLINGTON, W. 1843. *Reliquae Baldwinianae*. Kimber & Sharpless, Philadelphia, Pa.

HARSHBERGER, J. W. 1899. *The Botanists of Philadelphia and Their Works*. T. C. Davis & Sons, Philadelphia.

KELLY, H. A. 1914. *Some American Medical Botanists*. The Southworth Co., Troy, N.Y.

REDFIELD, J. H. 1883. Some North American Botanists, vi, Dr. William Baldwin. *Botan. Gaz.* 8: 233–237.

VIETS, H. R. *Dict. Am. Biog.* 1: 547–548.

John Banister

1650–1692

John Banister was born at Twigworth, Gloucestershire, England. He was graduated from Magdalen College, Oxford, where
he was granted the B.A. degree in 1671. Three years later he received his M.A. degree from the same University. By 1678, he had
established himself in Charles City County, Virginia and thereafter devoted himself to the study of natural science and of botany
in particular. In due course he obtained title to some land on the
Appomattox River and officially served as minister for what was
later known as "Bristol Parish."

While a resident of Virginia Banister made a painstaking study
of the plant life of the region with which he was best acquainted.
At the same time he corresponded with such men of science as
Ray, Bobart, Lister, and others interested in the flora and fauna of
Virginia and sent them specimens and illustrations. He devoted no
little time to his "Natural History of Virginia." However, because
of his premature death, this was never published. Some of his
botanical papers were published posthumously in the "Philosophical Transactions." His catalogues of Virginia plants were published
in Ray's "Historia Plantarum" and in Petéver's "Memoirs." Then
there were his "Observations on the Natural Productions of Jamaica" and "A Description of the Snakeroot, Pestilochia or Serpen-
taria Virginiana."

Although Banister was not a botanist of major importance, he
enjoyed a good reputation among those of his fellows who were
best qualified to appraise his knowledge and grasp of his subject.
It should be remembered that at the time of Banister's greatest
interest and activity, botany was in its infancy in America. Ray,
who probably was best acquainted with Banister, rated him as
"*eruditissimus vir et consummatissimus botanicus*" and Campbell,
the historian, ranks him with John Bartram. In May 1692, he died
from an accidental gun wound.

BRETTON, J. 1885. *Dict. Nat. Biog.* 3: 119–120.
GORDON, A. C., JR. *Dict. Am. Biog.*
GORDON, A. C., JR. *Virginia Mag. Hist. Biog.* 11: 163–164.

Charles Reid Barnes

1858–1910

Charles Reid Barnes was born September 7, 1858, in Madison, Indiana. His early education was obtained from private schools and from the Madison High School. He then attended Hanover College, from which he was graduated in 1877 with a Bachelor of Arts degree. He was a pupil of John Merle Coulter, with whom he was associated from 1883 through the remaining years of his life.

Following his graduation from Hanover, Barnes entered Harvard University, where he pursued advanced courses in botany, a subject of major interest to him. In recognition of his accomplishment at Harvard, he received an honorary A.M. degree from Hanover College in 1880. Following a second period of graduate study at Harvard, he was awarded the Ph.D. degree by Hanover College in 1886.

While in pursuit of studies leading to advanced degrees Barnes held teaching positions, first as instructor of natural science in Lafayette (Indiana) High School (1880). Subsequently (1882), he accepted a professorship at Purdue University, where he taught courses in botany and geology until 1885. In 1887, he accepted an offer from the University of Wisconsin, where he became a prominent figure in the department of botany. In 1892, he returned to Harvard briefly to do research in botany; in 1898, he was offered and accepted the newly created position of professor of plant physiology in Chicago University, an appointment he filled until the day of his tragic death in 1910.

Throughout his scholarly career, Barnes was an active participant in the affairs of botanical societies. His intimate and relatively long association with Professor Coulter contributed not a little to his eminence as a teacher and made possible his contribution to the importance of the "Botanical Gazette." Within the field of his profession he was an uncompromising perfectionist, as he was in the use of his mother tongue. Hence we owe to him the editorial excellence and high standard of scientific accuracy of not only his own published papers, but of the journal over which he so conscientiously presided.

Professor Barnes first became known to the botanical public through his bryological papers, in which he added not a little to our knowledge of the taxonomic relationships of the mosses. His first important publication in this field was "An Analytical Key to the Genera and Species of North-American Mosses." This was followed in 1887 by his "Revision of the North-American Species of Fissidens." Other and equally significant bryological contributions to the clarification of the facts on the taxonomy of North American mosses were forthcoming in 1890 and 1897. He did much to popularize the mosses and bring them within the range of the layman's interest in plant life. He wrote as he spoke, not voluminously but exceptionally well, with a precision and accuracy that left no doubt as to the meaning of either line or paragraph.

As a plant physiologist Dr. Barnes was perhaps best known as a critical and exacting reviewer and teacher, a very helpful guide to those of his students engaged in research. Those men and women whose good fortune it was to come within the pale of his influence and sense of scholarship were sure to come away from such experience reflecting the high ideals and rare excellence of a great and kindly teacher.

The death of Dr. Barnes followed an accident that befell him while he was in his prime and full of promise of still more important work as a botanist. It was known to his most intimate associates that he had in mind the publication of the substance of his lectures relating to "Plant Physics" and of similar lectures on plant chemistry and on plant growth and its dynamics. Few men have had as wide a range of intellectual interest or have given greater promise of accomplishment.

ANON. 1910. Charles Reid Barnes. *Botan. Gaz.* 49: 321–324.
COWLES, H. C. 1910. Charles Reid Barnes, A brief appreciation. *Science* n.s. 31: 532–533.
HOWE, M. A. 1910. *Bryologist* 13: 66–67.
PEATTIE, D. C. *Dict. Am. Biog.*

Elam Bartholomew
1852–1934

Elam Bartholomew, son of George E. and Fanny (Bowman) Bartholomew, was born June 9, 1852, at Strasburg, Pennsylvania. He was a descendant of Henry Bartholomew, who came to America from the Netherlands and settled in Lancaster County, Pennsylvania in the early years of the eighteenth century. The boy, Elam, attended rural school for several winters while living on his father's farm at Farmington, Illinois. Later (1876) he moved to Stockton, Kansas, where he acquired a homestead of 160 acres. Here, in addition to his active farm life, he participated in politics and education. He also showed a lively interest in matters of church and religion.

At thirty, Bartholomew decided to make a herbarium of the phanerogamic plants of northwestern Kansas. His innate sense of accuracy and thoroughness led to his collection of specimens of every flowering plant of his part of Kansas. In due course his botanical ambition expanded to include a study and collection of fungi, with the result that he became a world figure in mycology. He was the discoverer of upwards of five hundred species of fungi. His ever-enlarging herbarium contained specimens of fungi from many parts of the world, specimens he acquired through exchange. He traveled widely throughout the United States, Mexico, and Canada, with the result that he assembled a collection comprising 292,380 specimens. From 1891 to 1893, he was employed by the U.S. Department of Agriculture to undertake a project for control of cereal rusts through spraying and soil treatment. From 1908 to 1913, he conducted a series of agronomic studies of promising types, varieties, and strains of alfalfa, corn, and cotton from several parts of the world. Much of this testing was carried out on his own farm.

In 1898, the Kansas State College at Manhattan granted Bartholomew the M.Sc. degree for his thesis, "The Plant Rusts of Kansas" and in 1927 the same institution conferred on him the

D.Sc. degree for his thesis "The Fungus Flora of Kansas." His "North American Uredinales" comprising the rust fungi of continental North America and neighboring islands appeared from 1911 to 1926. His "Fungi Columbiana," published between 1901 and 1917, included North American fungi of every kind. His most important contribution, "North American Plant Rusts," was published in 1928 and again in 1933.

Dr. Bartholomew was a member of the American Association for the Advancement of Science, The American Phytopathological Society, the Kansas Academy of Science, and the Delta Upsilon honorary scientific society. He was married, June 14, 1876, to Rachel Isabel Montgomery of Farmington, Illinois. Four sons and a daughter were born to this union. He died in Hays, Kansas on the eighteenth of November, 1934.

BARTHOLOMEW, E. T. 1935. Elam Bartholomew. *Mycologia* 27: 91–95, with portrait.
RANKINS, MELCHERS WILSON. 1935. *Trans. Kansas Acad. Sci.* 38: 29.

Benjamin Smith Barton
1766–1815

Benjamin Smith Barton, son of the Rev. Thomas Barton and Esther (Rittenhouse) Barton, daughter of David Rittenhouse, the astronomer, was born in Lancaster, Pennsylvania, February 10, 1766. His father's avocation was the study of botany, and it was therefore quite natural that the son should be inspired by a like interest in nature. At an early age he spent much time in the woods, studying and collecting plants, and not neglecting such birds and insects as came under his observation. His preparatory school days were spent in York (Pennsylvania) Academy.

Benjamin's mother passed away while he was a boy of eight, and his father died in 1780, when he was but fourteen. He moved to Philadelphia to reside with his eldest brother, but not until he had completed nearly two years of classical study in York Academy. During his stay in Philadelphia he spent some time as a student in the College of Philadelphia, and then, at eighteen took up the study of medicine.

Barton later went to Edinburgh for further preparation for his profession. There he won, as a member of the Royal Medical Society at Edinburgh, the Harveian prize of that Society for his dissertation on the *Hyoscyamus niger* of Linnaeus, commonly known as black henbane, a medicinal plant endowed with an alkaloidal principle known as *hyocine*. From Edinburgh he went to Göttingen and from there returned to America in 1789 and commenced the practice of medicine.

The College of Philadelphia had decided to add to its required courses one in natural history and botany and appointed Barton, then twenty-four years old, to the chair. The following year the College of Philadelphia merged with the University of Pennsylvania, and he retained this position as long as he lived. Dr. Barton was the first instructor of natural history in Philadelphia, if not the first in any college in North America.

Barton suffered much from ill health and was eventually induced to travel and try the recommended advantages of a sea voyage. He sailed for France in the spring of 1815 and returned in November, still without restoration of his health. Becoming rapidly worse, he died December 19, 1815. Just three days before his death he wrote a memoir on *Bartonia*, a genus of plants named in his honor by the botanists Pursh and Nuttal.

Though Barton produced relatively little as a botanist, he was industrious, and it is believed that his plant and other scientific collections have been and will continue to be helpful to students of the natural sciences. He enjoyed the acquaintance and correspondence of eminent naturalists in Europe and at home. He married, in 1797, a daughter of Edward Pennington of Philadelphia by whom he had two children, a son and a daughter.

BARTON, W. P. C. A biographical sketch read pursuant to appointment before the Philadelphia Medical Society . . . 16 February 1810 (sic) of their late president, Professor Barton. (Philadelphia 1816?). 1938. Journal of Benjamin Smith Barton on a visit to Virginia in 1802. *Castanea* 3: 85–117.

KELLY, H. A. 1914. *Some American Medical Botanists.* The Southworth Co., Troy, N.Y. Pp. 88–96.

PENNELL, F. W. 1926. *Bartonia* 9: 17–34.

YOUMANS, W. J. 1896. *Pioneers of Science in America.* D. Appleton & Company, Inc., New York.

John Bartram

1699–1777

John Bartram, eldest son of William and Elizabeth (Hunt) Bartram, was born March 23, 1699, at Marple, near Darby, Delaware (then Chester) County, Pennsylvania. He inherited a farm bequeathed to him by his uncle, Isaac Bartram, and it was here that he first conceived the idea that he might some day become a botanist. Endowed with the aptitudes of a scholar, he very early acquired such learning as the country schools of his day and community provided. They taught him little if anything of natural history, and such knowledge of botany or zoology as he did acquire resulted directly from an insatiable scientific desire to know the facts about his environment. He apparently shared his enthusiasm for botany with James Logan, one-time governor of Pennsylvania, who was inspired to procure for Bartram a copy of Parkinson's *Herbal,* a work well designed to enable the young enthusiast to decide whether he should cast his lot with the botanists or with the farmers. But whether or not his decision was influenced by Logan,[*] the following is Bartram's account of how he became a botanist:

One day I was very busy in holding my plough . . . and being weary, I ran under the shade of a tree to repose myself. I cast my eyes on a *daisy;* I plucked it mechanically, and viewed it with more curiosity than common country farmers are wont to do, and observed therein very many distinct parts, some perpendicular—some horizontal. *What a shame, said my mind, or*

[*] In John Bartram's own account of how he became a botanist no reference is made to James Logan. In Harshberger's "The Botanists of Philadelphia," Logan is credited as probably having been the first seriously to interest John Bartram in botany.

something that inspired my mind, that thee shouldst have employed so many years in tilling the earth, and destroying so many flowers and plants, without being acquainted with their structures and their uses! This seeming inspiration suddenly awakened my curiousity, for these were not thoughts to which I had been accustomed. I returned to my team, but this new desire did not quit my mind; I mentioned it to my wife, who greatly discouraged me from prosecuting my new scheme, as she called it; I was not opulent enough, she said, to dedicate much of my time to studies and labors which might rob me of that portion of it which is the only wealth of the American farmer. However, her prudent caution did not discourage me; I thought about it continually,—at supper, in bed, and wherever I went. At last, I could not resist the impulse; for on the fourth day of the following week, I hired a man to plough for me, and went to Philadelphia. Though I knew not what book to call for, I ingenuously told the bookseller my errand, who provided me with such as he thought best, and a Latin grammar beside. Next, I applied to a neighboring schoolmaster, who, in three months, taught me Latin enough to understand *Linnaeus*, which I purchased afterward. Then I began to botanize all over my farm. In a little time I became acquainted with every vegetable that grew in my neighborhood; and next ventured into Maryland, living among the Friends. In proportion as I thought myself more learned, I proceeded farther, and by a steady application of several years, I have acquired a pretty general knowledge of every plant and tree to be found in our Continent. In process of time I was applied to from the old countries, whither I every year send many collections. Being now made easy in my circumstances, I have ceased to labour, and am never so happy as when I see and converse with my friends.[*]

It has been generally accepted that Bartram was one of the first Anglo-Americans to conceive the idea of establishing a botanical garden. Be that as it may, he purchased at a sheriff's sale— Owen Owen, Sheriff—on September 30, 1728, a tract of land where, shortly afterward, about five acres were laid out as a botanical garden. This garden, on the Schuylkill River about three miles from Philadelphia, was beautifully and very appropriately situated as to soil, its proximity to those who most needed its influence, and lastly, its convenience to its owner and director. Here with the passing years he assembled many native and exotic plants. Traveling at his own expense, he made carefully planned excursions into Maryland, Virginia, the Carolinas, and the far reaches of Florida.

Bartram's renown as a botanist and collector spread beyond the Atlantic. Through Joseph Breintnall, a Philadelphia merchant, he learned of Peter Collinson of London with whom he struck up a

[*] Recorded by William Darlington in his "John Bartram and Humphry Marshall," 1849.

lifelong correspondence and a lasting friendship. Collinson, writing to Dr. Cadwallader Colden on March 7, 1741, says of John Bartram:

> I am persuaded you would have been pleased with him; you would have found a wonderful natural genius,—considering his education, and that he was never out of America, but he is an husbandman. . . . His observations and accounts of all natural productions that happen in his way (and I believe few escape him) are much esteemed here for their accuracy.

Dr. Colden, in a letter to Peter Collinson, dated November 13, 1744, says:

> I had the pleasure of seeing Mr. Bartram at my house, this summer. It is really surprising what knowledge that man has attained merely by the force of industry and his own genius. He has a lively fancy, and a surprising memory and indefatigable disposition.

ANON. 1895. John Bartram. *Asa Gray Bull.* 3: 15.
DARLINGTON, W. 1849. *Memorials of John Bartram and Humphry Marshall.* Lindsey & Blakiston, Philadelphia.
EARNEST, E. 1940. *John and William Bartram, Botanists and Explorers, 1699–1823.* University of Pennsylvania Press, Philadelphia.
HARSHBERGER, J. W. 1899. *The Botanists of Philadelphia and Their Works.* T. C. Davis & Sons, Philadelphia.
HERBST, J. 1954. *New Green World.* Hastings House, Publishers, Inc., New York.
YOUMANS, W. J. 1896. *Pioneers of Science in America.* D. Appleton & Company, Inc., New York.

William James Beal

1833–1924

William James Beal, botanist and teacher, was born on the eleventh of March, 1833, in Adrian, Michigan. He was the son of William and Rachel (Comstock) Beal, and belonged to that period of our history when men and women dressed in homespun, lived in log houses, read or sewed by candlelight, and plowed their fields with primitive farm gear. Thus it was that the son of William and Rachel learned his lessons of economy and acquired an ability to derive much from so little.

Being a man of almost superhuman energy and an enthusiasm that would give him no rest, William burned with a desire to attend school. It was his privilege to live relatively near the University of Michigan (about 30 miles), easily within range of its influence, and it is not unexpected to find that he enrolled there in the class of 1859. As an undergraduate he acquired a smattering book knowledge of botany and zoology.

On receiving his A.B. degree, Beal moved to Union Springs, New York, where he served as a teacher in the Howland Institute for nine years. He devoted his vacations to study at Harvard University, where it was his great good fortune to meet Louis Agassiz, who gave point and purpose to Beal's ambition to become a botanist. Here also he had the opportunity to study botany under Asa Gray, who gave him what was then the best possible grounding in taxonomy and plant physiology available in any American university. From Harvard Beal received his B.Sc. degree in 1865, and his M.Sc. in 1875 from the old University of Chicago, where, in 1868, he had gone as a teacher of botany, zoology, and geology. In 1871, he was called to the Michigan College of Agriculture as professor of botany and horticulture. There he remained until 1910, when he retired.

In certain respects Beal was a remarkable figure in the galaxy of American botanists. He was one of a few pioneer American students of plant science who emerged from the "old botany" and successfully labored to bring forth the new. He was eminently successful as a teacher and was one, if not the first, of our botanists to strive for and obtain a building intended for and devoted to botany alone, and this at a time when in most of our American colleges and universities the biological sciences were, as children, permitted to fare at second table, if indeed so well.

Professor Beal was the author of some 1,200 published papers, books, etc., including a work entitled "The New Botany," and a two-volume treatise on North American grasses. These major contributions enjoyed a marked popularity, as did also his treatise entitled "Seed Dispersal," published in 1898. Through his effort he inspired legislation that authorized the creation of the State Forestry Commission. In 1875, he founded the College forest preserve; and in 1906 was successful in his realization of the "Pinetum." To Professor Beal the State of Michigan is indebted also for its excellent botanical garden. On September 2, 1863, Professor Beal married Hannah Proud, a friend of his youth. He died on the twelfth of May, 1924.

BAKER, R. S., and J. B. BAKER. 1925. An American Pioneer of Science. *Michigan Alumnus*, May 22, 1924: 946–947.
BESSEY, E. A. 1925. W. J. Beal. *Botan. Gaz.* 79: 103–106.
BESSEY, E. A. 1926. *Mich. Acad. Sci.*
McKIBBEN, C. W. 1924. W. J. Beal, Michigan Pioneer Forester. *Am. Forests and Forest Life*, Apr., 216–217.

Charles Edwin Bessey
1845–1915

Charles Edwin Bessey, celebrated American botanist, was born on May 21, 1845, in Wayne County, Ohio. His paternal forbears were of French Huguenot descent, who, because of religious persecution, fled from Alsace to England and thence to Pennsylvania. His father, Adnah Bessey, an Ohio school teacher, married Margaret Ellenberger, one of his pupils, in 1841. Charles Edwin received his elementary schooling from his father and in time attended an academy at Seville, Ohio. This important stage in his educational experience was interrupted by the death of his father, and we next hear of the son as a teacher in a school at Wadsworth, in a county adjoining that of his birth and well within the Connecticut Reserve where good schools and equally good teaching were traditional. It was not long before he returned to the Seville Academy, only to be a witness to its dissolution.

With this rather sketchy, catch-as-catch-can schooling, supplemented by the results of his own personal effort to prepare for college, in 1866 the young man entered Michigan Agricultural College at twenty-one. There, in 1869, he received his Bachelor of Science degree. When Bessey entered college it was with the intention of specializing in civil engineering, but he early discovered his penchant for plant life. His growing devotion to this absorbing interest caught the attention of certain of his teachers, among whom was Albert Nelson Prentiss, professor of Botany for several years at Michigan Agricultural College, and later at Cornell, who advised him to study botany. At first hesitating to accept such counsel, he finally yielded, and botany prevailed over engineering. His industry and devotion to his specialty were in due season rewarded by his appointment to an assistantship in horticulture, whereupon he was put in charge of the college greenhouse.

Bessey was not long at Michigan State College when he received an offer of a position in Iowa's College of Agriculture as instructor in botany and horticulture. This was in 1869. For the next fifteen years he served the college with honor and distinction, rising in rank from an instructorship to a full professorship. In June, 1884 he was notified of his appointment as professor of botany at the University of Nebraska. Before accepting the position he visited the university that he might the more carefully look into the status of the department he had been selected to preside over. Finding himself faced anew with the prospect of building from scratch another department of botany, he declined to accept the position. Unwilling to let the matter drop, a second attempt to win him over was made by the regents of the university. After further consultation, Bessey accepted the offer in August, 1884 and delivered his inaugural address in September.

It was in the winter of 1870–1871 that he attended and participated in the first farmers' institute ever held in Iowa. This incident is of historical significance, for these Iowa meetings were among the first to be held anywhere in the United States.

Bessey first met Dr. Asa Gray while attending a meeting of the American Association for the Advancement of Science in August, 1872. This meeting of the two botanists ripened into a most fruitful acquaintance, and led to opportunities for the younger man to profit professionally through subsequent visits to Harvard University for needed training under the master botanist. These rare hours of precious contact must have meant much to both master and disciple. What the latter carried away from his teacher was to be reflected again and again in those who went out into the world from the Nebraska laboratory and lecture hall.

Dr. Bessey was one of a small but exceptional group of Americans who contributed importantly to the foundation of what we recognize as the botany of the twentieth century. It was he who introduced at Iowa State College in 1873 the teaching of botany by the laboratory method, requiring use of the compound microscope, apparently quite unaware of the fact that this method had been inaugurated at Harvard the year before and by Thomas J. Burrill at the University of Illinois in 1869. In July, 1881, Bessey was asked to teach a course in botany at the University of Minnesota, the first time in the history of that institution that such a course had been presented by the laboratory method. The university had no microscopes of its own, so an arrangement was made whereby the required number of instruments was borrowed from the Iowa State Agricultural College. Thus we find Bessey, one of a few pioneers in the field of plant science, to whom credit is due for much of the spade work necessary to laying a good foundation for North American botany, at work to the end of his days. He was a master builder of the superstructure of his chosen science, a man of vision and of creative leadership.

Aside from Bessey's remarkable genius as a teacher, much of his influence and success in his profession is attributable to his series of textbooks on botany: "Botany for High Schools and Colleges," published in 1880; "The Essentials of Botany" (1884), a text that went through several editions, the seventh and final one coming out in 1896. This textbook enjoyed wide popularity, and was one of the most extensively used in North America. His "Essentials of College Botany" (1914), written in collaboration with his son, Ernst Bessey, was, in fact, but another edition of the more elementary "Essentials of Botany."

Dr. Bessey was married on December 25, 1873 to Miss Lucy Athearn of West Tisbury, Martha's Vineyard, Massachusetts. To this union were born three sons, Edward, Ernst, and Carl.

COULTER, J. M. 1915. Charles Edwin Bessey. *Botan. Gaz.* 60: 72–73.
POOL, R. J. 1915. A Brief Sketch of the Life and Works of Charles Edwin Bessey. *Am. J. Botany* 2: 505–518, with portrait.
SHEAR, C. L. 1896. Charles Edwin Bessey. *Asa Gray Bull.* 4: 223–224.

Jacob Bigelow
1786–1879

Jacob Bigelow, botanist and physician, was born February 27, 1786, the son of Jacob Bigelow, Congregational minister, and Elizabeth (Wells) Bigelow. He entered Harvard College at the age of sixteen. Seven years later (1809), he matriculated at the University of Pennsylvania as a student of medicine. It was then that he became interested in botany. He received his M.D. degree in 1810 and returned to Boston, where he established his practice of medicine.

In 1812, Dr. Bigelow gave a series of botanical lectures and undertook an intensive study of the flora of Boston and vicinity within a radius of 10 miles. This was published in 1814 under the title of "Florulae Bostoniensis." Ten years later, Bigelow, with Francis Booth, conducted botanical exploratory work in the mountains of New Hampshire and Vermont. A second edition of "Florula Bostoniensis" included the results of these explorations. Enlarged and corrected, but under the same title, this manual remained the popular standard of New England botany until 1848, when Asa Gray's "Manual" more than replaced it.

Bigelow's most important contribution to botany was his "American Medical Botany" (3 vols.), 1817, 1818, and 1820. He was also an important contributor to the first American pharmacopaeia (1820). In his memory, De Candolle gave to a genus of compositae the name *Bigelovia*.

Dr. Bigelow married, in 1817, Mary Scollay, the daughter of Col. William Scollay. He died in 1879.

BAILEY, L. H., JR. 1883. Some North American Botanists. I. Jacob Bigelow. *Botan. Gaz.* 8: 217–222.

ELLIS, G. E. 1880. *Memoir of Jacob Bigelow, M. D.* A. Williams & Co., Boston.

GRAY, A. 1879. Dr. Jacob Bigelow. *Am. J. Sci.* 3rd Ser. 17: 263–266.

KELLY, H. A. 1914. *Some American Medical Botanists.* 120–128. The Southworth Co., Troy, N.Y.

MUMFORD, J. G. 1902. Jacob Bigelow, a Sketch. *Johns Hopkins Hospital Bull.* 13: 1–8.

Albert Francis Blakeslee

1874–1954

An outstanding botanist was lost to the world of science in the passing on November 16, 1954, of Albert Francis Blakeslee. Born in Geneseo, New York, on November 9, 1874, he died in Northampton, Massachusetts, a few days after his eightieth birthday. During his professional life he was a tireless and productive worker, contributing over three hundred technical articles singly or with collaborators. His studies in the field of genetics were highly original and constituted some of the most valuable contributions to that field that were made during his generation. Using the genus *Datura* as a medium for plant breeding research, he carried on extensive studies designed to determine how evolution occurs.

Albert Francis Blakeslee was the second son of Francis Durbin and Augusta Miranda Blakeslee. At the time Albert was born his father was principal of East Greenwich Academy, East Greenwich, Rhode Island. He was also a Methodist minister and, in addition to being an educator, had been at various times newspaper correspondent, lecturer, and university president. Albert attended the academy while his father was principal, then continued his university education at Wesleyan University, in Middletown, Connecticut. In addition to graduating *cum laude*, he received prizes in chemistry and mathematics, was elected to Phi Beta Kappa, and won recognition for athletic ability in both football and tennis.

After receiving his bachelor's degree in 1896, Blakeslee taught science for four years, part of the time at the East Greenwich Academy and part at Montpelier Seminary in Montpelier, Vermont. Feeling the need for additional education and training in the field of botany, which he had elected as his major interest, he entered the graduate school at Harvard in 1900 and was granted his Ph.D. four years later. While at Harvard he received valuable training and financial assistance by serving as instructor in botany at Radcliffe College and as teaching fellow in botany at Harvard.

His doctoral thesis, "Sexual Reproduction in the Mucorineae," was a botanical milestone in its discovery of sexual reproduction in the lower fungi and the light thus thrown on reproduction in the lower plants. A grant from the Carnegie Institution of Washington permitted a two-year continuation of these studies in Germany. On returning to the United States, he was appointed instructor in botany at Harvard and Radcliffe. He had been in this position for but a single year when he received an appointment as professor of botany from Connecticut Agricultural College at Storrs. Here he established a reputation as an inspiring and natural teacher that was to stay with him throughout his life. It was at Storrs, also, that he developed a method for identifying trees, using their winter vegetative characteristics, and produced a hybrid pine, one of the first to be grown in this country.

The academic year 1912–13 was spent on leave from the Agricultural College, at the Carnegie Institution's Department of Genetics. The impression made there, added to his previous record, resulted in an offer to return on a permanent basis. This he elected to do, despite his love of teaching, and, in 1915, Blakeslee left the academic fold, not to return until his retirement thirty-six years later. He kept intending to get back to his teaching, but the genetics research in which he became increasingly engrossed at the Cold Spring Harbor Laboratory exerted too much of a pull for him to give it up.

In 1923, eight years after his initial appointment as resident investigator, Blakeslee was promoted to Assistant Director of the Laboratory. During 1934–35 he became Acting Director and the following year, Director. During his entire stay with the Carnegie Institution his genetics research centered around jimson weed (*Datura stramonium*) and the other species of the genus. Using these plants as media, he and his co-workers, through cytologic and genetic studies, discovered fundamental features of inheritance and hitherto unknown mechanics of chromosome behavior. Variations from the usual diploid that were discovered included a tetraploid, a trisomic mutant, and a haploid plant. This was the first report of a haploid flowering plant and a sporophyte at that, not a gametophyte. These, in addition to other highly original investigations of extra-chromosomal types, and his studies made jointly with the late Dr. John Belling on segment interchange between non-homologous chromosomes, won him international acclaim.

In 1937, Blakeslee soaked some jimson weeds in the alkaloid colchicine. The plants appeared to have received a stimulus of some sort and, on examining the chromosomes, they were found to have doubled in number. He recognized the importance of this in its application to germinating seeds which might have the chromosomes in the center cell layers numbers doubled or quadrupled. As these tissues retained their extra chromosome numbers and consequent differentiation during the life of the plant, this technique had definite value in tracing tissue derivation.

Blakeslee's interest in genetics led him to an investigation of the inheritance of taste. He noted during the course of his work that a *Verbena* of a certain color possessed a definite fragrance to his assistant but not to him, while one of a different color had an odor that he could detect but that his assistant could not. These initial observations led him to an extensive study of smell and taste and the inheritance of these abilities. Definite inherited differences were discovered.

After retiring as Director of the Cold Spring Harbor Laboratory in 1941 at the age of sixty-eight, Blakeslee was asked to serve at Smith College as the William Allan Neilson Research Professor of Botany. He accepted the invitation and during the next twelve years continued his highly productive professional life. He directed the activities of graduate students and nine received their master's degrees and four their doctor's degrees under him during this period. In addition to his teaching he obtained funds for and organized the Smith College Genetics Experiment Station. Two of his former colleagues at Cold Spring Harbor became staff members of the new Experiment Station and continued their work with their former director. The new station was highly productive both as to quantity and quality of research. The earlier genetic studies on *Datura* were continued but were expanded to include research on the embryology and physiology of the genus. More than seventy technical papers were published by the staff of the Experiment Station during this period.

In 1919, when Blakeslee was forty-five, he married Margaret Bridges. Although both were no longer young, the marriage was a happy one, and she was a great asset to him in helping to handle the social responsibilities of his position as laboratory director. He never fully recovered from her unexpected death in 1947. They had no children.

Throughout his life Blakeslee had a participating interest in the activities of those around him and of the scientific or academic community in which he lived. At Smith College, in particular, he took part in a variety of school activities. These included the presidency of Phi Beta Kappa, Sigma Chi, and the Smith Faculty Club. In each of these offices he contributed by energetic participation in the organization's activities and by ideas for improvement. In his later years, while at Smith College, he was impressed with the need for means of stimulating the activities and morale of the older, retired faculty and staff members. As a consequence he organized the OBND Club (Out But Not Down). The group assembled once each month for a luncheon meeting and twice annually for a dinner.

Blakeslee had a wide variety of interests and a genuine warmth of feeling for his fellow man. He enjoyed the company of children and his liking for them was spontaneously reciprocated. His natural warmth and generosity were expressed in his professional relations with his co-workers. As an indication of this, most of his published papers appeared with his name only as co-author, thus giving his associates credit for their share in the research that was being carried on.

Many honors came to Blakeslee during his life. Six universities or colleges granted him the honorary Doctor of Science degree; one the Doctor of Laws. He was elected to membership in three American honor societies, the American Academy of Arts and Sciences, the American Philosophical Society, and the National Academy of Sciences. Five American scientific societies, including the American Association for the Advancement of Science, elected him to presidency. In addition he was awarded honorary membership in twelve foreign scientific societies.

ANON. 1943. Blakeslee, A[lbert] F[rancis] *Current Biography, 2nd Annual Volume.* Pp. 86, 87.

AVERY, AMOS G., SOPHIA SATINA, and JACOB RIETSEMA. 1959. *Blakeslee: The Genus Datura.* The Ronald Press Company, New York.

DARLINGTON, C. D. 1954. Prof. A. F. Blakeslee. *Nature* 174: 1037.

LIVINGSTON, BURTON E. 1940. Newly elected president of the American Association. *Sci. Mon.* 50: 182–185.

SINNOTT, EDMUND W. 1959. Albert Francis Blakeslee; November 9, 1874–November 16, 1954. *Nat. Acad. Sci. Biog. Mem.* 33: 2–38.

SMITH, HAROLD H. 1955. Albert Francis Blakeslee. *Bull. Torr. Club* 82: 305–308.

Ezra Brainerd

1844–1924

Ezra Brainerd, botanist, geologist, and educator, was the son of Lawrence Robbins Brainerd and Catherine (Wood) Brainerd. He was born at St. Albans, Vermont, December 17, 1844. There he received his preparatory schooling. He went on to Middlebury College where he was awarded the A.B. degree in 1864. Four years later he was graduated from Andover Theological Seminary, though not ordained. Following graduation from Andover, he served Middlebury College as a teacher of rhetoric. Thereafter he taught physics and mathematics and, from 1885 to 1906, served as president of the college.

Brainerd's scientific bent leaned decidedly toward geology and botany, his first published contribution to botany being "The Blackberries of Vermont," published in 1900. This in due season was followed by the "Flora of Vermont," the work of Brainerd and two collaborators, L. R. Jones and W. W. Eggleston. Four years later his initial paper on the genus *Viola* appeared. From that time to the end of his active career he worked ceaselessly on this genus and its multitudinous natural hybrids in an endeavor to disclose their pure parental species. To this end he grew them under controlled conditions and, according to Mendelian principles, studied their unit characters as revealed in subsequent generations. He collected extensively specimens peculiar to different parts of the United States. Through a wide correspondence he extended his knowledge of the genus and published, all told, fifty papers, the most important of which were those of a series entitled: "Hybridism in the Genus *Viola.*" The quantity and quality of his published work on violets won for him a deserved international reputation. With A. K. Peiterson he published in 1920 Vermont Bulletin 217 on "Hybridism in the Genus *Rubus*." His last published papers were "Violets of North America," and "Some Natural Violet Hybrids of North America." Throughout his life he maintained an enthusiastic and profound interest in natural science.

Prof. E. C. Jeffrey, botanist, of Harvard University has this to say of Dr. Brainerd as the American scientist whose contribution to our knowledge of the laws of hybridism in plants is of outstanding importance: "We owe the most important results which have yet (1927) been produced on this continent, in this direction, to the studies of Brainerd."

Dr. Brainerd's botanical research was not confined to the genus *Viola* for, very early in his career, he founded an herbarium. He became interested in the sedges (the genus *Carex*), and wherever his botanical or other excursions took him, he would seek out the sedges. He kept in constant touch with such botanists as L. H. Bailey, M. L. Fernald, and other specialists on the genus *Carex*. Thus did his own study of the sedges become more and more critical. He was twice married: first, to Frances Viola, the daughter of Sylvester B. Rockwell, born December 1, 1868, deceased January 11, 1893; and second, on December 25, 1897, to Mary E. Wright, the daughter of Alvah S. Wright. He was the father of six children by his first wife and of two by his second. He died December 8, 1924.

BARNHARD, J. H. 1925. Ezra Brainerd. *Am. Fern J.* 15: 127–128.
EGGLESTON, W. W. 1928. *Bull. Torrey. Club* 55: 91–104, with portrait and list of scientific papers.
HOWE, M. A. 1925. *J. N.Y. Botan. Gard.* 26: 12–13.
WRIGHT, C. B. 1927. *A Memorial of Ezra Brainerd*. Privately printed. Middlebury, Vt.

Townshend Stith Brandegee

1843–1925

Townshend Stith Brandegee was the son of Elishama and Florence (Stith) Brandegee. He was born February 16, 1943 in Berlin, Connecticut. His father, a physician, was fond of natural history. In 1866, the son entered the Sheffield Scientific School of Yale, where he was graduated in 1870. Although he prepared himself for a career in engineering, he found time to study botany under Prof. A. A. Eaton and became keenly interested in the collection and study of the ferns.

In 1871, Brandegee qualified as a county surveyor, and was appointed city engineer of Canon City, Colorado. Here he devoted his spare hours to collecting ferns for John Redfield, a Connecticut botanist. In the course of events, some of his specimens came to the notice of Dr. Asa Gray, a fact that led to Gray's recommending Brandegee as botanical collector and topographical assistant to the Hayden Expedition to southwestern Colorado and adjoining parts of Utah. Later, he was appointed engineer to the Royal Gorge and Santa Fe Surveys and to the northern Transcontinental Survey, across Wyoming to Oregon and Washington.

All this time Brandegee missed no opportunity to collect plants, among which were many new or hitherto non-described species. For Prof. C. S. Sargent he assembled an enviable lot of timber samples under the authority of the Bureau of the United States Census, a collection which was later to become part of the Jessup Collection as installed in the American Museum of Natural History in New York City.

Although up to this time (1886) he had not declared himself for botany, Brandegee accepted a commission that year that took him to Santa Cruz island, off the coast from Santa Barbara, California. Here he could devote himself freely to the study of an island flora. He then and there declared his consuming interest in botany and from that time on devoted himself to the collection and study of plants. He gave up engineering as such, though he occasionally made forest topographical maps.

In 1889, Brandegee made a botanical exploration of Baja California, Mexico, volunteering his service in the interest of the California Academy of Sciences. That experience marked the beginning of his intermittent visits to Baja California and to the Mexican states of Sonora, Sinaloa, Veracruz, and Puebla. He became recognized as an authority on the flora of Baja California and of the islands of the Gulf of California. Incidentally, he made exploratory studies of the plant life of southern California.

At first he sent his specimens to certain eastern authorities for identification but, in due time, came to depend more and more on his own ability to identify his plants. He published many notes contributing to our knowledge of the life histories, habitats, and other characteristics pertaining to the plants he observed and studied. From 1909 to 1924 he applied himself to his major undertaking, "Plantae Mexicanae Purpusianae," a work comprising twelve fascicles describing the new species collected by Dr. C. A. Purpus in Mexico.

In May, 1889, Brandegee married Dr. Mary Katherine (Layne) Curran (Oct. 1844–Apr. 1920), known to botanical science as Katherine Brandegee, curator of the herbarium of the California Academy of Sciences. Brandegee was among the last of the self-trained American botanists and one of the first of the pioneer plant collectors of the West. He died on April 7, 1925.

SETCHELL, W. A. 1926. Townshend Stith Brandegee and Mary Katherine Brandegee. *Univ. Calif. Publ. Bot.* 13: 155–178, with portrait and bibliographies.

Elizabeth Gertrude Knight Britton
1858–1934

Elizabeth Gertrude Knight Britton, beloved wife of Nathaniel Lord Britton, was born in New York City on January 9, 1858. She was the daughter of James and Sophie Ann (Compton) Knight.

During much of her youth she dwelt in Cuba, where her father and her grandfather were interested in the manufacture of mahogany furniture and in the sugar industry. Following her graduation from what was subsequently known as Hunter College in New York, Miss Knight continued to serve as a teacher at her alma mater from 1875 to 1883 and as a tutor of natural science from 1883 to 1885, when, in August, she and Nathaniel Lord Britton were married.

As Mrs. Britton, she continued her service as tutor until 1895. With an ever-increasing interest in botany, she joined the Torrey Botanical Club in 1879 and engaged in a special study of the bryophytes. In time she became internationally recognized as a specialist in that phylum, and was unofficially recognized as botanist in charge of that part of the Hunter College herbarium devoted to the mosses.

For a time Mrs. Britton served as editor of the "Bulletin of the Torrey Botanical Club," was a frequent contributor of reviews and critiques, and published there an enumeration of Rusby's collection of South American ferns. In 1889, she contributed through the Bulletin her first of a series of papers entitled, "Contributions to American Bryology," followed by another series, "How to Study the Mosses," which appeared in "The Observer." Although Mrs. Britton published a number of important papers on the ferns, such as her "Revision of the North American Ophioglossaceae," "Life History of the Curlygrass Fern (*Schizaea pusilla*)," and "Life History of *Vittaria lineata*," it was her work in the field of bryology that caused her to become known as a botanist. Mrs. Britton was a founder of the Wild Flower Preservation Society of America and of the Sullivant Moss Society. She died on February 25, 1934.

Barnhart, J. H. 1935. The published work of Elizabeth Gertrude Britton. *Bull. Torrey Club* 62: 1–17.
Grout, A. J. 1935. Elizabeth Gertrude (Knight) Britton. *Bryologist* 38, No. 1: 1–3.
Howe, M. A. 1934. Elizabeth Gertrude Britton. *J. N.Y. Botan. Gard.* 35: 97–103, with portrait.

Nathaniel Lord Britton

1859–1934

Nathaniel Lord Britton was born January 15, 1859, at New Dorp, Staten Island, New York. He was the son of Alexander Hamilton and Harriet Lord (Turner) Britton, and was a descendant of James Britton, who came to America from London, England, in 1635. His higher education was obtained in the School of Mines of Columbia College, where he was prepared for the profession of mining engineering and from which he received his M.E. degree in 1879 and his Ph.D. degree in 1881. His outdoor experience in geology resulted in a growing interest in things botanical and, in 1879, he and a college classmate compiled and published a treatise entitled "The Flora of Richmond County."

For seven years, Dr. Britton served as assistant to John S. Newberry, then lecturing in geology and botany to Columbia students. Britton became daily more interested in botany, and was appointed instructor in botany at Columbia University in 1886. Four years later he was promoted to the position of adjunct professor and, in 1891, was raised in rank to a full professorship. While at Columbia he reorganized and classified the herbarium and labored to include the collection of rare plant specimens and valuable books that had been stored away for many years, more or less buried under an ever-deepening blanket of dust. During his official connection with Columbia University he served for five years as chief botanist and assistant geologist of the New Jersey geological survey. For a short time he was a field assistant for the United States Geological Survey.

In 1902, on establishment of the Carnegie Institution of Washington, Dr. Britton was a member of the advisory committee charged with the responsibility of planning its botanical research. As early as 1896 he was called to the directorship of the recently established New York Botanical Garden. He resigned his position at Columbia University and was named professor emeritus.

Britton, at the time, was editor of the "Bulletin of the Torrey Botanical Club" and was one of the incorporators of the New York

Botanical Garden, authorized by the New York State Legislature in 1891. It was through the initiative of the Torrey Botanical Club that the Botanical Garden had become an accomplished fact. Under authority of the act of incorporation, the New York City park commissioners were empowered to set aside "not to exceed 250 acres in some public park north of the Harlem River." This was conditioned on the proviso that the corporation secure within seven years the sum of 250,000 dollars. The funds were raised in less than the required time, the acreage of the garden was subsequently increased to approximately 400 acres, and the New York Board of Estimate appropriated the sum of half a million dollars for necessary buildings. Arrangements were made whereby the Columbia College herbarium was transferred, along with the botanical library, to the museum. This worked to the advantage of students and teachers, for all of the facilities of the Botanical Garden were made available to them.

Dr. Britton devoted more than thirty years of his life to the development of the Garden and lived to see it become one of the three largest in the world. The herbarium, built around a nucleus comprising the Torrey collection, is now surpassed in North America only by that of the Smithsonian Institution.

Doctor Britton retired in 1929 at the age of seventy years. At that time the Garden's endowment amounted to 2.5 million dollars, and it had expended, over and above city funds, somewhat more than 2.6 million dollars of its own money.

Britton's life-long passion for botanical exploration led him into the West Indies, a region he visited more than thirty times. He was particularly interested in the forest flora of Puerto Rico where, on his recommendation, the government established a forest preserve and planted as a reforestation project as many as 900,000 trees.

Problems of botanical nomenclature came in for their share of his attention, and he was one of the first of those who worked for the adoption of the Rochester and American codes, which stood out for the principle of priority in the selection of plant names for both species and genera. Several plants pay honor to the name of Britton, and the same may be said of three animal species. Dr. Britton's published works are many, the more important being his "Catalogue of Plants Found in New Jersey," "Illustrated Flora of the Northern United States and Canada," "North American Trees," "The Cactaceae," 4 vols. (with J. N. Rose), "The Bahama Flora" (with C. F. Millspaugh), and "The Botany of Porto Rico and the Virgin Islands," 2 vols. (with Percy Wilson).

The honorary degree of D.Sc. was conferred upon Britton in 1904 by Columbia University in recognition of his many years of preeminent service as a botanist. In 1924, the University of Pittsburgh honored him with the degree of Doctor of Laws. He was a member of several scientific societies, including the Botanical Society of America, The Natural Science Association of Staten Island, The National Academy of Sciences, The American Philosophical Society, The American Academy of Arts and Sciences, The New York State Forestry Association, The Linnean Society of London, and The Czechoslovakian Society of Botany.

In August, 1885, he was married in New York City to Elizabeth Gertrude Knight, daughter of James Knight. He died, without issue, June 25, 1934.

FERNALD, M. L. 1934. *Proc. Am. Acad. Sci.* 70: 504–505.
HOWE, M. A. 1934. *J. N.Y. Botan. Gard.* 35: 169–180, with portrait.
MERRILL, E. D. 1938. *Nat. Acad. Sci. Biog. Mem.* 19: 147–202, with portrait and bibliography compiled by John Hendley Barnhart.
MERRILL, E. D. 1935. *Proc. Linn. Soc.* (London). 161–165.
RUSBY, H. H. 1934. Nathaniel Lord Britton. *Science* n.s. 80: 108–111.
SPRAGUE, T. A. 1934. *Bull. Misc. Inform. Kew* No. 6: 275–279.

Arthur Henry Reginald Buller

1874–1944

Arthur Henry Reginald Buller was born on the 19th of August, 1874 in Birmingham, England and his early education was obtained in England. He then entered the University of London where he was awarded the B.S. degree in 1896. The award of an 1851 Exhibition Scholarship in recognition of his ability and promise made possible his matriculation at the University of Leipzig, where he pursued his graduate studies in botany under the direction of Professor Pfeffer and was granted the Ph.D. degree in 1899. At Munich he studied under Professor Hartig and then was for a year a student at the Naples Marine Biological Station. On returning to England he served as lecturer in botany at the University of Birmingham from 1901 to 1904.

Buller then went to Canada, where he had accepted a professorship in the University of Manitoba (Winnipeg). This position he held until 1936, when he retired and became professor emeritus. Although he remained loyal to the country of his birth, he spent nearly forty years in Canada. He labored diligently in the interests of the University of Manitoba and for the establishment of the Dominion Rust Research Laboratory, which subsequently became known as the Dominion Laboratory of Plant Pathology.

Although Buller was a man of diverse intellectual gifts, he was ever the botanist. He possessed an insatiable scientific curiosity and a passion for research. As a teacher he was gifted; he was a rare perfectionist; he was also friend and scientific counselor. He is perhaps best known for the excellence and volume of his published research on the fungi, but his contribution as a teacher of botany becomes increasingly recognized for its far-reaching and inestimable value.

From his birth Buller was an inquisitive naturalist. He was ever sounding the depths and seeking the answers, that he might know and understand. His monumental six-volume work, "Researches on Fungi" (1909–1939) is regarded as Buller at his best in research and in scientific exposition. In addition to his "Researches on Fungi," were his "Essays on Wheat" (1919), his "Practical Botany" (1929), and a considerable number of mycological articles published in numerous technical journals; in collaboration with Messrs. G. R. Bisby and John Dearness, he prepared the "Fungi of Manitoba"; and, subsequently, with W. P. Fraser and R. C. Russell, "The Fungi of Manitoba and Saskatchewan" (1938). With C. L. Shear he was a coeditor of W. B. Groves' translation of "Selecta Fungorum Carpologia" of the Brothers Tulasne (1931), and had a prominent part in securing its publication. This and other botanical classics appealed to him as being of the utmost importance to the graduate student, and he never ceased to advocate their careful consideration.

Buller clearly understood and appreciated the practical importance of the fungi to the human economy. Being a man of vision, he did not fail to point out the significance of basic research to our success in the control of plant-disease epidemics. He manifested a more than casual interest in geology and ornithology and earnestly sought to keep abreast of the advance of knowledge along fronts other than the strictly botanical. Buller's gifts as a lecturer were well known. As with his laboratory appointments, he took the utmost care to prepare the subject matter of his lectures and so to present the facts as to assure their clarity and the validity of their interpretation.

Many were the honors bestowed upon Dr. Buller in recognition of his preeminence as a botanist and scholar. The following is a list of the more distinctive testimonials to the significance of his accomplishments in research and as a teacher. He was president of the British Mycological Society in 1913; president of Section IV, Royal Society of Canada, 1914–1915; president of the Canadian Phytopathological Society, 1920; president of the Mycological Section of the American Botanical Society, 1921; associate member of the Société Royale de Botanique de Belgique, 1921; Hon. LL.D., University of Manitoba, 1924; president of the Botanical Society of America, 1928; president of the Royal Society of Canada, 1927–1928; Flavelle Medal of the Royal Society of Canada, 1929; Hon. D.Sc., University of Pennsylvania, 1933; corresponding member of the Netherlands Botanical Society, 1935; president of the Section for Mycology and Bacteriology, Sixth International Botanical Congress (Amsterdam) 1935; vice president of the Mycological Society of America, 1935; Medal of the Manitoba Natural History Society, 1936; Royal Medal of the Royal Society, 1937; visiting professor of botany at the Louisiana State University, 1941; Hitchcock Visiting Professor of botany at the University of California, 1942; and Schiff Foundation Lecturer at Cornell University, 1942.

Dr. Buller remained single throughout life. It was his intention on visiting America in 1939 to return finally to England and there remain permanently. Due to the hazards of ocean travel in wartime, however, he remained in Canada, where he died in 1944.

ANON. 1938. *Am. Men Sci.*
BISLEY, G. R. 1944. A. H. Reginald Buller. *Nature* (London). Aug. 5, 1944.
BRODIE, H. J., and C. W. LOWE. 1944. *Science* n.s. 100: 305–307.
HANNA, W. F., C. W. LOWE, and E. C. STAKEMAN. 1945. *Phytopath.* 35: 577–584,
    with portrait and list of publications.
THOMSON, R. B. 1945. A. H. Reginald Buller. *Trans. Roy. Soc. Canad.*, 3rd Ser. 39:
    79–81.

Thomas Jonathan Burrill
1835–1916

Thomas Jonathan Burrill, botanist and horticulturist, was born near Pittsfield, Massachusetts on April 25, 1835, the son of John and Mary (Francis) Burrill. While Thomas was a child, the family moved to Stephenson County in northwestern Illinois. His early education was such as was offered by the primitive midwestern country schools of a hundred years ago. At the age of nineteen he entered high school in Freeport, a painfully shy and self-conscious boy. His misery drove him home; yearning for further schooling, he tried again, enrolling at Rockford. When twenty-three years old, he entered the Illinois State Normal School, from which he was graduated in 1865. From Northwestern University he received his M.S. degree in 1876, and from the University of Chicago, the Ph.D. degree in 1881, the L.L.D. from Northwestern in 1893, and from the University of Illinois in 1912.

From 1865 to 1868 Burrill served as the Superintendent of Schools in Urbana. On July 22, 1868, he married Sarah H. Alexander of Seneca Falls, New York. That same year he was appointed assistant professor of natural history at the University of Illinois. The following year he organized and conducted, with his students, a natural history survey extending from Cairo on the Ohio to Chicago. Throughout this survey, plant collections were made and note taken of climatological, geographical, and other factors. Burrill served as professor of botany from 1903 to 1912. On retirement in 1912, he was made professor emeritus. He was dean of the graduate school from 1894 to 1905, and botanist of the Illinois Agricultural Experiment Station from 1888 to 1912.

During forty years of service to his university, Burrill contributed richly and variously to its improvement as a public service institution. He was among the first American botanists to introduce and use the compound microscope as an adjunct to biological laboratory equipment. In the early part of his career as a botanist he undertook a survey of the cryptogamic flora of Illinois. This extended to consideration of certain disease-inducing bacteria, and he was subsequently able to demonstrate that bacteria as a "cause" of disease were not confined to animals. His published results were at first regarded with caution, even scorn, by botanists at home and abroad. Eventually, however, they were accepted, as also were his predictions as to the possible relation of bacteria to numerous other plant maladies.

Thus did Burrill establish himself as a pioneer in the then embryonic offshoot of botany, subsequently to be known as plant pathology. His final work was a study of soil bacteria in which he sought to purify and domesticate them by means of culture technique. Although not famous as a teacher, Burrill possessed those qualities that go to make up the genuine scientist, satisfied only with the truth.

BARRATT, J. T. 1918. Thomas Jonathan Burrill. *Phytopath.* 8: 1–4, with portrait.
DAVENPORT, E. 1917. Memorial Address. *Trans. Ill. Hort. Soc.* n.s. 50: 67–97.
TRELEASE, W. 1916. *Botan. Gaz.* 62: 153–155.

Douglas Houghton Campbell
1859–1953

Douglas Houghton Campbell, son of Judge James Valentine and Cornelia (Hotchkiss) Campbell, was born in Detroit, Michigan, December 16, 1859. There he received his early education from his parents and his Aunt Valeria Campbell. Subsequently he attended the Detroit High School. Before entering it, he had the beginnings of an herbarium and a considerable collection of insects. His inclination toward nature study was encouraged by his parents, and at no time could he recall having thought of any other career. His father, a man of many interests and profound scholarship, had built up around himself and family an environment reflecting such interests as science, literature, and the arts. His son Douglas became acquainted with the family library and with its books of travel and biology in particular, chief among which were Alfred Russel Wallace's "The Malay Archipelago," Menault's "The Intelligence of Animals, with Illustrative Anecdotes," and other equally serious works. When he was eleven years old, he received a copy of Stainton's "British Butterflies and Moths." Subsequent additions to his growing collection were Benjamin Waterhouse's "The Botanist," William Jardine's "The Naturalists Library," and Agassiz's "Introduction to the Study of Natural History."

On graduating from the Detroit High School, Campbell enrolled at the University of Michigan, where, in 1882, he was awarded the Ph.M. degree. While at Ann Arbor he received instruction from the eminent zoologist, Joseph B. Steere, Volney Morgan Spalding, the botanist, and Calvin Thomas, whose scholarship in the classical and other languages was most helpful to the young aspirant for the doctorate. Thomas, perhaps more than others, advised Campbell in his pursuit of an education. But lately returned from Germany, he counseled him to continue his postgraduate studies at the University of Michigan to fulfill the requirements for the doctorate, and then go abroad.

Campbell obtained his Ph.D. degree in 1886 and shortly thereafter left for Europe, where he spent two years. At Bonn he met Professor Strasburger under whose direction he studied cell structure and microtechnique. From Bonn, he went to Tübingen. There he met Professor Pfeffer and engaged in a study of the technique of staining living plant tissues, possibly the first study of its kind. Before returning to the United States, Campbell went to Berlin, where he spent some months with Professor Kny. There, with equipment obtained from England, he introduced the paraffin-embedding method of sectioning delicate plant material. Before he left Berlin, he was supplied with enough material of *Pilularia* by Kny to enable him to ascertain the basic facts of one of his most

important papers ("The Development of *Pilularia globulifera* L."
(1888).

Having been recommended to Dr. David Starr Jordan as a man
worthy of consideration for appointment to a botanical professorship at Indiana University, Campbell was offered the position and
forthwith accepted it. Here until the spring of 1891 he served as a
teaching and research botanist. In due season he applied himself
also to the task of writing his "Elements of Structural and Systematic Botany" (1890). This textbook was no mere laboratory manual; it reflected in very large measure Dr. Campbell himself at
work as teacher and explorer. With this text he vitalized his teaching to an extent seldom observed in botanical laboratories; he inspired his students with an interest and zeal born of facts and de-
ductions he himself had realized from his own research.

In 1891, Dr. Campbell was offered an opportunity to join the
teaching staff at Stanford University. The offer appealed to him because of the wealth of cryptogamic plant material available there
for the research he was prepared to conduct. He accepted the offer
and in due season brought out papers of fundamental worth on
Isoëtes, Osmunda, Marsilia, Azolla, and other ferns and mosses in
chronological order, until he had accumulated enough for a comprehensive summation of his results and their interpretation. This,
his second book, came out in 1895 under the title, "The Structure
and Development of the Mosses and Ferns." It was widely hailed
as a work of first importance and did much to establish Campbell's
leadership in North American botany. In 1902 Campbell published
his "University Textbook of Botany." It was the opinion of some
that his interest in research would prejudice the worth of such a
textbook. But here again much of the subject matter and nearly all
of the illustrations were his own. Devoted as he was to research,
he was inspired by a vital teacher-interest in producing a comprehensive textbook that was more than a dry-as-dust laboratory
manual.

Dr. Campbell combined happily his love of travel with that of
research. Following the publication of his textbook he visited, in
1906, the Buitenzorg Botanical Gardens in Java, Krakatau, Ceylon,
and Capetown, where he found much new and interesting bryo-
phytic material, as witness his papers on the Ophioglossaceae, the
Anthocerotaceae, *Pandanus, Angiopteris,* and *Kaulfussia* during a

period of four years. In 1911, he published "Plant Life and Evolution," which was of more popular interest. In 1912, he visited Barbados, British Guiana, Surinam, and Trinidad, and a year later the Malay Peninsula, the Philippines, Borneo, and Sumatra. The two years (1912 and 1913) spent in Caribbean and Malayan environments enabled him to add much of very substantial interest to life-history studies on a number of such plants as *Treubia*, *Aglaonema*, and *Podomitrium*. Over the years, however, his botanical interests broadened to the extent that he participated in discussions of plant geography and plant distribution. In 1926, his "Evolution of the Land Plants" came off the press, a work that in a sense assembled the fruit of his lifetime. Here was a work of 731 pages and 351 illustrations, an account of his opinions and conclusions regarding a number of controversial matters. Completed in his eightieth year, it was dedicated to Dr. F. O. Bower, a contemporary British morphologist.

Dr. Campbell was author of six books, about ninety papers of major importance to our knowledge of morphology and life history, and ninety notes and lesser papers. From the start he worked alone, collaborating in the writing of but two papers. By way of recognition of the output and quality of his scholarship and research, he was the recipient of many honors and of election to honor societies. He was a member of the National Academy of Sciences, the American Philosophical Society, the Royal Society of Edinburgh, and of the Linnaean Society of London. In addition to his professional interests he was ever interested in the arts, especially in painting and music.

Dr. Campbell passed away February 24, 1953, in his ninety-fourth year.

CAMPBELL, D. H. 1953. Autobiographical Fragment and Letters to Dr. H. B. Humphrey 1953. *Asa Gray Bull.* n.s. 2: 103–106.
HAYES, M. C. 1953. Douglas Houghton Campbell, Family, Boyhood, Youth, and Travels. *Asa Gray Bull.* n.s. 2: 107–120.
SMITH, G. M. 1956. Douglas Houghton Campbell. *Nat. Acad. Sci. Biog. Mem.* 29: 45–63, with portrait and bibliography prepared by William Campbell Steere.
STEERE, W. C. 1953. Douglas Houghton Campbell and especially his work on Bryophytes. *Asa Gray Bull.* n.s. 2: 137–140.
STEERE, W. C. 1956. *Bryologist* 56: 127–133.
WIGGINS, I. L. 1953. Twenty-eight years with Douglas Houghton Campbell. *Asa Gray Bull.* n.s. 2: 121–128.
WIGGINS, I. L. 1953. Douglas Houghton Campbell, in the Classroom and on the Campus. *Am. Fern J.* 43: 97–103.

Alvan Wentworth Chapman
1809–1899

Alvan Wentworth Chapman, botanist and physician, was born September 28, 1809, at Southampton, Massachusetts. He was a son of Paul and Ruth (Pomeroy) Chapman, of British ancestry, and was educated in local centers of schooling. At the age of sixteen he entered Amherst College, where he was graduated in 1830 with the degree of Bachelor of Arts. Shortly thereafter he moved to Georgia, where he was employed as a tutor for a family on Whitemarsh Island. In 1833, he accepted the principalship of an academy in Washington, Georgia and there commenced his study of medicine. Later, he moved to Quincy, Florida, where he engaged in the practice of surgery and continued in this capacity for more than fifty years, first at Quincy, then at Marianna, and for several years in Apalachicola. In November, 1839, he married Mrs. Mary Ann Hancock, the daughter of Benjamin Simmons of New Bern, North Carolina.

Though he was deeply interested in plant science, Chapman had received no training in any aspect of it. He collected specimens of plants that were peculiar to the semitropical complex of western Florida, which he sent to Asa Gray and John Torrey for identification. Chapman's enthusiasm and interest mounted to new heights when he realized that he was a pioneer laboring in a little-known field. For half a century he strove to acquaint himself with its plant population, and he became a recognized leader in Southern botany as Asa Gray was for that of the North. He retired from medical practice in 1880 and thenceforth devoted his entire time and energy to his favorite botanical interests. Even while still practicing medicine, he published in 1860 his "Flora of the Southern United States." The genus *Chapmania* of the family Leguminosae was named in his honor by Torrey and Gray (*see* "Flora of North America" I: 355. 1840) who, in an appended note, stated:

We dedicate this interesting genus to our friend Dr. A. W. Chapman, an accurate and indefatigable botanist, who has largely contributed to our knowledge of the plants of middle Florida.

After a long and productive life, Dr. Chapman died on April 6, 1899.

BAIN, S. M. 1928. Southern Contributions to Natural History. *J. Tenn. Acad. Sci.* 3 No. 3: 27.
KELLY, H. A. 1914. *Some American Medical Botanists Commemorated in Our Botanical Nomenclature.* The Southworth Company, Troy, N.Y. Pp. 163–164.
LAMSON-SCRIBNER, F. 1893. Southern Botanists. *Bull. Torrey Club* 20: 331–332.

Frederick Edward Clements
1874–1945

Frederic Edward Clements, son of Ephraim G. and Mary Angeline (Scoggin) Clements, was born September 16, 1874, in Lincoln, Nebraska. His parental grandparents were George and Harriet (Richards) Clements. Considering the circumstances under which he grew to boyhood and mature manhood, Frederic Edward was evidently destined to become a botanist, and by all odds an ecologist. His education was obtained in the schools and in the open country of the Great Plains of his native Nebraska. On completing his college-preparatory training, Clements entered the University of Nebraska, where he received his B.Sc. degree in 1894. Two years later he was awarded the M.A. degree and in 1898 the Ph.D. degree.

Early in his university experience it was Clements' good fortune to become a member of that dynamic group of men known as the "Botanical Seminar," under the leadership of Prof. Charles E. Bessey. The "Seminar," comprising such young men as Clements, Pound, Rydberg, Shear, Webber, Williams, and Woods, ranged far and wide over the Nebraska prairies in the interest of a "Nebraska Flora," which they had planned and, in part, had accomplished, a project ambitious and sufficiently comprehensive to include "a description of every species of plant in the state, from the simplest water-slimes to our highest and most complex flowering plants." By the time Clements was nineteen years old his

botanical interest had so widened as to include structure and nomenclature of lichens, North American hyphomycetes, plant geography, taxonomy, morphology, and plant physiology.

From 1894 to 1907, Clements distinguished himself at the University of Nebraska as instructor, then as associate professor of
botany, and as professor of plant physiology. He was then appointed professor of botany and head of the department of botany
at the University of Minnesota, responsibilities which he fulfilled
until 1917 when he was offered a research associateship in the
Carnegie Institution in Washington.

In 1899 Dr. Clements married Edith Schwartz. During the
years of their collaboration, Mrs. Clements rendered devoted assistance in the preparation and joint publication of "Rocky Mountain Flowers" (1913) and "Flower Families and Ancestors" (1928).
From 1917 until the termination of his active career, Dr. Clements
devoted himself to research in ecology under the auspices of the
Carnegie Institution of Washington. From 1917 to 1925 he and
Mrs. Clements established winter quarters in Tucson, where they
carried on their ecological research. The winter nights, however,
proved too cold for certain of their studies, so they moved to Santa
Barbara, where the climate was more equable. During the summer
they conducted research on Pikes Peak in Colorado with a view to
determining facts bearing upon the origin of plant species exposed
to the impact of physical factors peculiar to alpine environment.
In addition to his Carnegie Institution assignment, Dr. Clements
served as a consultant to the National Highway Research Board in
1935.

Clements believed that the study of the vegetation or "earth
cover" afforded the most satisfactory indicator of not only the climate but also of the climax. It is probable that one of the most important of his more debatable contributions to our knowledge of
vegetation and its ecological classification is his "The Nature and
Structure of the Climax" (Jour. Ecol. 24: 252–284, 1936). Equally
important is his "The Relict Method in Dynamic Ecology" ("Jour.
Ecol." 22: 39–68, 1934). Careful study of these two papers leaves
one with the conclusion that climax and climate are inseparably
interdependent. The climax is not merely a response to a particular climate but an indicator of it. It has been aptly said that "Dr.
Clements has given us a theory of vegetation which has formed an

indispensable foundation for the most fruitful modern work" and that he "is by far the greatest individual creator of the modern science of vegetation."

Dr. Clements was honored with membership in many scientific and professional societies in the United States and abroad, for example: the Ecological Society of America, the British Ecological Society, the Societas Phytogeographica Suecana of Sweden, Reale Academia Agricoltura of Italy, the American Association for the Advancement of Science (Fellow), the American Geographical Society, the Botanical Society of America, The American Society of Plant Physiologists, Phi Beta Kappa, and Sigma Chi. In 1940 his Alma Mater, the University of Nebraska, conferred upon him the honorary degree of LL.D. He died on July 26, 1945, in Santa Barbara, California.

ALLRED, B. W. 1945. Frederic Edward Clements. *Soil Conserv.* 11: 94.
PHILLIPS, J. 1954. A tribute to Frederic E. Clements and his concepts in ecology. *Ecology* 35: 114–115.
POOL, R. J. 1954. A memorial, Frederic Edward Clements. *Ecology* 35: 109–112, with selected publications and portrait.
POUND, R. 1954. Frederic E. Clements as I knew him. *Ecology* 35: 112–113.
SHANTZ, H. L. 1945. *Ecology* 26: 317–319.

Jane Colden

1724–1766

Jane Colden, daughter of Cadwallader and Alice (Christie) Colden, was the first woman in America to win distinction as a botanist. If we consider her background, it becomes apparent that she came naturally by her love of nature and her particular aptitude for botany. Her father was a graduate of the University of Edinburgh. He was also a correspondent of the Swedish botanist, Linnaeus, and became well known as a stateman and a man of scientific attainment. Her mother was the daughter of a Scottish clergyman.

The Coldens established themselves at Coldenham near Newburgh, New York, in 1728. Jane was then four years of age, and there she grew up. Her father, being an enthusiatic botanist, devoted considerable time to a study of the flora of Orange County, New York, that part of the state with which he was best acquainted. In this work he had the collaboration of his daughter. John and William Bartram botanized the neighboring hills and made a survey of the plant life of the Catskills. They were familiar with Coldenham, the estate of the Coldens, to which also the distinguished botanist and explorer, Peter Kalm, favorite disciple of Linnaeus, repaired.

Of a family of ten children, Jane was the fifth. Her education was obtained in its entirety from her parents. Very early she manifested an absorbing interest in botany and soon acquired, as had her father, a genuine interest in the life and career of Linnaeus. In due course she mastered the Linnaean system of plant identification and classication. Proof of this fact is borne out in many letters of that period of her life. Peter Collinson, writing to Linnaeus in May, 1756, said: "I but lately heard from Mr. Colden. He is well; but what is marvellous, his daughter is perhaps the first lady that has so perfectly studied your system. She deserves to be celebrated." John Ellis wrote to Linnaeus (April 25, 1758), that "she [Jane Colden] has drawn and described 400 plants in your method only." How many other articles should be credited to her is not known. Slender as the evidence may be, there can be but little if any doubt that her career as a botanist is worthy of note.

Jane Colden married Dr. William Farquhar, March 12, 1759; they had one child. Death claimed both the mother and child in 1766.

EAGER, S. W. 1861. Account of Jane Colden. *Newburgh Telegraph*. April 25.

CALLAHAN, S. T. 1846–1847. *An Outline History of Orange County* (*N.Y.*), Newburgh.

PURPLE, E. R. 1873. *Genealogical Notes of the Colden Family in America*. Referred to in *Dictionary of American Biography* 4: 288–289. Charles Scribner's Sons, New York. 1930.

Frank Shipley Collins
1848–1920

Frank Shipley Collins, son of Joshua Cobb and Elizabeth (Carter) Collins, was born in Boston, Massachusetts February 6, 1848. His formal education was interrupted by ill health. As a consequence, his limited contacts with nature did not favor his becoming acquainted with plant life. Much of his education was obtained at home from two aunts who were interested in botany along with certain other branches of learning. Their pupil then attended the local high school and graduated in 1863.

Aware of the desirability of earning a living, he made several more-or-less futile attempts at small mercantile opportunities. Still suffering from ill health, however, he occupied his time with the study of music. In 1875, he married Anna Lendrum Holmes. Short of money, he borrowed a considerable sum from his grandfather and spent several months in Europe, where he attended concerts in centers of musical culture. Shortly after his return from Europe, he found employment as a bookkeeper for the Malden Rubber Shoe Company. Thereafter his advancement was rapid, and he ultimately became manager of the concern. This position he held until 1913, when he retired. In 1918, he was recalled by the Company as its efficiency expert.

Collins' interest in matters botanical arose from a seemingly accidental incident during a visit to Magnolia, Massachusetts, when his perfectionist sense was aroused by some postal-card specimens of marine algae offered for sale as souvenirs. These were so obviously incorrectly named that he sought to please his fancy by trying to correct them. This sufficed to spur his interest, and he soon became engrossed in a deepening interest in the algae as a whole, a branch of botany that for many years had received little serious study in North America. Collins first familiarized himself with such species as he found in the nearby tide pools.

During the ensuing forty-five years his progress as an algologist was little short of phenomenal. His study of the taxonomy and geographic distribution of the algae extended up and down the Atlantic seaboard and included the algae of the Bermudas. Studying the collections of other students, he widened and intensified his knowledge of the algae from every American coast and became generally recognized as an authority on the marine species. He began to lecture and write about them in 1879 and, from 1899 to 1911, published a series of his algological studies in *Rhodora*. His "The Green Algae of North America," with subsequent supplemental papers, was first published by Tufts College in 1909. In 1918 the same College issued his "Working Key to the Genera of North American Algae." Collins won recognition in Europe as the leading American algologist of his time. His work had gained for him the respect of botanists in such institutions as Harvard, the Missouri Botanical Gardens, the Marine Biological Laboratory at Woods Hole, and others. His life-history studies of the algae were important examples of pioneering research in a field involving biological theories of sex.

Although Collins had never enjoyed the privilege of college training, his originality, his love of scientific accuracy, and his facility in languages made of him a valued staff member of whatever institution was fortunate enough to obtain his service. Such names as *Collinsiella tuberculata* Setchell & Gardener, a genus of green algae, and *Phaeosaccion Collinsii* Farlow, a species of brown algae, commemorate the years of consecrated study and labor of Frank Shipley Collins in his chosen field of scientific endeavor. He passed away May 25, 1920.

SETCHELL, W. A. 1925. Frank Shipley Collins, with portrait and bibliography of works. *Am. J. Botany* 12: 54–62.

John Merle Coulter
1851–1928

John Merle Coulter, son of Moses Stanley and Caroline (Crowe) Coulter, was born in Ningpo, China, on November 20, 1851. Shortly after the death of his father, his mother, with her children, returned to the United States and established her residence in Hanover, Indiana, the home of her father.

John Coulter attended the schools of Hanover, and eventually enrolled as a student at Hanover College, from which he obtained his B.A. degree in 1870 and M.A. in 1873. Nine years later the Ph.D. degree was conferred upon him by Indiana University.

It is quite probable that the most important event in Coulter's long scientific career came out of his appointment to a position as assistant geologist for the Hayden Survey of the Yellowstone country in 1872. Although his official interest in this position was geological, he found time to scout the hills and valleys for plants while his colleagues indulged in leisure-consuming activities of little or no interest to him. His keen appreciation of and interest in the plant life encountered in the survey was brought to the attention of Dr. F. V. Hayden, director of the survey, who at the moment stood in need of a botanist. He forthwith appointed Coulter to fill the position.

On terminating his obligation to the survey, Coulter accepted an appointment as professor of natural sciences at Hanover, a position he held from 1874 to 1879. During this interval he and his brother Stanley founded the "Botanical Bulletin," in its humble beginnings a monthly journal of four unpretentious pages. On completion of its second volume the "Botanical Bulletin became the Botanical Gazette," under the editorial management and direction of John Merle Coulter, who was to preside over the new journal's destinies until 1926.

Coulter's extraordinary interest in plants and all that pertained to them led him first in the direction of exploration and thence into projects of a taxonomic character. This was quite natural because it was in a field where American botanists, with few exceptions, had labored prior to the 1890's. The results of his service as botanist for the Hayden Survey gave him the opportunity to prepare and publish, in 1874, in collaboration with T. C. Porter, his "Synopsis of the Flora of Colorado." A year later his report on "The Botany of Montana, Idaho, Wyoming, and Utah" appeared. The year 1885 marked the advent of his "Manual of the Botany of the Rocky Mountain Region." It was in the early 1880's that he went to Washington to study his western collections, and there for the first time he met Asa Gray. A most happy and productive acquaintance grew out of this chance meeting which, for Coulter, was one of the crowning events of his life.

Dr. Coulter was a lifelong friend of David Starr Jordan who, on assuming the presidency of Leland Stanford, Jr., University, persuaded Coulter to accept the presidency of Indiana University (1891). The necessity of soliciting funds from state politicians proved so distasteful to him that after a term of two years he resigned to accept the presidency of Lake Forest College, an endowed institution that seemed to promise freedom from pecuniary annoyance. But here again he found that the university's financial problems absorbed too much of the time and energy he felt necessary for the pursuit of his botanical studies. Hence, after three years at Lake Forest, he accepted a call to head the department of botany at the University of Chicago (1896), where he was free to devote the next thirty years of his life to the development and usefulness of his school of botany.

Even under the weight of administrative responsibilities, Coulter did not neglect his scientific interests. In 1891–1894 his monograph, entitled, "A Manual of the Phanerogams and Pteridophytes of Western Texas," appeared. In 1909, he brought out his "North American Umbelliferae," which had been preceded by four other papers on the same family, done in collaboration with his pupil, J. N. Rose. In the same year, also, Coulter's "Manual of Rocky Mountain Botany" was published, prepared in collaboration with Aven Nelson of the University of Wyoming.

Early in Professor Coulter's career he became interested in the morphology and function of plants. This urge became increasingly pronounced, to the end that many papers and books of outstanding importance appeared as the product of his genius for research.

Chief among these were his "Morphology of Spermatophytes" (1901); "Morphology of Angiosperms" (1903); "Embryogeny of Zamia," in collaboration with C. J. Chamberlain. Then came "Development of Morphological Conceptions"(1904); "Gametophytes and Embryo of Torryea taxifolia(1905); Relations of Megaspores to Embryo Sacs in Angiosperms" (1908); "An American Lepidostrobus"(1911); "Origin of Monocotyledony" (1914); "Fundamentals of Plant Breeding (1914); and, in 1916, a text on "Evolution, Heredity, and Eugenics."

Great and far reaching as was Dr. Coulter's influence as a contributing botanist, his importance as a teacher was transcendent. Many were those whom he inspired with an unfailing zeal for botanical research, and it is commonly agreed that he was one of a significant school of American botanists whose attainments in research and as teachers of their chosen science made graduate study abroad no longer necessary. Such was his influence at Hanover, at Crawfordsville and Lake Forest, and at Indiana University. Especially was it true of his term of service at the University of Chicago, where no restrictions were imposed upon his opportunity to teach. Because of his deep interest in research and his long participation in it, he vitalized his teaching and touched off in his students the spark of intelligent endeavor.

In 1925, Doctor Coulter established his residence in Yonkers, New York, seat of the Boyce Thompson Institute for Plant Research. He had been called there by Boyce Thompson, the founder, to help organize the Institute. He spent his remaining years as its dean and chief advisor, dying in 1928.

CALDWELL, O. W., H. C. COWLES, W. CROCKER, L. R. JONES, and R. A. HARPER. 1929. John Merle Coulter. *Science* n.s. 70: 299–301.

COWLES, H. C. 1929. *Botan. Gaz.* 87: 211–217.

FULLER, G. D. 1929. *Science* n.s. 69: 177–180.

ROGERS, A. D. III. 1928. *John Merle Coulter, Missionary in Science.* Princeton University Press, Princeton, N.J.

TRELEASE, W. 1932. Biographical Memoir of John Merle Coulter. *Nat. Acad. Sci. Biog. Mem.* 14: 97–123, with bibliography by J. C. Arthur.

Frederick Vernon Coville
1867–1937

Frederick Vernon Coville, for forty-four years botanist of the U.S. Department of Agriculture, was born in Preston, Chenango County, New York on March 23, 1867. He was a son of Joseph Addison and Lydia Smith (More) Coville. His father was well known as a successful farmer in Preston and at one time was supervisor of the town and adjutant of his company in the Civil War. The son Frederick attended the Oxford (N.Y.) Academy, where he prepared for college. Following a year at Hamilton College, he obtained a transfer to Cornell University. There he devoted most of his time and effort to the study of botany and received his A.B. degree in 1887. In addition to acquitting himself with distinction as a scholar, as indicated by his election to Phi Beta Kappa and Sigma Chi, he acquired much fame in athletics and in 1887 was awarded the intercollegiate medal as "the best general athlete in New York State."

Immediately following his graduation from Cornell, Coville was appointed botanist with J. C. Branner in the geological survey of Arkansas. This appointment enabled him to prepare and publish "A List of the Plants of Arkansas." In the autumn of 1887 he returned to Cornell as an instructor in botany, but resigned in 1888 to accept the position of assistant botanist in the U.S. Department of Agriculture. On the death of Dr. George Vasey, then botanist of the Department, Coville was appointed his successor and at the same time was made curator of the National Herbarium.

His most notable achievement as a field botanist followed his appointment in 1891 as botanist of the Death Valley Expedition. His published report, entitled "Botany of the Death Valley Expedition," was one of the earliest of the critical studies of desert plant life and is widely accepted as a classic. A dozen years later, as an authority on desert vegetation, he was an able counselor to the Carnegie Institution of Washington in its founding of the Desert Botanical Laboratory at Tucson, Arizona.

Another of Coville's authoritative contributions to botanical knowledge was his paper on the Juncaceae of America. This and a similar treatise on the family Grossulariaceae (currants and gooseberries) were published as a part of Britton and Brown's "Illustrated Flora of the Northern United States and Canada."

Coville's botanical interests were sufficiently broad to encompass the field in a number of its more practical aspects, as witness his establishment of a seed laboratory for the sake of seed purification and standardization. He did much also to help shape the policies affecting the use of national forest lands for grazing purposes and to build up an excellent scientific library in the Department of Agriculture.

From 1910 until his death, his chief interest was the experimental culture and improvement of blueberries. Most of the improved varieties now found in commercial production are the result of Coville's initiative and sound, discriminatory judgment and his twenty-five years of hybridization and varietal selection of wild species. At the time of his death, most of these varieties, known as *Coville hybrids*, were known to the trade as "Tru-Blu-Berries" and were grown and marketed by the Blueberry Cooperative Association in New Jersey and North Carolina.

Coville was also actively interested in the standardization of plant names and was to a large extent responsible for "Standardized Plant Names" as published under the editorship of Harlan P. Kelsey and Frederick Law Olmstead, a book of value to workers in many plant fields. He wrote many of the botanical definitions for the "Century Dictionary" and was the author of two hundred or more technical papers. In 1921, George Washington University conferred upon him the honorary degree of D.Sc. Ten years later the Massachusetts Horticultural Society, in recognition of his "outstanding work for horticulture," awarded him the George Robert White medal of honor.

Coville held membership in a number of scientific societies, notable among which were the American Association for the Advancement of Science, the Washington (D.C.) Academy of Sciences, the Botanical Society of America, and the National Geographic Society, of which he was for several years a director. He also was a member of the Cosmos Club, the Biologists' Field Club, and the Arts Club (Washington, D.C.).

Dr. Coville was married at Lockport, New York, on October 4, 1890, to Elizabeth Harwood. To this union were born five children. Death claimed their father on January 9, 1937.

Maxon, W. R. 1937. Frederick Vernon Coville. *Science* n.s. 85: 280–281.
Pieters, A. J. 1895. Sketch of Mr. F. V. Coville. *Asa Gray Bull.* 3: 37.

Henry Chandler Cowles
1869–1939

Henry Chandler Cowles was born on February 27, 1869, at Kensington, Connecticut. He received his elementary and high school training in the schools of his native state and then attended Oberlin College. He graduated from Oberlin in 1893 and was appointed an instructor of natural science at Gates College (Waterloo, Iowa) for the year 1894–1895. In 1895 he was granted a graduate fellowship at the University of Chicago. He followed geology as his major interest until the appointment of John Merle Coulter as head of the department of botany in 1896. Cowles then became one of the first graduate students in Dr. Coulter's department. It was at this time that Warming's epochal text on plant ecology became available, a book that provided Cowles with the inspiration that led him to prepare for a career in botany rather than geology.

In 1898, Cowles was awarded the Ph.D. degree, for which he presented his monumental thesis on the vegetation of the sand dunes of Lake Michigan. Subsequently his "Physiographic Ecology of Chicago and Vicinity" appeared, a paper in which he presented an ecologic concept, the principle of which maintained that a classification, to be valid, must be dynamic and genetic. These two monographs were of such basic importance as to serve as models of excellence and scientific soundness for many students of ecology of that and later generations.

Dr. Cowles became a member of the botanical faculty of the University of Chicago in 1897. He was several times promoted and, in 1911, became a professor in the department. In 1925 he was honored with the chairmanship of the department, a position he continued to hold to the day of his retirement in 1934.

As a leader in his chosen branch of plant science, he was an international figure. As a teacher he had few rivals, a fact testified to by the many able students who went out from his laboratory. His classroom was the great outdoors, where the dynamics of plant life in relation to environment was worked out. Recognition of his leadership was made manifest in 1930, when, on the occasion of the International Botanical Congress held in Cambridge, England, he was chosen president of the section on plant geography and ecology.

William S. Cooper of the University of Minnesota had this to say of his great teacher, Dr. Cowles:

He may relinquish his active labors secure in the consciousness of work well done, confident of achievement beyond the ordinary lot. He has laid the foundation for a new and useful branch of science, he has constructively influenced the thought of hundreds of investigators and teachers, and in his professional and personal contacts he has made for himself a multitude of devoted friends. Fortunate and happy is the man with a record of accomplishment so thoroughly satisfying. Such good fortune and such happiness are the undoubted right and privilege of Henry Chandler Cowles.

Dr. Cowles passed away in Chicago on September 12, 1939.

Cooper, W. S. 1935. Henry Chandler Cowles. *Ecology* 16: 281–283, with portrait.
Fuller, G. D. 1939. *Science* n.s. 90: 363–364.
Kraus, E. J. 1940. *Botan. Gaz.* 101: 241–242.

Moses Ashley Curtis
1808–1872

Moses Ashley Curtis was born May 11, 1808 at Stockbridge, Massachusetts and died at Hillsborough, North Carolina on April 10, 1872. He was the son of the Rev. Jared and Thankful (Ashley) Curtis, daughter of Gen. Moses Ashley, for many years chaplain of the state prison at Charlestown, Massachusetts. The college-preparatory education of son Moses was obtained in his father's private school, where he was fitted for entrance to Williams College; he graduated from there in 1827. Three years later he moved to Wilmington, North Carolina, where he found employment as a tutor in the household of Governor Dudley until 1833. He then returned to Massachusetts to study for the ministry. In 1834 he married Mary de Rosset of Wilmington, North Carolina, and, in 1835, was ordained for the ministry. In 1837 he tried his hand at teaching and, for two years, served in that capacity in an Episcopal school at Raleigh, North Carolina.

Because of poor health he abandoned his adventure into pedagogy and took to the nearby mountains, there to recuperate and, incidentally, to acquaint himself with the mountain flora. This he did to an extent attained by few, if any, of those who had gone before him. His interest in botany had been aroused by Prof. Amos Eaton at Williams College, and his first paper, a rather remarkable document entitled "Enumeration of Plants Growing Spontaneously Around Wilmington, N.C." ("Boston J. Nat. Hist.," May, 1833) was the more interesting because of the author's seemingly limited training in taxonomy and floristics. The paper was an account of a survey of the Coastal Plain plant life within a radius of two miles of Wilmington; the author recorded his discovery of as many phanerogamic species as had been recorded for the state up to that time.

Until that time very little attention had been given the lower forms of plant life such as the fungi, lichens, algae, etc. As early as 1845, Curtis became interested in the lichens and began collecting them for Tuckerman, the lichenologist. Work in this field soon led Curtis into the exploration of the much richer and more rewarding study of the fungi. Shortly thereafter he was corresponding with the Swedish botanist, Fries of Upsala. Even though Curtis covered the same region that a few years earlier had been covered by De Schweinitz, Curtis discovered many species then new to science. He developed an excellent herbarium from which the herbaria of Farlow, Peck, and Bessey were enriched.

In 1847 he began corresponding with Berkeley, the British authority on the fungi, and thus there grew a devoted friendship of more than ordinary importance to the progress of mycology in America and elsewhere in the world. The series of papers, published under title of "North American Fungi," had its beginning in 1872, after Professor Curtis' death. Based as it was on the fruits of a joint undertaking of many years' duration, this contribution was much more than a collection of fungi, for the specimens were accompanied by annotations of the utmost value to the study of the collection.

In 1860 Curtis saw the publication of his "Geological and Natural History Survey of North America," Part III, "Botany: Containing a Catalogue of the Plants of the State, with Descriptions and History of the Trees, Shrubs, and Woody Vines." This was followed in 1867 by what may be considered the most comprehensive and scholarly treatise on the state flora that had been published up to that time. This work was accompanied by a list of the phanerogamic species and much that was and is of interest to students of the fungi.

The death of Professor Curtis occurred on April 10, 1872.

GRAY, A. 1873. Botanical necrology. *Am. J. Sci.* 3rd Ser. 5: 391–393.
SHEAR, C. L., and N. E. STEVENS. 1919. The mycological work of Moses Ashley Curtis. *Mycologia.* 11: 181–201.
YOUMANS, W. J., ed. 1889. Sketch of Moses Ashley Curtis. *Pop. Sci. Monthly* 34: 405–410.
LAMSON-SCRIBNER, F. 1893. Southern botanists. *Bull. Torrey Club* 20: 321–324.

Otis Freeman Curtis

1888–1949

Otis Freeman Curtis, plant physiologist, son of William Willis and Lydia Virginia (Cone) Curtis, was born February 12, 1888, in Sendai, Japan, and died July 4, 1949, while on vacation at Cape Cod, Massachusetts. He left Japan at the age of seven and received his early education in various places in the United States. Having completed his college entrance requirements, he registered at Oberlin College, where he received his Bachelor of Arts degree in 1911. While at Oberlin he was led, through the influence of Susan Percival Nichol, to engage in a serious study of botany.

Having received a scholarship at Oberlin, he devoted the summer of 1911 and 1912 to botanical study at Woods Hole. For further postgraduate study he entered Cornell University where, in 1916, he received his Ph.D. On August 27, 1913, he and Lucy Marguerite Weeks were married. From 1913 to the day of his death, Dr. Curtis remained at Cornell, first as instructor and later as assistant professor of botany and, from 1922, as plant physiologist at the State Agricultural Experiment Station.

Although he devoted much time and effort to teaching while at Cornell, he found time for research and publication of its results. Altogether about thirty papers, chiefly in the field of plant physiology, are to his credit. He and his graduate students devoted much time to the study of translocation, and his monograph on the subject was an outstandingly useful contribution.

Dr. Curtis was a visiting professor at the University of Leeds, England, 1926–1927, and at Ohio State University, 1930–1931. He was a member of the American Association for the Advancement of Science, the Botanical Society of America, and The American Society of Plant Physiologists. He died at the age of 61, leaving a wife, two sons, and a daughter.

KNUDSON, L., and D. C. CLARK. 1949. Otis Freeman Curtis 1888–1949. *Plant Physiol.* 24, No. 4: ix, x.

William Darlington
1782–1863

William Darlington, son of Edward and Hannah (Townsend) Darlington, was born April 28, 1782, near the ancient village of Dilworth (now Dilworthstown), Chester County, Pennsylvania. As a boy he lived on a farm, where he cultivated the soil and developed his powers of observation. His boyhood teacher was John Forsythe, an exceptionally able man and pedagog. In due course, Darlington studied medicine under John Vaughn of Wilmington, Delaware, and in 1804 received his M.D. degree from the University of Pennsylvania. At this institution he received unusually thorough instruction in medical botany, a fact that no doubt sharpened his resolve to devote more and more of his leisure time to the collection and study of plants and to botany in general.

In 1808 William Darlington and Catherine, the daughter of Gen. John Lacey, were married. This event took place after his return from Calcutta, where he had gone while serving for two years as a surgeon on a ship. On the outbreak of the War of 1812 he was appointed major in the Army but saw no active service. He devoted the rest of his life to the practice of medicine, at times taking an active part in politics and finance. But it was as a botanist that he became best known. Here was the one life pursuit that singled him out from among his fellows. His contributions to the then none-too-voluminous knowledge of botany, were highly esteemed. Of particular note were his "Florula Cestrica" (1826) and "Flora Cestrica," published eleven years later. His "Reliquiae Baldwinianae," a biographical treatise and collection of the writings of William Baldwin, the naturalist, appeared in 1843 and his "Memorials of John Bartram and Humphry Marshall" in 1849. In 1859, he published his "American Weeds and Useful Plants," a work of considerable practical worth to agriculture and of interest to arts and crafts.

The true stature of Dr. Darlington the botanist is not fully reflected in published works. Any adequate measure of the man calls for the testimony of those who knew him and who were familar with his total performance. He enjoyed a wide correspondence with naturalists of his day and was highly respected by those who became acquainted with his integrity and character. Asa Gray referred to him as the "Nestor of American Botany." One cannot rightly say that he was a leader of it, even in his own day; yet he was then, and is even today, held in high esteem as a botanist.

A pitcher plant, then new to science, was discovered in 1841 by W. D. Brackenridge, assistant botanist, U.S. Exploring Expedition under Captain Wilkes, who at the time was on duty in northern California. This plant was identified by Dr. John Torrey and dedicated by him in 1853 under the generic name *Darlingtonia*, in honor of Dr. Darlington.

In addition to his service as a physician, and his political and business activities, Dr. Darlington amassed an herbarium of some 8,000 species of plants, which he bequeathed to the Chester County (Pa.) Cabinet. The entire collection and most of his private library later became the property of the West Chester State Normal School. In 1848 Yale College conferred upon Dr. Darlington the degree of Doctor of Laws. He passed away April 23, 1863.

HARSHBERGER, J. W. 1899. *The Botanists of Philadelphia and Their Works.* T. C. Davis & Sons, Philadelphia.

JAMES, T. P. 1862–1864. *Proc. Am. Philos. Soc.* 9: 330–342.

KELLY, H. A. 1914. *Some American Medical Botanists.* The Southworth Company, Troy, New York.

SHARPLESS, W. T. 1932. Dr. William Darlington, Physician and Botanist. *Bartonia* 14: 1–13.

Chester Dewey

1784–1867

Chester Dewey, botanist, clergyman, and educator, was born October 25, 1784, in Sheffield, Massachusetts. He was the son of Stephen and Elizabeth (Owen) Dewey and was a descendant of Thomas Dewey, one of the earliest settlers of Dorchester, Massachusetts. He grew to early manhood on a farm, with its rigors and occasional emergencies that called for ready initiative. Young Chester early manifested an interest in plant and animal life as he found it all about him on the farm; minerals and ways of the weather fascinated him and surely revealed his scientific aptitude.

Having completed his elementary schooling, Dewey entered Williams College at eighteen and was graduated in 1806, prepared to enter the ministry. After a brief pastorate, however, he returned to Williams as a teacher. From 1810 to 1827 he occupied a professorship in mathematics and natural philosophy. During this time he devoted much effort to the development of laboratory courses in physics and chemistry and to building up museum collections in geology and botany. Through his own personal effort and by resort to exchange of specimens by way of correspondence, he was able to develop well-organized collections of basic importance to the excellent museum of his Alma Mater.

From 1827 to 1836 he was principal of the Pittsfield, Massachusetts, Gymnasium and from 1836 to 1850 of the Rochester, New York, High School, later known as the Collegiate Institute. The University of Rochester was founded in 1850 and Dewey was that year selected professor of chemistry and natural sciences. By experience and natural aptitude he was well qualified for the position and continued in it until his retirement in 1861 as professor emeritus. He was a gifted teacher and popular lecturer in chemistry and botany. For years he recorded meteorological information of first interest to residents of Rochester—information based on daily weather readings from 1837 until the day of his death.

His published botanical papers included a series of contributions on the sedges entitled "Caricography." Never assembled in a single volume, these were referred to by Asa Gray as an "elaborate monograph patiently prosecuted through more than 40 years." It is worthy of note also that Dr. Gray classed Dewey with De Schweinitz and Torrey in his botanical attainment, saying that "they laid the foundation and insured the popularity of the study of sedges in this country." Dewey also prepared for publication a report on the herbaceous plants and on the quadrupeds of Massachusetts, which was published by the state in 1840. His work as a botanist was memorialized in the naming of the genus *Deweya*, a genus of plants belonging to the family Umbelliferae.

Professor Dewey was twice married: first, to Sarah Dewey in 1810, and again, in 1825, to Olivia Hart Pomeroy. Five children were born to the first union and ten to the second.

ANDERSON, M. B. 1870. Sketch of the Life of Prof. Chester Dewey. *Smithsonian Inst. Ann. Report* 231–240.

GRAY, A. 1868. Obituary. *Am. J. Sci.* 2nd Ser. 45: 122–123.

SEELYE, C. W. 1900. A Memorial Sketch of Chester Dewey. M.D., D.D. *Proc. Rochester Acad. Sci.* 3: 182–185.

SPRING, L. W. 1917. *History of Williams College.* Houghton Mifflin Company, New York.

William Russell Dudley
1849–1911

William Russell Dudley, a descendant of New England forbears, was born at North Guilford, Connecticut, March 1, 1849. The home of his youth was a farm, and here it was that he early acquired an insatiable taste for nature and particularly for things botanical. He early determined to obtain an education and, in 1870, applied for admission to the then young Cornell University, where for a time he paid his way by milking cows at the University farm. In due course he was appointed botanical collector, and, from the day of that appointment, he did not cease to grow in his chosen profession. Dudley was graduated from Cornell in 1874, and two years later he received the degree of Master of Science. In 1876 he was promoted to the rank of assistant professor of botany, which he held until 1892. That year he was offered the headship of systematic botany at Stanford University, a position he held until 1911.

While Professor Dudley was yet at Cornell he was granted leave of absence for one year (1880) to serve as acting professor of biology at Indiana University, in the absence of David Starr Jordan, then head of the department of biology there. In 1887, he was again granted leave to pursue graduate study, chiefly on the fungi, at the universities of Strassburg and Berlin. A man of quiet but nonetheless real enthusiasm, he began at the outset of his career at Stanford to build up a well-ordered and comprehensive collection, which may be considered his most important contribution to our knowledge of the plant life of California. This extensive herbarium he donated to the University, there to become the nucleus of its ever-growing botanical collection, today known as the Dudley Herbarium.

Professor Dudley early became actively interested in problems of forest preservation and was frequently consulted by Gifford Pinchot, then United States forester, for information and counsel regarding matters pertaining to the development of national forests in California. He took an active interest in the organization and activities of the Sempervirens Club, devoted to the protection and preservation of the Coast redwood (*Sequoia sempervirens*) and was instrumental in bringing about the establishment of the California Redwood Park, until then known as the Big Basin, a forested tract of 2,500 acres in the Santa Cruz Mountains.

Most important among Dudley's published works are: "The Cayuga Flora" (1886); "A Catalogue of the Flowering Plants and Vascular Cryptogams found in and near Lackawanna and Wyoming Valleys" (1892); "The Genus *Phyllospadix*"; and "Vitality of the *Sequoia gigantea*." All of his published work was characterized by extreme care and accuracy, a fact largely accounting for the rather slender output of a botanist who lacked neither diligence nor originality.

As a teacher Professor Dudley had few equals. His great enthusiasm and his wholesome influence led his students to come away from his laboratories with superior preparation and promise in research and teaching. For many years Dudley was in poor health and died in Los Altos, California on June 4, 1911.

Campbell, D. H. 1911. *William Russell Dudley*. Dudley Memorial Volume, Leland Stanford Junior University publication. University Series. Stanford University Press, Stanford, Calif.

Jordan, D. S. 1911. William Russell Dudley. *Science* 34: 142–145, with bibliography.

Pierce, G. J. 1911. *Plant World* 14: 200–202.

Benjamin Minge Duggar
1872–1956

Benjamin M. Duggar was one of the country's outstanding botanists. Although primarily a mycologist and pathologist, he came to be recognized also as an authority in physiology, primarily, though by no means exclusively, physiology of the fungi.

He was born September 1, 1872, in Gallion, Alabama, the fourth of six sons of Reuben H. and Margaret Louisa (Minge) Duggar. His grade- and high-school education was obtained at a private school and from tutors, and he entered the University of Alabama at the youthful age of fifteen. He remained there only two years before transferring to the Mississippi A. & M. College. This move was apparently prompted by an increasing interest in the general field of botany. Two years later, in 1891, he graduated with first honors. While at the Mississippi school, Duggar assisted in research involving introduction of exotic forage grasses, displaying an interest and ability in plant research unusual in an undergraduate.

The next year, at nineteen, Duggar enrolled as assistant in mycology and plant pathology at Alabama Polytechnic Institute to work toward his Master of Science degree. This degree was granted the next year and was followed almost immediately by an opportunity to continue the agrostology research initiated at Mississippi in the form of an offer of the assistant directorship of the Canebrake Agricultural Experiment Station at Uniontown, Alabama. This was accepted and, during the brief stay of one year there, he continued his research on introduced grasses. The problems encountered, however, must have convinced the young scientist that he needed additional and broader training. In any event, he enrolled at Harvard University to work toward his Master of Arts degree. Additional basic courses were required for this degree, which when completed made him eligible for a B.A. from Harvard College. This was granted in 1894 and the M.A. the following year.

While at Alabama Polytechnic Institute, Duggar was working under the eminent botanist George F. Atkinson. Atkinson was soon to move to Cornell University, where he was followed not long after (1896) by Duggar to work on his doctorate. While working toward this degree, he was on the Cornell staff as assistant cryptogamic botanist and instructor in botany. The Ph.D. was granted in 1898, for which he wrote a thesis in cytology. The next two years (1899–1900) were spent largely in Europe continuing studies on the physiology of fungus-spore germination that he had initiated at Cornell.

On Duggar's return to Cornell in the fall of 1900 he was appointed assistant professor of plant physiology. The appointment was of short duration, however, as he accepted a position as plant physiologist with the U.S. Bureau of Plant Industry the following year. In this capacity he initiated studies of cotton diseases and mushroom culture in the South. Again, the appointment proved to be a brief one, and the next year (1902) he was appointed professor of botany and head of the department at the University of Missouri. The studies initiated with the Bureau of Plant Industry were continued, however, in his new joint capacity as professor of botany and collaborator with the Bureau.

Duggar remained at Missouri only five years, but during this period he began and essentially completed the text, "Fungous Diseases of Plants," the first textbook on the subject to be published in this country. In 1907, two years before the book was published, he was tendered the chair in plant physiology at Cornell University. Another text, "Plant Physiology," was completed while there, prior to his leaving in 1912. In that year he moved again to a new position, where he apparently felt the opportunity to contribute and serve was greater. The move was to Washington University and the Missouri Botanical Garden at St. Louis. He was appointed research professor of plant physiology in charge of graduate work in the Henry Shaw School of Botany.

Duggar remained at St. Louis until 1927, a period that saw his interests turning more and more into physiological channels. His lines of investigation, though dealing to a considerable extent with various phases of plant physiology, were broad, ranging from tomato pigmentation to nitrogen fixation, transpiration, salt requirements of phanerogams, and techniques for the determination of hydrogen-ion concentration in plant and animal fluids. Several publications resulted from these studies, as well as several from a study of tobacco-mosaic virus. This latter research, which was pursued primarily after 1920, resulted in his major contribution during the Washington University period.

Duggar left St. Louis in 1927 to accept a position at the University of Wisconsin as professor of plant physiology and economic botany. Here he remained until his retirement to emeritus status in 1943 at the age of seventy-one. Still extremely active, both mentally and physically, and with a wealth of knowledge and experience useful in medical research, he was employed as consultant in mycological research and production by the Lederle Laboratories division of the American Cyanamid Company. The research that he pursued involved development of antibiotics and led to his discovery of chlortetracycline, the first broad spectrum antibiotic made available for the treatment of disease. Under Duggar's able leadership aureomycin was isolated and became available for commercial use. This final phase of his career as a scientist was to last for twelve years until his death in 1956. It constituted a fitting final chapter to a life dedicated throughout to finding new facts through the scientific method and the application of these facts to human needs.

Duggar's active participation in scientific affairs and the esteem in which he was held by his fellow workers is indicated by the organizations to which he belonged, the offices held in many of them, and the other honors he received during his scientific career.

He was a Fellow of the American Association for the Advancement of Science (V.P. Section G, 1925); member of the National Academy of Sciences, American Philosophical Society, Philadelphia Academy of Science, Botanical Society of America (Pres. 1923), American Society of Plant Physiologists (Pres. 1946–47), American Society of Agronomy (V.P. 1908), American Phytopathological Society, American Chemical Society, American Society of Naturalists (V.P. 1928), Society of Experimental Biology and Medicine, Society for Industrial Microbiology (Pres. 1952), American Public Health Association, Torrey Botanical Club, National Research Council (Chairman, Division of Biology and Agriculture, 1925–26), Phi Beta Kappa, Sigma Xi, Phi Sigma; Chairman of Organizing Committee and General Secretary, International Congress of Plant Sciences, Ithaca, New York, 1926; Editor for Physiology, Botanical Abstracts, 1917–26, and Biological Abstracts, 1926–33; Editor, Biological effects of radiation, 2 v. McGraw-Hill, New York, 1936. 2019 p.; Trustee, Woods Hole Marine Biological Laboratory, Woods Hole Oceanographic Institution, and Bermuda Biological Station. He was an honorary fellow of the International College of Surgeons, an honorary member of La Societa Lancisiana di Roma. He was awarded the honorary LL.D. degree by the University of Missouri in 1944, the Sc.D. by Washington University in 1953 and by the University of Wisconsin in 1956, the Medal of Honor of Public Education of Venezuela and a medal from The Pasteur Institute in 1951, and in the same year a decoration from Pope Pius XII for his services to mankind (Keitt).

About the time Duggar joined the Bureau of Plant Industry staff in 1901, he and Marie L. Robertson were married. She died in 1922, but to them were born five children, two sons and three daughters. He was married a second time to Elsie Rist on June 6, 1927, and they had one daughter.

Duggar had a variety of interests in addition to his scientific pursuits. Like most botanists he liked to be out of doors, doing instead of merely looking on. He was an ardent fisherman, an enthusiastic gardener, and he enjoyed the outlet provided by golf, tennis, and bowling.

The personal facets of a man's life are best known by his friends. The following excerpt from a letter addressed to the author by Dr. Paul E. Hoppe, reveals Duggar as a man with a zest for living and a keen interest in many things.

Dr. Duggar was a man of widely varied interests—"you name it, and he had it." He was endowed with an unusual capacity to keenly enjoy menial tasks. We were fishing partners for about 20 years and jointly owned a row boat which we calked and painted each spring to make it second to none in durability and appearance when we shoved it in the water on opening day. No academic problem could interfere when that pleasurable time came for getting our fishing boat ready for the season's activities.

Duggar was an excellent cook. He always took over on those duties on our fishing trips to the North Woods. Yes, we fared well at the table when Ben Duggar was the chef. His real specialty though was making jellies and jams. We frequently went berry picking in the woods and he would then make an assortment of those sweets to serve on those pre-dawn breakfasts we enjoyed at his home prior to taking off for the early morning fishing on Lake Mendota.

I have been a stamp collector all my life and believed this to be one activity of interest that Dr. Duggar somehow had overlooked. One evening while I was working over some stamps Duggar happened to drop in and I was surprised at the knowledge he had of matters in the philatelic field. He told me that while at Harvard he had sold Confederate stamps and covers for an uncle on a commission basis. The commission he realized from the stamp sales about paid for his expenses while at Harvard.

The same evening Dr. Duggar said he thought he still had some odds and ends—remnants of the Harvard material in his basement and that if he could find it would bring it over. The following evening Duggar brought over a dust-covered shoe box filled with 19th Century philatelic material that would make any stamp collector's heart throb.

AINSWORTH, G. C. 1950. Professor B. M. Dugger. *Nature* 178: 834–835.
KEITT, G. W. 1957. Benjamin Minge Duggar: 1872–1956. *Mycologia* 49: 434–438.
STAKMAN, E. C. 1957. B. M. Duggar, Pioneer in Precise Plant Research. *Science* n.s. 126: 690–691.
WALKER, J. C. 1958. Benjamin Minge Duggar: September 1, 1872–September 10, 1956. *Nat. Acad. Sci. Biog. Mem.* 32: 113–131.
WALKER, J. C. 1957. Benjamin Minge Duggar, 1872–1956. *Phytopath.* 47: 379–380.

Élie Magloire Durand

1794–1873

Élie Magoire Durand, pharmacist and botanist, though a native of France, spent the greater part of his life in the United States, where he was known as Elias Durand. He was born in Mayenne, France, the youngest of fourteen children. His father, André Durand, was a recorder of deeds in Mayenne, where Élie's school days began. He early showed ability in chemistry, and at fourteen was apprenticed to a chemist and pharmacist in Mayenne. On completing his apprenticeship, he finished his technical training with a year's study in Paris. He was then commissioned as a pharmacist in the French army, in 1813, which commission he resigned in April, 1814, after a year and two months of service. He again joined the army and, following Napoleon's defeat at Waterloo, returned to Nantes, where he had earlier established himself.

From Nantes he embarked for America on April 16, 1816, and landed in New York two and a half months later. For some years he led a roving existence, met several men of science, found employment that made demands on his knowledge of chemistry, studied English, and finally, in Baltimore, entered into partnership with Edme Ducatel. There he began his career as a botanist. He withdrew from the partnership in 1824 and in 1825 established an apothecary shop in Philadelphia the like of which had not been seen in America. To make it resplendent and attractive, he went to Paris, where he purchased heavy glass furnishings, porcelain ware, mahogany cabinet cases, and marble counters. He had collected many valuable books, and of these he made a library to which he added a number of technical journals.

His was something other than the commonplace drugstore; it was a rendezvous for botanists as well as for physicians. He gave financial aid to an occasional botanical explorer and in return sometimes accepted their plant collections. Thus, for example, he acquired the herbarium of Thomas Nuttall and the rat-gnawn collections of Rafinesque. To satisfy his own instinct for exploration and discovery, he explored the Dismal Swamp of Virginia in 1837, the Appalachians of Pennsylvania in 1862, and made several lesser excursions with some of his scientist friends, including Joseph Bonaparte of Bordentown, New Jersey.

He made his drug business over to his son and thereafter was free to devote the rest of his time to his botanical activities. In 1868 he went again to Paris and took with him his herbarium of more than 10,000 species and 100,000 specimens. This he presented to the Musée du Jardin des Plantes, where it was placed in a special room as the Herbier Durand. From his own collections he added materially to the herbarium of the Philadelphia Academy of Natural Sciences. He also gave his botanical library to the Academy; and to the Philadelphia College of Pharmacy he donated his collection of published works on pharmacy and chemistry and a herbarium of medicinal plants. To this same College of Pharmacy he had earlier given a general herbarium of some 12,000 specimens.

Élie Magloire Durand was twice married: first, in November, 1820, to Polymnia Rose Ducatel, who died on February 18, 1822. Again he married, October 25, 1825, Marie Antoinette Berauld, who died in 1851. Durand himself lived until August 14, 1873. His published writings on botany and chemistry are listed in the "Catalogue of Scientific Papers Compiled by the Royal Society of London," Volumes II, VII, and IX.

Anon. 1873. Elias Durand. *Bull. Torrey Bot. Club* 4: 45–47.
Gray, A. 1873. *Am. J. Sci.* 3rd Ser. 6: 316–317.
Harshberger, J. 1899. *The Botanists of Philadelphia and Their Works.* T. C. Davis & Sons, Philadelphia.

Daniel Cady Eaton
1834–1895

Daniel Cady Eaton, born September 12, 1834, at Fort Gratiot, Michigan, was the son of Gen. Amos B. and Elizabeth (Selden) Eaton. His paternal grandfather, Amos Eaton, was a scientist and educator, author of an early manual of botany and other texts of interest to botanists. He was a teacher of botany at Yale College and was well known for his versatility and his power to inspire and develop somewhat more than a superficial interest in whatever subject it was his duty to present to his pupils.

His grandson, Daniel Cady Eaton, early aspired to become a teacher of botany and to be a student at Yale, where his grandfather had taught. Even as an undergraduate at Yale, he corresponded with such men as Gray, Torrey, and Sullivant and made considerable progress in acquiring a basic knowledge of cryptogamous plants. His plant collections formed the foundation of what later became the large herbarium that today bears the name of its founder. In his third year in college he had progressed so far as to be able to describe a number of hitherto unidentified ferns from California. Eaton was graduated from Yale in 1857 and thereupon matriculated at Harvard College, where he spent three years. At that time Alvan Wentworth Chapman was at work on his "Flora of the Southern United States." The section of it on the ferns was assigned to and adequately executed by Professor Eaton. In addition to this, Eaton published a number of papers describing ferns collected in Venezuela, Cuba, Japan, and territory along the Mexican boundary.

On the outbreak of the Civil War, Eaton joined the Union Army and served in the commissary department with headquarters in New York City. On the establishment of a professorship of botany in Yale College in 1864, he was chosen to fill the position and in it continued his research and teaching for the rest of his active life. He is best and most widely known for his work on the taxonomy of the ferns. His "Ferns of North America" (1877–1880) is a monumental contribution, beautifully illustrated and of comprehensive scope. His later active years were devoted to a study of mosses and liverworts and to contributing botanical definitions to "Webster's International Unabridged Dictionary." Throughout Eaton's career as a botanist his work was characterized by scrupulous devotion to accuracy in portrayal and description.

Professor Eaton married Caroline Ketcham of New York City on February 13, 1866. He died in his sixty-first year, June 29, 1895.

BRITTON, N. L. 1895. *Science*. n.s. 2: 57–58.
DAVENPORT, G. E. 1895. Daniel Cady Eaton. *Botan. Gaz.* 20: 366–369.
SETCHELL, W. A. 1895. *Bull. Torrey Club* 22: 341–351, with portrait and bibliography.

Job Bicknell Ellis
1829–1905

Job Bicknell Ellis, son of Freeman and Sarah Ellis, was born in a farm home near Potsdam, New York, January 21, 1829. As a boy he found only intermittent leisure for school attendance, being occupied much of the time with farm duties. He early manifested an innate urge to study and was from his early youth interested in nature. His parents encouraged him to make the most of his opportunity to acquire an education. At sixteen he was appointed to teach in a country school at Stockholm, New York, at a salary of 10 dollars per month, one-half of which he received in cash and the balance in grain.

He worked his own way through the local academy and thereupon registered at Union College in Schenectady at the age of twenty. Two years later he was granted the B.A. degree. At Union College he received his introduction to college botany and was so favorably impressed that he resolved to continue his pursuit of the subject. He was a diligent collector, and he devoted much attention to the collection and study of the fungi while engaged in teaching at Germantown, Pennsylvania, and while stationed at Albany, New York.

At Albany he became acquainted with George H. Cook, a gifted and competent teacher of natural science, who did much to inspire Ellis's interest in botany. Up to this time, Ellis had had little access to the literature on the fungi; but, in 1857, he chanced upon a published announcement of a book, "Fungi Caroliniani Exsiccati" by H. W. Ravenel. Thereafter he began corresponding with Ravenel, who exchanged specimens with him and gave him much valued aid. Ellis, in 1856, was teaching in the South, but, due to an unhappy incident in which he was informed that because he was from the North he would not succeed as a teacher in the South— and he did not—he returned to Potsdam. There on April 15, 1856, he married Arvilla J. Bacon, whose interest in botany enabled her to be of manifest assistance to her husband in his mycological studies. In 1864 he enlisted in the United States Navy and did not resume his active interest in mycology until after the close of the Civil War.

At Newfield, New Jersey, he purchased a home, where he spent much of his time on the fungi—collecting, studying, and exchanging them, and devoting attention to an ever-increasing correspondence. In 1878 he undertook the preparation and distribution of sets of North American fungi and thereafter devoted much time and energy to his mycological research. This undertaking proved to be an engrossing one, and out of it grew one of the most comprehensive of all the mycological collections that had been made up until that time in America. It is now in the Herbarium of the New York Botanical Garden, where it is available to mycologists from all parts of the world. Through his published works and his other mycological activities, Ellis contributed much to our knowledge of the fungi and won for himself widespread recognition as an authority in his chosen field of scientific endeavor. With the collaboration of B. M. Everhart, he published his most important work, "The North American Pyrenomycetes." He passed away December 30, 1905, at his home in Newfield, New Jersey.

ANDERSON, F. W. 1890. A biographical sketch of J. B. Ellis. *Botan. Gaz.* 15: 299–304, portrait p. 241.
KELLERMAN, W. A. 1906. Obituary, Job Bicknell Ellis. *J. Mycol.* 12: 41–45.

George Engelmann
1809–1884

George Engelmann, American botanist and man of science, was born February 2, 1809, in Frankfurt am Main, Germany. He was the eldest of thirteen children. As to parentage he was a favored child: his father, George Engelmann, was a doctor of philosophy from the University of Halle, who, though educated for the ministry, devoted much of his life to education, a choice largely to be credited to his wife's influence. The mother of a large household and daughter of an artistic and cultured family, Julia (May) Engelmann had been a teacher prior to her marriage. George's early education was chiefly directed by his parents at Frankfurt am Main, where the Engelmann family had established a school for girls.

He remained there until 1827, when he received a scholarship that made possible his registration at the University of Heidelberg, where he became acquainted with Alexander Braun and Karl Schimper. It is not to be inferred from this, however, that Engelmann's interest in botany had its origin in this acquaintance, for according to Engelmann's own statement, he had experienced a deep interest in plants as early as 1824, when he was fifteen. Due to a student row in 1828, he left the University of Heidelberg and enrolled at the University of Berlin. But his democratic tendencies were not graciously received there; and, after two years he became a student of medicine at the University of Würzburg, where, in July, 1831, he was granted his M.D. degree. His graduation thesis, entitled "De Antholysis Prodromus," was an important treatise on the morphology of animal and vegetable monstrosities. The author illustrated it by his own carefully executed pencil drawings. The original manuscript is in the care of the custodian of the Harvard University herbarium.

In 1832, Engelmann went to Paris where he became acquainted with Louis Agassiz. There, too, he met such men as Braun, Constadt, and others. Towards the close of that same year he set out for the United States, enthused by the prospect of discovering new species of plants and thus of being able to contribute something of interest to man's knowledge of New World botany. Incidentally, he was also seeking opportunity for profitable investment in America of some money entrusted to him by his uncle.

Engelmann arrived in St. Louis in 1833 and found domicile on a farm a score of miles east of St. Louis. From this farm as his headquarters, he spent the better part of the next two years prospecting for minerals and searching for new plants and geologic specimens. In 1835 he settled in St. Louis, where he engaged in the practice of medicine with distinctive success. He did not neglect his botanical research. Not the least of his contributions were his observation of the pollination of the yuccas by the pronuba moth and his discovery of immunity of the American wild-grape from *Phylloxera*.

Plant research afforded Engelmann his most satisfying occupation. His collected notes, drawings, and data on plants of various kinds comprise more than sixty volumes; but, exceeding these in comprehensiveness and importance, is the memorial volume of "Botanical Works of the late George Engelmann Collected for Henry Shaw" (1887).

In 1856 he organized the St. Louis Academy of Science. In 1837 he engaged in a botanical exploration of the state of Arkansas, which, in 1842, resulted in the publication of his first botanical contribution, "A Monograph on North American Cuscutaceae." He further published work which included his *Plante Fendlerianae*, his study of the Cactaceae, and his painstaking study of American species of *Vitis* (wildgrape).

Engelmann was a tireless traveller. His excursions took him into such remote parts of America as the Rocky Mountains of Colorado, the Appalachians of Tennessee, to New Mexico, and what are now known as the Pacific Coast states. He was ever on the alert for new and undiscovered plants. Engelmann's interest included not only botany, medicine, geology, and mineralogy, but also meteorology. His final published paper was a digest of his thermometrical readings made during certain of his botanical explorations. His plant collection, containing much type material, was donated to Shaw's Botanical Garden in St. Louis, a gift that did much to bring about the realization of the Shaw School of Botany. Engelmann returned to Germany in 1840 and, at Kreutznach, married Dorothea Horstmann, a cousin who, since the age of eleven, had lived as a member of the Engelmann family. Doctor Engelmann died in St. Louis, Missouri, February 4, 1884, at the age of seventy-five.

GRAY, A. 1884. Obituary, George Engelmann. *Am. J. Sci.* 3rd Ser. 28: 61–67.
KELLY, H. A. 1914. *Some American Medical Botanists.* The Southworth Company, Troy, N.Y. Pp. 137–162.
SARGENT, C. S. 1884. *Science* 3: 405–408.
SPAULDING, P. 1909. A Biographical History of Botany at St. Louis, Mo. Pop. Sci. Monthly 74: 124–133.
WHITE, C. A. 1902. Memoir of George Engelmann. *Nat. Acad. Sci. Biog. Mem.* 4: 3–21.
YOUMANS, E. L., AND W. S., eds. 1886. *Pop. Sci. Monthly* 29: 260–265.

William Gilson Farlow

1844–1919

Dr. Farlow was born of humble parents on December 17, 1844, in Boston, Massachusetts. There he spent his youth until the age of fourteen, when, with the family, he moved to Newton, Massachusetts. The greater part of his early education was obtained in the Boston schools. Those who best knew him in his youth were impressed by his mental and physical vigor, his enthusiasm for and keen interest in nature, and his devotion to botany in particular. He early developed a rival interest in music and, with it, no ordinary skill in playing the piano. This penchant for music prevailed throughout his life, and his deeper understanding of the art undoubtedly enriched his life immeasurably. A collateral interest that claimed a part of his devotion to the arts was participation in private theatricals. It is not surprising, therefore, that a young man of his talents and pronounced enthusiasm, once he had made his decision, should have become, as he did, one of the greatest of American botanists and a leading figure in world botany.

Early in his career as a student of natural history in Harvard

College, it was his good fortune to come under the guiding influence of Asa Gray with whom he formed an intimate friendship. Even though he was well grounded in botany at the time of his graduation, he declared that he had "no definite plans for life." Dr. Gray, himself a Doctor of Medicine, advised Farlow to study medicine, for at that time, the pursuit of botany as a profession promised scant advancement. Although Farlow acquitted himself brilliantly as a student of medicine and received his medical degree in May, 1870, he continued his botanical studies with Dr. Gray and was appointed Dr. Gray's assistant by the University. In this position he acquired a thorough knowledge of cryptogamic botany and of taxonomy in particular. His interest lay unquestionably in the cryptogams, as was clearly evident from his work on the marine algae.

On the advice of Dr. Gray, he sailed for England in June, 1872, and thence proceeded to the Continent, visiting Norway, Denmark, Sweden, and Russia, where he met many celebrated botanists, some of whom were recognized authorities in the field of algology. From Russia he traveled to Germany and established himself at Strassburg, where, at the university, he studied with Anton De Bary, then generally recognized as the outstanding authority in cryptogamic botany. Farlow's initial European experience lasted over two years, most of which time he devoted to study in De Bary's laboratories. He did, however, spend some weeks in other laboratories, notably those of Müller of Geneva and Thuret of Antibes, where he had opportunity for intensive study of lichens and the algae.

On returning to America, greatly enriched by all that he had gained through association with preeminent botanists of the European school, Farlow was without a peer in cryptogamic botany. Following his appointment as assistant professor of botany at Harvard University, he became the first American botanist to assume charge of a cryptogamic laboratory. This was in 1874. During the first years following his return from Europe, he was a member of the staff of the Bussey Institution where he carried on research in plant pathology and instructed specialists interested in the economic aspects of botany. Here he prepared the ground for the growth and permanence of plant pathology, that lusty scion of botanical science.

In 1879 Dr. Farlow returned to the university proper as professor of cryptogamic botany, where he enjoyed the freedom necessary to follow out his departmental plans to a realization that apparently would not have been possible at the Bussey Institution. Here also he was free to develop the great herbarium that bears his name, one of the most remarkable of its kind to be found anywhere. Here, too, his reputation for research and as a teacher drew to the Harvard laboratories such young men as B. D. Halsted, James Ellis Humphrey, H. M. Richards, William Trelease, W. A. Setchell, and many more who proved to be a credit to their great teacher, men who as teachers and investigators passed along to their students a new and amplified concept of plant science. North American botany, thanks to De Bary, Thuret, Hofmeister, Zimmermann, Marshall Ward, Strasburger, Bower, Pfeffer, and other eminent European botanists, produced its own great school of botanists, free of the need to serve a term of apprenticeship in European schools or laboratories.

BLAKESLEE, A. F., R. THAXTER, and W. TRELEASE. 1920. William Gilson Farlow. *Am. J. Botany* 7: 173–181, with portrait and publications.
CLINTON, G. P. 1920. William Gilson Farlow. *Phytopathol.* 10: 1–8, with portrait.
LINDER, D. H. 1945. In Honor of William Gilson Farlow. *Farlowia* 2: 1–7.
SETCHELL, W. R. 1926. William Gilson Farlow. *Nat. Acad. Sci. Mem.* 21: (4th Memoir) 1–22, with portrait and bibliography as given in *Amer. J. Botany* 7, 1920.
THAXTER, R. 1920. *Botan. Gaz.* 69: 83–87.
WESTON, W. H., JR. 1945. Dr. Farlow's influence on Mycology. *Farlowia* 2: 84–95.

Merritt Lyndon Fernald

1873–1950

In the field of taxonomic botany, few have approached the eminence attained by Merritt Lyndon Fernald. His long and fruitful life was devoted with religious zeal to a study of the plants of northeastern North America, specifically the area covered by Gray's "Manual." This included those portions of the United States and Canada north of the southern boundary of Virginia, east of the Mississippi River, and extending as far northeast as the Maritime Provinces and Newfoundland.

Fernald was born October 5, 1873, in Orono, Maine. He died September 22, 1950, in Cambridge, Massachusetts. As a growing boy, he was exposed to academic and scientific influences, since his father was president of Maine State College at Orono. His interests turned at an early age to botany, and, by the time he registered at the state college as a freshman at seventeen, he was thoroughly committed to making botany his life's work. Before his first year at the college had been completed, he received a letter from Sereno Watson, director of the Gray Herbarium, asking if he would be interested in a position in the herbarium, with the opportunity to continue his academic education. Young Fernald accepted with enthusiasm, and thus began a career at the Gray Herbarium that was to continue throughout his life. During the next fifty-six years he served the herbarium in one capacity or another, including that of curator, and ultimately (1937–1947) as director. From 1915 until he retired to emeritus status in 1947, he held the chair of Fisher Professor of Natural History at Harvard University. The rank of full professor was attained after a series of promotions from his original status of assistant (1891–1902), instructor (1902–1905), and assistant professor (1905–1915).

Fernald enrolled in the Lawrence Scientific School at Harvard University in the fall of 1891. He combined work at the Gray Herbarium with his course of study, graduating *magna cum laude* with a Bachelor of Science degree in 1897. This was to be his only earned degree, although he later received two honorary degrees, the D.C.L. from Acadia University in 1932 and the D.Sc. from the University of Montreal in 1938.

Fernald felt that the time he would have to spend working toward an advanced degree could be spent more effectively working in the herbarium and the field with his plants. Certainly his lifetime accomplishments indicated no inadequacy in his botanical training. From the first he knew what he wanted to do and how to do it. Throughout his life he demonstrated a singleness of purpose and the industry requisite to reach the goal toward which he was striving. This industry is indicated in part by the more than 800 publications that appeared under his name.

The eighth edition of Gray's "Manual of Botany," published in 1950, is a monument to Fernald. He spent much of the last forty years of his life working on the "Manual," largely in the field at first but later increasingly in the herbarium and at his desk, writing and rewriting.

Fernald was a careful, exact, and critical writer. He was equally critical of the work and writing of others. He was not averse to giving criticism where he felt it was needed, a trait that did not always endear him to his colleagues. It did, however, do much to elevate and maintain a high level of thinking and expression in botanical writing.

The available record does not indicate that Fernald had any interests except botany. "Actually it should be clear that this greatly gifted field botanist can be described as a one-pointed, one-sided botanical machine. Fernald lived, thought, and talked botany," (Griscom). Had he been otherwise constituted, he could not have made such great contributions to the field.

Although presumably possessed of a weak heart, he was a tireless collector and would go all day with little or no food at a pace that would wear out many a younger, less enthusiastic person. A considerable part of his early field work was done in the Gaspé Peninsula of Quebec, a region of rough topography and dense brush that was enough to exhaust even those of rugged constitution. In later years when it was necessary to make some concessions to his more limited endurance, field work was largely restricted to the tidewater regions of Virginia. Even here, however, he set a rugged pace for all except the most seasoned.

Fernald seemingly possessed all the characteristics, mental and physical, required to make a great botanist. He had an unusual memory for details that would combine or separate groups of plants. Combined with this was the ability to remember years later not only the general area where a given plant had been collected but almost, or quite, the exact spot. And, of course, he had the all-absorbing interest that largely prevented disturbance by outside distractions. Physically he appears to have kept in good condition, a fact that must largely have counteracted any inherent cardiac weakness. He was also possessed of phenomenal eyesight that enabled him to detect plants glimpsed even fleetingly from a car window.

He married Margaret Howard Grant of Providence, Rhode Island, in 1907. Two of his children survived him, Katherine (Mrs. H. G. Lohnes) and Henry Grant Fernald. A second daughter, Mary, died in 1927.

Fernald was a member of many professional societies. These included:

New England Botanical Club (president 1911–1914); the American Society of Plant Taxonomists (president 1938); the Botanical Society of America (vice president 1939, president 1942); the American Association for the Advancement of Science (vice president 1941); the Societas Phytogeographica Suecana; the Linnaean Society (London); the Botanical Society and Exchange Club of the British Isles; and the Torrey Botanical Club. He was a fellow of the American Academy of Arts and Sciences; the American Philosophical Society; a member of the National Academy of Sciences; a corresponding member of the Academy of Natural Sciences (Philadelphia), the Société Linneane de Lyon, and of the Norske Videnskaps Academi; a member of the International Committee on Botanical Nomenclature (1930–1935) and the Association of American Geographers, and various other organizations. He was awarded the honorary degree of D.C.L. by Acadia University (1933) and that of D.Sc. by the University of Montreal (1938); also the Leidy Gold Medal of the Academy of Natural Sciences at Philadelphia (1940), a Gold Medal from the Massachusetts Horticultural Society (1944), and the Marie-Victorin Medal, given by the Foundation Marie-Victorin for outstanding services to botany in Canada (1949). (Pease)

BARTLETT, H. H. 1951. Fernald as a reviser of Gray's *Manual. Rhodora* 53: 56–61.
FOGG, JOHN M., JR. 1951. Fernald as a teacher. *Rhodora* 53: 39–43.
GRISCOM, LUDLOW. 1951. Fernald in the field. *Rhodora* 53: 61–65.
MERRILL, ELMER D. 1951. Merritt Lyndon Fernald 1873–1950. *Am. Philos. Soc. Yearbook* 1950: 287–295.
MERRILL, ELMER D. 1954. Merritt Lyndon Fernald, 1873–1950. *Nat. Acad. Sci. Biog. Mem.* 28: 45–98.
PEASE, A. S. 1951. Merritt Lyndon Fernald 1873–1950. *Rhodora* 53: 33–39.
RAUP, HUGH M. 1950. Merritt Lyndon Fernald, 1874–1950. *Annals of Assoc. Am. Geographers* 40: 354–355.
ROLLINS, R. C. 1951. Merritt Lyndon Fernald. 1873–1950. *Bull Tor. Club* 78: 270–272.
SANDWITH, N. Y. 1950. Professor M. L. Fernald. *Nature* 166(4229): 848–849.

Charles Stuart Gager
1872–1943

Charles Stuart Gager, son of Charles Carroll and Leora Josephine (Drake) Gager, was born on December 23, 1872, in Norwich, New York. His preparatory education was obtained in the schools of his native state. From high school he went to Syracuse, New York, where he entered Syracuse University, and he received his A.B. degree in 1895. In 1897 he was the recipient of the bachelor and master of pedagogy degrees from the New York State Normal College at Albany. Later he attended Cornell University, where he completed the requirements for the Ph.D. in 1902. In 1920 the honorary degree, D.Sc., was awarded him by Syracuse University, and a year later he was honored by award of the degree, doctor of pedagogy, by the New York State Normal College. In 1902 he and Bertha Woodward Bagg were married.

Gager's career as a botanist began with his appointment as a laboratory assistant at Syracuse University in 1894. In 1895 he was appointed to the position of vice principal of the Ives Seminary in Antwerp, New York. A year later he became professor of biological sciences and physiography at the New York State Normal College, in which position he remained until 1905. We next find him as director of laboratories at the New York Botanical Garden from 1906–1908. Thereafter, he was (1908–1910) professor of botany at the University of Missouri. For brief intervals he taught at Morris High School in New York City; New York University, and at Cornell and Rutgers universities.

With this varied pedagogic experience as a background, he was called to the directorship of the Brooklyn Botanic Garden in 1910. He accepted the offer and there devoted his remaining years to the development of one of America's most important institutions of its kind. His vision of and keen insight into the educational importance of such a garden inspired him to supreme endeavor. Under his direction the Garden became something more than a beauty spot, important as that may have been. Gager was aware of its potential importance as an educational agency, as a source of intellectual satisfaction as well as mere pleasure. Here provision was afforded for botanical research and for education of children through their daily contact with the soil and with living plants, the product of the little gardener's own husbandry.

Gager's interest in botanical science lay chiefly in the field of plant physiology. While stationed at the New York Botanical Garden (1906–1908), he engaged in a study of the effect of radium on plant behavior. Because of the exacting requirements of administrative duties he was unable to carry to completion the research he had undertaken. He was ever in demand for participation in committee and board meetings. He devoted such time as was left him to the writing and publication of articles on genetics and to the publication of botanical and pedagogic texts. He served also as editor and business manager of certain technical journals, such as the "American Journal of Botany" and related periodicals. Gager was a member of the American Botanical Society; the Torrey Botanical Club; the Royal Agricultural and Horticultural Society of India; the Pennsylvania Horticultural Society, and the School Garden Association. Ever responsive to calls for his counsel and assistance in matters botanical, he was able and willing to serve constructively and intelligently. Dr. Gager died at Waterville, Maine, on August 9, 1943.

CONKLIN, M. E., and BOTANIC GARDEN STAFF. 1944. C. Stuart Gager and the Brooklyn Bot. Garden. *Brooklyn Botan. Gard. Record.* 33: 69–168.
REED, G. M., and A. H. GRAVES. 1944. *Bull. Torrey Club* 71: 193–198, with portrait and selected writings.
ROBBINS, W. J. 1943. *Science* n.s. 98: 234–235.
SVENSON, H. K. 1944. *Ecology* 25: 1–2, with portrait.

William Francis Ganong
1864–1941

William Francis Ganong, botanist and historian, was born at St. John, New Brunswick, February 19, 1864, son of James Harvey and Susan Elizabeth (Brittain) Ganong. His earliest American ancestor was Jean Guenon, an Huguenot who migrated from France to North America in 1657 and settled in New York. Both the paternal and maternal ancestors of Professor Ganong were loyalists, and they therefore moved to Canada where they settled in New Brunswick. It was there that the botanist was born; he was subsequently educated in the schools of St. John and St. Stephen. At twenty he graduated from the University of New Brunswick, Fredericton, and received his M.A. there two years later (1886).

In 1887 he was a student at Harvard, where he served as assistant in botany and was in due course appointed instructor. He then went to Germany, where he continued his botanical studies at the University of Munich and, in 1894, received his Ph.D. in botany. On returning from Europe, he was appointed professor of botany and director of the botanic garden at Smith College, Northampton, Massachusetts. This joint responsibility he held until his retirement in 1932. As a botanist he served with distinction as teacher and investigator.

Among his several published works, the following should be mentioned as important to both teacher and student alike: "The Teaching Botanist" (1899); "A Laboratory Course in Plant Physiology" (1901); "The Living Plant" (1913); and a "Text Book of Botany for Colleges" (1916). He was the author of several botanical papers and an important treatise on the natural history and archaeology of New Brunswick, published in scientific journals and in Transactions of the Royal Society of Canada. Ganong was a corresponding member of the Royal Society of Canada and a member of the Botanical Society of America, of which he was president in 1908. For nine years he was secretary of the Society for Plant Physiology and Morphology, merged since with the Botanical Society of America. Professor Ganong was married, April 4, 1888, to Jean Murray, daughter of William Carman of Fredericton, New Brunswick. He died September 7, 1941 at St. John, New Brunswick, in his seventy-eighth year.

ANON. 1941. William Francis Ganong. *Plant Physiol.* 16: 215–216. *Life Membership Award.* 16: 842, portrait.

SMITH, F. G., and H. A. CHOATE. 1941. *Science* n.s. 94: 317–318.

WEBSTER, J. C. 1942. William Francis Ganong. *Trans. Roy. Soc. Canad.* 3rd Ser. 36: 91–92.

Nathaniel Lyon Gardner
1864–1937

Nathaniel Lyon Gardner was born in Keokuk, Iowa, on February 26, 1864 and died at Berkeley, California, on August 15, 1937. His elementary and college-preparatory education he obtained in the public schools of Iowa, following which he taught school for a short time in that state and then moved to Tacoma, Washington, where he entered upon a business venture with his brother. Following the financial panic of the early 1890's, he again engaged in teaching. He had already been graduated from the Ellensburg (Wash.) State Normal School, so he proceeded to the University of Washington at Seattle, where he subsequently received his Bachelor of Science degree.

We next hear of Dr. Gardner as a post-graduate student at the University of California, where, in 1903, he received his M.S. He found it possible there to continue his studies for the doctorate and, in 1906, was awarded his Ph.D. As a public-school teacher, it was his good fortune to obtain an appointment at Coupville, in Island County, Washington. This position afforded him opportunity to continue his plant-life studies, which resulted in his collecting and preparing many herbarium specimens of land and marine plants. These he sent away for identification by recognized authorities until he himself became thoroughly acquainted with the plants of the Pacific Northwest.

In the course of time he came to know Dr. William Albert Setchell, head of the department of botany at the University of California and a widely known student of marine algae. Largely because of a common interest shared by the two men, there grew up a friendship that proved richly productive in its contributions to our knowledge of the marine botany of the Pacific littoral. This cooperative urge continued until the two men were separated by death, which first claimed Dr. Gardner. Up to that time, he had published many papers of which he was the sole author and several under joint authorship with Dr. Setchell.

Gardner was an acknowledged authority on the blue-green algae of the world, and, though his knowledge of the green algae was less extensive, it was nevertheless considerable. Notable among his published papers were those on the morphology and development of several species of the Chlorophyceae. But it was in his study of the brown algae that he made many significant additions to our knowledge. Just prior to his death, he was engaged in a study of the polymorphic forms of the rhodophyceae.

The term of Dr. Gardner's service at the university breaks down in the following order: From 1900 to 1906 he was an assistant in botany; from 1909 to 1910 he served as acting assistant professor; from 1913 to 1923 he was assistant professor of botany; 1923 to 1934 he served as associate professor and then retired as associate professor emeritus. From 1920 to his retirement in 1934, he was curator of the herbarium of the University of California. From 1906–1909 and 1910–1913 he was head of the department of biology in the Los Angeles Polytechnic High School. Dr. Gardner married Edith Jordan, the daughter of David Starr Jordan in 1915.

SETCHELL, W. A. 1937. Nathaniel Lyon Gardner. *Science* n.s. 86: 300–301.

George Lincoln Goodale
1839–1923

George Lincoln Goodale, son of Stephen Lincoln and Prudence Aiken (Nourse) Goodale, was born in Saco, Maine, August 3, 1839. As a boy he enjoyed the advantage of superior parenthood. His father, a man of much ability and versatility had been trained in pharmacy and chemistry and achieved recognition as a man of some importance. He was much interested in arboriculture and especially in fruit culture. Although he was not a botanist, he undoubtedly was influential in directing his son's interest toward things scientific.

After spending a year in his father's pharmacy, George Goodale became a student at Amherst College, where he received instruction in botany from Edward Tuckerman, America's foremost lichenologist, and in geology from Edward Hitchcock. While at Amherst, Goodale took up the study of medicine. He continued his work at the Portland (Maine) School for Medical Instruction and at the Harvard Medical School and graduated with distinction in 1863. During his years as a medical student, it was his privilege to cooperate in a scientific survey of his native state, a project interrupted by the Civil War. This survey included consideration of the botanical, chemical, and geological resources of the state and the publication of reports on all of these aspects. These reports brought Goodale into fruitful contact with such eminent scientists as Hitchcock, the geologist, Packard, the entomologist, and with Asa Gray.

Dr. Goodale's three years' experience as a practicing physician was sufficiently engrossing to leave him little time to devote to serious botanical work. Because of ill health, he traveled in 1866 and went to California by way of Panama. This enabled him for the first time in his life to observe plant life in the tropics and to acquaint himself with the diverse and highly interesting flora of the Far West. Returning from California, Dr. Goodale again visited his native Maine.

He next became professor of natural science at Bowdoin College, a position that necessitated his services as instructor of classes in botany, zoology, chemistry, and geology. This position he held until 1872, a period of approximately four years, when he accepted an offer to go to Harvard as an instructor under Dr. Asa Gray and thus to relieve him of a very considerable burden of teaching. He was subsequently promoted in rank to an assistant professorship and, in 1878, he became professor of botany.

Along lines suggested by the works of Eichler and Sachs and by Gray's "Structural Botany," Goodale developed a textbook "Physiological Botany" of new content for an American botany text. Here he brought together much pertaining to physiological behavior of plants and treated with marked clarity such subjects as transpiration, respiration, assimilation, reproduction, etc.

Although Dr. Goodale's record in research was in no sense spectacular, his service to his chosen science was of very real and great importance. Much credit is due him for his success in obtaining funds for the erection of the botanical section of the Harvard University museum. Here adequate provision was made for laboratory and lecture-room facilities and space for the housing and proper display of illustrative botanical material. He it was who negotiated the acquisition of the Blaschka collection of glass models of plants, flowers, vegetable structures, and fruits. The collection represents 160 families of flowering plants and more than 3,200 enlargements of anatomical details.

Dr. Goodale, in addition to his superior ability as a teacher and his gifts as a lecturer, traveled extensively and made a thorough-going study of botanical gardens. Through his influence the Harvard Botanical Garden succeeded in establishing near Cienfuegos, Cuba, a tropical garden and experiment station. In December, 1866, he married Henrietta Juell Hobson of Saco, Maine, by whom he had five children. His death occurred April 12, 1923.

BAILEY, L. H. 1923. George Lincoln Goodale. *Rhodora* 25(286): 117–120, with portrait.
JACKSON, R. T. 1923. *Harvard Grad. Mag.* 32: 54–59, with portrait.
ROBINSON, B. L. 1926. *Nat. Acad. Sci. Memoirs* (6th Memoir) 21: 1–19, with portrait and bibliography by Robert Tracy Jackson.
TRELEASE, W. 1923. *Science* n.s. 57: 654–656.

Asa Gray
1810–1888

Asa Gray, American botanist and explorer of new trails into the plant kingdom, was born on November 18, 1810, in Sauquoit Valley in the township of Paris, Oneida County, New York. He was the eldest of eight children born to Moses and Roxana (Howard) Gray. His father, a thrifty farmer and tanner, and his mother were of Scotch-Irish and English lineage, respectively. Their ancestors had moved to Oneida County from Massachusetts and Vermont.

The boy Asa attended school at Clinton, nine miles from his home, and later at Fairfield Academy for a term of four years. It is not reported that he was precocious in his studies or that as a boy he was more interested in natural history than in other subjects such as history, geography, higher mathematics, or literature. At Fairfield Academy he met Dr. James Hadley, professor of materia medica and chemistry, from whom he received his introduction to the natural sciences.

Gray's first interest was in mineralogy. He had heard of botany, but not until he had read an article on the subject in Brewster's "Edinburgh Encyclopoedia" was his curiosity aroused to the point of desiring to learn more about the plant life in his environment. The following spring, while still in Fairfield, he came upon the common wildflower popularly known as spring beauty. With characteristic thoroughness and the aid of Amos Eaton's "Manual of Botany," he identified the plant as *Claytonia virginica*. Encouraged by his success, it was not long before he had collected and identified many of the plants he had observed near Fairfield and within the vicinity of Sauquoit Valley. As Professor Hadley's pupil, he continued his materia medica studies and at the end of four years was granted the M.D. degree, an event that was at once to become the beginning and the end of his career as a doctor of medicine. Notwithstanding the fact that he opened an office, he never actually practiced the profession. Even while primarily devoted to his medical studies, he managed to find time to collect many plants for this, his first herbarium, and to add materially to his collection of minerals. Quite naturally these interests led to a growing and encouraging correspondence with Dr. Lewis C. Beck of Albany, New York and with Dr. John Torrey of New York City.

On graduation from Fairfield Academy, Gray received an appointment as instructor in botany, chemistry, and mineralogy in Bartlett's High School in Utica, New York. Later he offered a course in botany and mineralogy at Hamilton College. With his earnings from these activities, he financed his botanical explorations of the vicinity of Niagara Falls and elsewhere in New York and in New Jersey.

In the autumn of 1833, he received a call to go to New York, there to become Dr. John Torrey's assistant in chemistry. Fortunately for Gray he found Torrey deeply interested in plants. Their combined interest centered upon botany, and it was not long before Gray witnessed the publication of his first botanical papers, of which his "Monograph of the North American Species of Rhynchospora" (1835) was the more significant and his first wholly botanical contribution. Deficient funds made impossible the continuance of his appointment beyond 1833. Notwithstanding this interruption in his career, he became curator and librarian of the Lyceum of Natural History in New York and was thereby enabled to undertake the writing of his first textbook, his "Elements of Botany" (1836). During that summer he collaborated with Dr. Torrey on the "Flora of North America" and was appointed botanist of the Wilkes Exploring Expedition. The enterprise was two years late in getting under way. Meanwhile, Gray, having wearied of waiting, accepted appointment to the chair of botany in the then new University of Michigan. For financial reasons he never entered upon the duties of this appointment, and accepted, instead, a professorship of natural history at Harvard University, the responsibility of which position he assumed in 1842.

On May 4, 1848, he married Jane Lathrop Loring, who survived him. Assured of lucrative employment in a field of his own choice, there was more than a promise of uninterrupted devotion to botany and to the realization of his fondly entertained dream, the creation of a botanical establishment at Harvard, a department the development of which it may truthfully be said was peculiarly his own. It was he who assembled there the books, the herbarium, and the students and who, single-handed and alone, continued the good work. He gathered around him young men and those not so young, men eager to profit from his inspiration and absorb his knowledge of the vegetable kindom; men such as Liberty Hyde Bailey, Charles Edwin Bessey, John Merle Coulter, Charles Reid Barnes, William Gilson Farlow, David Penhallow, and many more destined to win distinction and preeminence as botanists. They, like their greater teacher, passed on to their disciples their heritage of love for and devotion to the plant sciences and added their contribution to the sum total of botanical knowledge and scientific culture.

Gray's contribution as a teacher, far-reaching as it was in its impact upon American education, was the more so because of the quantity and quality of his botanical research. He was above all a systematist; yet, he was conscious of the worth and importance of morphology, plant anatomy, and physiology; he encouraged men of scientific promise to study these and other branches of botany.

In 1856 Gray published his "Statistics of the Flora of the Northern United States," his first paper on plant distribution, a subject that at the time was of intense interest to him. In his comparison of the floras of Eastern and Western North America, the one with the other and with that of Japan, as well as of all with the Tertiary flora of North America, he presented to us a historical outline of the plant life of the North Temperate Zone in relation to its past and present geographic features, from the Cretaceous period to the present.

Gray's study of plants collected during the Ringgold and Rodgers Expedition into the North Pacific did more than all else to establish his reputation as an authority on plant distribution and culminated in his masterly paper entitled: "On the Botany of Japan and Its Relations to that of North America and of Other Parts of the North Temperate Zone." Within the span of thirty years (1857–1887) he produced the following textbooks, each important in its own way: "First Lessons in Botany and Vegetable Physiology"; "How Plants Grow"; "Field, Forest, and Garden Botany"; "How Plants Behave"; and another "Elements of Botany" (1887), the first one having appeared in 1836.

In the words of William Gilson Farlow in his appreciation of his great teacher, Asa Gray:

His whole life was as beautiful as it was fortunate. He found a country in which a few botanists were struggling against general neglect and popular ignorance. He left a great nation in which, very largely through his exertions, the value of botany had become generally recognized and in which a crowd of young workers had arisen anxious to carry out the good work even in the most remote regions. ("Biog. Mem. Nat. Acad. Sci." III, 1895)

GRAY, ASA. *Memoirs and Bibliography 1888–1890.*
BRADFORD, G. 1929. *As God Made Them.* Portraits of some Nineteenth Century Americans. Houghton Mifflin Company, Boston.
DANA, J. D. 1888. Asa Gray. *Am. J. Sci.* 3rd Ser. 35: 181–203.
DEAN, W. 1888. *Bull. Torrey Club* 15: 59–72.
FARLOW, W. G., 1895. Memoir of Asa Gray. *Nat. Acad. Sci. Biog. Mem.* 3: 163–175.
FARLOW, W. G. 1888. *Botan. Gaz.* 13: 49–52.
GRAY, J. L., Editor. 1893. *Letters of Asa Gray.* 2 vol. Houghton Mifflin Company, New York.

Edward Lee Greene

1843–1915

Edward Lee Greene was born in Hopkinton, Rhode Island, August 20, 1843. He was the son of William and Abby (Crandall) Greene and is reported to have moved with his parents to Illinois when he was about twelve years old. From Illinois, the family moved to Wisconsin and settled near Janesville, where the boy Edward acquired some knowledge of the Norwegian language from his Norwegian neighbors and became acquainted with the Swedish naturalist, Thure Ludwig Theodore Kumlien.

Edward attended Albion Academy, but his experience there was interrupted by three years of service in the Civil War (1862–1865), during which he served as a private in a regiment detailed for garrison, guard, and like duties. He was, however, able to collect and study many of the plants of Alabama, Tennessee, and Kentucky. In July, 1865, he returned to Albion Academy and finished his requirements for graduation.

After limited service as a teacher, he moved, in 1870, to Colorado, where he collected plants for Asa Gray and George Engelmann. At Golden City he entered Jarvis Hall, an Episcopal Seminary, where, in 1873, he was ordained for the ministry. He then served as a clergyman in Colorado and later in California. As a missionary he covered much of Wyoming and the Southwest. In 1882 he was called to the rectorship of St. Mark's in Berkeley, California but resigned in 1885 to become a Roman Catholic layman and thereafter devoted himself more assiduously to botany.

It was at this time that he inaugurated a new epoch in his career as a botanist. In 1879 he traveled on foot from San Diego to Santa Fé. As he journeyed, he met, without being molested, Indians who by reputation were known to have been less considerate of wayfaring whites. At this time, an opportunity came to him from the University of California, where he was offered a position in the department of botany. Here he served during the academic year 1885–1886 as instructor.

Up to this time, Greene had published little, but from then onward more favorable conditions fostered his growth as a botanical contributor. His six papers "Studies in the Botany of California and Parts Adjacent" were, as has been said, "the first noteworthy contributions to western botany published in the west by a resident botanist." In 1887, Greene became assistant professor and, in 1892, was raised to the rank of associate professor. The following year he was promoted to the rank of professor. After ten years of service in the department of botany at the University of California, he resigned and moved to Washington, D.C., where he became head of the department of botany in the Catholic University of America and served in that capacity from 1895 to 1904 and, following this, as an associate in botany in the Smithsonian Institution from 1904 to 1914.

Among Greene's more noteworthy separate contributions to North American botany were "Pittonia: a Series of Papers relating to Botany and Botanists" (5 vols. 1887–1905); "West American Oaks" (Part 1, 1889; Part 2, 1890); "Flora Franciscana" (Parts 1–4, 1891–1897, incomplete); "Manual of the Botany of the Region of San Francisco Bay" (1894); "Plantae Bakerianae" (1901, incomplete); "Leaflets of Botanical Observations" (2 vols., 1903–1909), and "Landmarks of Botanical History" (Part 1 to A.D. 1562, 1909, discontinued). To give a complete bibliography of his published works would fill many pages.

Dr. Greene was noted for his originality, his profound knowledge of the classics, and his extensive and thorough grasp of the literature of his field of scientific endeavor. His originality, his radical views as to nomenclature reform and species limitations made it difficult, if not impossible, for the more conservative botanists to accept his botanical doctrine without reservation. He had many readers but few if any disciples. He was never married and, after a prolonged illness, died in Washington, November 10, 1915.

JEPSON, W. L. 1943. Edward Lee Green, The Individual. *Am. Midl. Nat.* 30: 3–5.
MAIN, A. K. 1929. Life and Letters of Edward Lee Green. *Trans. Wis. Acad. Sci.* 24: 47–185.

David Griffiths

1867–1935

David Griffiths, the son of David and Rachel (Lewis) Griffiths, was born in Aberystwyth, North Wales, August 16, 1867. At the age of three, he came with his parents to a farm in South Dakota. There he attended the public schools and Groton (S.D.) Academy. Subsequently he graduated from the high school in Aberdeen, South Dakota. He then entered the State College of Agriculture and Mechanic Arts at Brookings, whence he was graduated in 1892. The following year he received his Master of Science degree; and from 1893 to 1898 he served as a teacher of physics, chemistry, and biology in the Aberdeen High School, where but a few years before he had been a zealous student of those same branches of science. Even as a boy in high school his chief interest had led him more and more into a serious and absorbing study of botany and zoology, and he pursued these as a graduate student at Columbia University. There, in 1900, he was awarded his Ph.D.

On completion of his duties at Columbia, Dr. Griffiths was appointed professor of botany at the University of Arizona and botanist of the Agricultural Experiment Station. He forthwith initiated pioneer research on grasses and other range vegetation peculiar to the arid Southwest. With characteristic insight and thoroughness, he followed this line of research through the first fifteen years of his service as a botanist in the Bureau of Plant Industry, U.S. Department of Agriculture (1901–1916). He was fully aware of the importance of his assignment and continued his research with exemplary seriousness and integrity. He demanded much of himself and of his assistants. Everything to which he applied himself bore the mark of his scientific zeal and scholarship.

During the fifteen years of Dr. Griffiths' service in the Office of Grass and Forage Plant Investigations, he traveled widely from the far reaches of the northern Great Plains to Mexico and its interior, with the result that he became an authority on range research and range management. The results of his extensive studies have in all essential respects remained unchallenged. They are to be found in several department bulletins and other publications.

It was while conducting these studies that Griffiths came to realize the importance of the cacti as a possible source of forage for livestock. He then proceeded, through use of natural and experimental stands in Texas and California, to study the value and availability of certain species as sources of emergency forage. His objective in this was to ascertain the importance of so-called spineless prickly pear cacti and to determine whether the widely publicized claims of certain "experts" were truly valid. There followed from these studies numerous important contributions to our knowledge of the taxonomy, culture, and agronomic worth of the cacti.

Griffiths' increased enthusiasm for and interest in matters horticultural quite naturally resulted in his attraction to lily culture and to his ultimate assignment to the position of horticulturist in charge of that project, a responsibility that was his during most of the remaining twenty years of his life. Again his enthusiasm and scientific integrity soon resulted in his mastery of this field of horticulture and the ultimate recognition of David Griffiths as an authority in bulb culture. His most important published work on the subject was of an economic nature, touching upon bulb management and the development of practical methods of growing narcissi, hyacinths, tulips, Easter, tiger, Madonna, and other equally popular lilies. His research extended his interest to less well-known members of the lily family and to his publication of several technical and popular papers and bulletins, all of which helped to promote an ever-expanding interest in commercial bulb culture.

Here was a man of unquestioned stature and soundness as a botanist and one who was at the same time a horticulturist of eminence and great common sense. Added to these qualifications, Dr. Griffiths had an unusual appreciation of and love for the beautiful, whether that of the Great Plains or of our Southwestern desert, virtues that detracted not at all from his worth as a botanist or as a man among men. In 1905 he married Emigene Lily, who passed away in 1909. He died in Washington, D.C., March 10, 1935. He was survived by a daughter and a son, and his second wife, Louise Hayward Griffiths.

TAYLOR, W. A. 1935. David Griffiths. *Science* n.s. 81: 426–427.

Robert Almer Harper
1862–1946

Robert Almer Harper was born January 21, 1862, at Le Claire, Iowa. He was one of a family of three boys whose parents were Almer Sexton—Congregational minister and graduate of Oberlin— and Eunice (Thompson) Harper of New York and New Jersey. Both had been active in the field of education and had been reared in an environment of culture and scholarship. Robert's brother Edward, at first interested in plants, went to Leipzig to study theology. Here he completed his doctorate and was later appointed professor in the Chicago Theological Seminary. Robert, whose initial interest was botany, remained true to his first love, went to Oberlin College, and obtained there his A.B. degree in 1886.

For two years thereafter and before he registered at Johns Hopkins University for graduate study, he taught Greek and Latin at Neligh, Nebraska. This brief absence from his devotion to botany ended, he spent some months as master of science at Lake Forest Academy in Illinois, where his superiority as a teacher won for him, in the autumn of 1891, a promotion to Lake Forest College as professor of botany. He had received his M.A. from Oberlin and, in 1893, was granted a leave of two years (1894–1896) to pursue postgraduate study of botany in Germany. Harper's deep interest in the plant cell led him directly to Bonn where he, like Campbell, Fairchild, Swingle, Mottier, Humphrey, and other Americans learned their cytology from the immortal Strasburger, who, up to that time, had done more to shape the destiny of plant science in North America than any other botanist.

Harper's interest in the fungi quite naturally led him to Brefeld's laboratory. However, he found Brefeld a bit headstrong in his insistence on student acceptance of methods and conclusions no longer tenable. This disappointment again induced him to return to Bonn and to Strasburger's laboratory, where he worked among such research men as Fairchild, Swingle, Osterhout, and others. Here he studied the intimate structure and development of the plant cell to his heart's content. His was a master hand at depicting and interpreting the behavior and function of the fungus nucleus, especially in its relation to sex and the subsequent development of the ascus and its characteristic number of spores. Thus was he able to contribute much that was of basic importance to our knowledge of the Ascomycetes and their reproduction. His success at Bonn stimulated in him a desire to study spore development in *Mucor* and *Pilobolus*. Over and over again he returned to his study of the Myxomycetes in an attempt to reconcile their puzzling reproduction with more orthodox cell behavior.

Although Harper was at heart and by training a morphologist, he did not overlook the importance of plant pathology. He was well informed in all that was essential to a working knowledge of the subject. He was well informed in genetics but was critical of some of the hard and fixed conclusions of some of the more modern geneticists. He seemed unable to accept the idea that living plants or animals would invariably follow mathematical formulae.

Dr. Harper was a member of the National Academy of Sciences; the Botanical Society of America; the American Phytopathological Society; the American Association for the Advancement of Science; the American Academy of Arts and Sciences; the Torrey Botanical Club; corresponding member of the Deutscher Botanischen Gesellschaft; the Linnaean Society of London; the Wisconsin Academy of Sciences, Arts and Letters; the New York Academy of Sciences; the Washington (D.C.) Academy of Sciences; and the Century Association of New York City.

Harper was a teacher of botany for forty years. He spoke of himself as a botanist. He was not a voluminous contributor of botanical papers, but such as he did contribute were basically sound. He was well aware of the importance of the laboratory and classroom, but he knew also the out of doors and did not fail to acquaint his students with the yet unspoiled wilderness, the dunes and woodlands where they could learn of nature at her best. He served as professor and head of botany at the University of Wisconsin from 1898 to 1911 and was head of the department of botany at Columbia University from 1911 to 1930, when he retired and became professor emeritus. He passed away May 12, 1946, at Bedford, Virginia, where he had established a farm home for himself and family.

Dr. Harper married, in June, 1899, Alice Jean McQueen, who lived until 1909. In January 1918 he married a second time to Helen Sherman, of Washington, D.C., by whom he had two children, a daughter and a son.

Anon. 1948. Obituary. *Phytopath.* 38: 328.
Dodge, B. O. 1946. Robert Almer Harper. *Am. Philosoph. Yearbook* 304–313.
Stout, A. B. 1946. *J. N.Y. Botan. Gard.* 47: 267–269.
Thom, C. 1949. *Nat. Acad. Sci. Biog. Mem.* 25: 229–240, with portrait and bibliography by Miss Sally McDonald.

James Arthur Harris
1880–1930

James Arthur Harris, botanist and biometrician, was born near Plantsville, Ohio. He was the son of Jordon Thomas and Ida Ellen (Lambert) Harris. Both his paternal and maternal ancestors were of English origin. When James was but five years old, he and his parents undertook a covered-wagon journey across the Great Plains, an adventure that carried him into western Nebraska, thence to western Kansas, and ultimately to eastern Kansas, where they settled on a farm.

This migration was not without its hardships, reducing the family to severe financial straits. The boy James Arthur, at the age of thirteen, undertook the responsibility of self support, and, from that time on, further subsidy from his parents was unnecessary. This meant that his entire schooling was paid for from his own earnings, and also that of his sister was made possible through his aid. He attended the University of Kansas, where, in 1901, he was awarded his A.B. A year later he received his M.A. from the same institution and in 1903, the Ph.D. degree at Washington University, St. Louis.

His keen interest in botany very early attracted the notice of his superiors, and this won for him the opportunity to serve as an assistant on the staff of the Missouri Botanical Garden. From 1904–1907 he was librarian for the Garden, and, from 1903–1907, he was an instructor in the department of botany at Washington University. In 1907 he became a staff member of the Station for Experimental Evolution of the Carnegie Institution. This position bore the title of botanical investigator and was held by Harris until 1924, when he was called to the headship of the department of botany at the University of Minnesota. This position he maintained with eminent distinction until his death in 1930.

Possessor of an omnivorous mind, Dr. Harris felt that no branch of science was so unimportant as not to merit serious study. As a result of this mental attitude, he was more than superficially interested in the advance of agriculture and of population and the impact of these on environment. He was a firm believer in the study of plants *in situ* and of their effect on their native heath. Hence we find him visiting wherever possible the unspoiled boglands, the Dismal Swamp, and other like regions along the South Atlantic seaboard. These and other natural, wild areas called him repeatedly for serious study: the desert, the rain forest, the wilderness, all were of never-failing interest to him.

Thus he studied the plant associations of the basin of prehistoric Lake Bonneville in Utah for ten successive seasons. His precise habits of thought led him to adapt the methods of chemistry, physics, and mathematics to the solution and clearer understanding of biological problems. This helped to win for him the recognition of the U.S. Department of Agriculture, and he collaborated for the department with the Bureau of Plant Industry on problems of cotton and cereal production. As a biometrician he won singular distinction, and in 1921 he was the recipient of the Weldon Medal and Weldon Memorial Prize, the highest possible award for distinction in biometry. Dr. Harris was a member of several scientific societies, served on many commissions, and was president of the American Society of Naturalists. His scientific papers number in excess of three hundred on a large variety of subjects. He was married, on April 20, 1910, to Emma Lay of New York City, and was survived by her and their four sons. He died on April 24, 1930.

Anon. 1930. *Industrial & Engineering Chem.* June 23.

Davenport, C. B. 1930. *Science* n.s. 71: 474–475, 528–529.

Rosendahl, C. O., R. A. Gortner, and G. O. Burr. 1936. *J. Arthur Harris, Botanist and Biometrician.* University of Minnesota Press, Minneapolis.

John William Harshberger

1869–1929

John William Harshberger, son of Abram and Jane Harris (Walk) Harshberger, was born January 1, 1869, in Philadelphia, where he resided all his life. His father was the great-grandson of a German emigrant who came to America from Coblenz about 1735. His mother was of Scotch-Irish, English, and Slavic descent. Her family moved to Philadelphia after the burning of Chambersburg, Pennsylvania, during the Civil War. John Harshberger as a boy became interested in plants and, at twenty published his first paper, "a Few Pennsylvania Forestry Statistics," in *Forest Leaves* (April, 1889). He received his elementary and college-preparatory education in Philadelphia and graduated from the University of Pennsylvania in 1892 with the degree of Bachelor of Science. In 1893 he completed the requirements for the Ph.D., presenting a thesis entitled: " Maize: A Botanical and Economic Study."

He was presently appointed to fill a position as instructor in biology at the University of Pennsylvania, and he remained there until his death in April, 1929. He was promoted, in 1907, to assistant professor and to the rank of professor in 1911. In addition to his university responsibilities, he was a teacher of general science at Rittenhouse Academy, served in 1896 as a lecturer for the American Society for Extension of University Teaching, was a farmers' institute instructor for three terms, and was a director of nature study at the Pocono Pines Assembly from 1903 to 1908. From 1913 to 1922 he was professor of ecology at the marine biological laboratory at Cold Spring Harbor, Long Island, and in charge of botany at the Nantucket Maria Mitchell Association, 1914 to 1915.

In 1896 Harshberger visited Mexico, where he took copious notes on his botanical observations and subsequently published several of those pertaining to such native and domestic species as he had encountered. In 1899 appeared his: "The Botanists of Philadelphia and their Work." This was followed by a textbook: "Students Herbarium for Descriptive and Geographic Purposes," in 1901; then, in 1911, was published as Volume 13 of "Die Vegetation der Erde" (Engler and Drude) his "Phytogeographic Survey of North America." Other of his contributions to the literature on plant distribution were "The Vegetation of South Florida" (1914), and "Vegetation of the New Jersey Pine Barrens" (1916).

Although at heart a plant geographer, Harshberger was interested in mycology. In 1917 he published his textbook of "Mycology and Plant Pathology." This was followed in 1920 by a "Textbook of Pastoral and Agricultural Botany, for the Study of the

Injurious and Useful Plants of Country and Farm." His published
work, including about three hundred titles, covers a variety of subjects. He was a popular teacher and a zealous conservationist. He
traveled extensively in both North and South America and in
Europe. During his travels he collected much plant material, later
to be placed in the university herbarium.

Dr. Harshberger was married, June 28, 1907, to Helen B. Cole
who passed away in 1923, survived by her husband, who lived until April 27, 1929.

HARSHBERGER, J. W. 1928. *Life and Work of John Harshberger Ph.D.* An Auto-
    biography. T. C. Davis & Sons, Philadelphia.
NICHOLS, G. E. 1930. Obituary. John William Harshberger. *Ecology* 11: 443–444.
PENNELL, F. W. 1929. *Bartonia* 11: 51–55.

Albert Spear Hitchcock
1865–1935

Albert Spear Hitchcock was born in Owassow, Michigan, on
the fourth of September, 1865. He, though the son of Albert and
Alice (Martin) Jennings, was the adopted son of Mr. and Mrs.
J. S. Hitchcock. His higher education was obtained at Iowa State
College, where he graduated as a bachelor of science in agriculture in 1884. He received his M.S. in 1886 from the same institution. His high rating as a student of chemistry favored his appointment as assistant in that department in 1885 and subsequently as
instructor in chemistry at Iowa State College from 1886 to 1889.

He next took a position as an assistant in botany at the Missouri
Botanical Garden where he remained until 1892, when he was
called to Kansas State College of Agriculture as professor of
botany. Hitchcock occupied this position until 1901, when he accepted an opportunity to serve as assistant agrostologist in the
U.S. Department of Agriculture in Washington, D.C., where he
resided until he died in December, 1935. He was promoted to the

position of systematic agrostologist in 1905, and to senior botanist in the Bureau of Plant Industry in 1924. Subsequently he was advanced to the rating of principal botanist in charge of systematic agrostology.

Here he devoted much of his time and energy to the taxonomy of the grasses and served as custodian of that section of the National Herbarium. His ever-widening knowledge of the grasses extended to remote parts of the world, for his botanical explorations were wide ranging. Chief among the regions visited by him were Mexico, Central America, the West Indies, British Guiana, China, Japan, the Philippine Islands, Indochina, South America (a second time), New Foundland and Labrador, South Africa, and East Africa. He spent the summer of 1935 in Europe, where he made important examinations of herbarium specimens of grasses from England, Germany, the Netherlands, Belgium, France, and Switzerland.

Hitchcock's published contributions were many. The more important of these were his "Textbook of Grasses," "Genera of Grasses of The United States," "Manual of Farm Grasses," "Methods of Descriptive Systematic Botany," and "Manual of Grasses of the United States." To various scientific journals and bulletins he contributed more than one hundred and fifty papers on grasses and became recognized at home and abroad as a preeminent authority on the Gramineae.

Dr. Hitchcock was a member of the American Academy of Arts and Sciences, the National Research Council, the Botanical Society of America, the Washington (D.C.), Iowa, and Kansas academies of science, the Botanical Society of Washington, the Biological Society of Washington, the Washington Biologists' Field Club, the Cosmos Club, and corresponding member of the Bohemian Society of Botany. He was also a fellow of the American Association for the Advancement of Science. In 1920 he received from his Alma Mater (Iowa State College) the honorary degree of Doctor of Science and was similarly honored by Kansas State College in 1934.

Dr. Hitchcock was married March 16, 1890, to Rania Belle, daughter of Mallery Dailey, by whom he had five children. He passed away on board ship, while returning home from Europe, December 16, 1935.

Anon. 1936. *J. Washington (D.C.) Acad. Sci.* 26: 86.

Chase, A. 1936. Albert Spear Hitchcock. *Am. J. Botany* 74: 54–55.

Chase, A. 1936. *Science* n.s. 83: 222–224.

Fernald, M. L. 1935–1936. *Am. Acad. Arts Sci.* 71: 505–506.

McClure, F. A. 1936. Albert Spear Hitchcock, An Appreciation. *Lingman Sci. J.* 15: 305–306.

Dennis Robert Hoagland

1884–1949

Dennis Robert Hoagland, son of Charles Breckenridge and Lillian May (Burch) Hoagland, was born April 2, 1884, at Golden, Colorado, where he spent the first eight years of his youth. The rest of his childhood he lived in Denver, where he finished his elementary and college-preparatory schooling; he graduated from East Denver High School in 1903. During his high-school years, he became interested in science. From Denver he went to Stanford University, where, in 1907, he received his A.B. and was elected to Phi Beta Kappa and to Phi Lambda Upsilon, then known as the Chemistry Honor Society.

Having completed his undergraduate requirements, he chose to enroll for postgraduate work at Stanford, where, for one semester as a graduate student in physical chemistry, he acquitted himself with distinction. In January, 1908, however, he accepted an offer of a position as instructor and laboratory assistant in the Laboratory of Animal Nutrition at the University of California, in which position he served from 1908 to 1913. He did not, however, continue in this field of research.

In 1913, Hoagland was offered an opportunity to join the staff of the department of agricultural chemistry. This he accepted and soon found himself engaged in fundamental research problems relating to fertilizers and soil chemistry. Early in this chapter of his experience, he found opportunity for teaching. Due to the effect of World War I on American trade in potash fertilizers, we were forced to look elsewhere than to Germany for a source of such material. The kelps of the Pacific came in for their share of interest during the exploratory searching, but the results were not particularly rewarding. Hoagland's attention then turned to a study of the accumulation of ions by plants. He had already made a systematic study of the chemical composition of the kelps, and in a paper dealing with the subject he wrote as follows:

Of far greater interest to the plant chemist and physiologist [than their economic importance] is the study of the chemical composition and metabolism of these remarkable plants.

He noted with keenest interest the ability of these plants to accumulate potassium and iodine in amounts often exceeding the concentration of these elements found in sea water.

From 1913 to 1920 Hoagland was assistant professor of agricultural chemistry, from 1920 to 1925, associate professor of plant nutrition, and head of that division from 1922, when the division of soil chemistry and bacteriology were merged to form the division of plant nutrition. This bit of administrative reorganization having been effected, Dr. Hoagland returned with renewed zeal to his study of fundamental behavior of plants as absorbers and accumulators of ions. At that time there was much need of a clarification of just how plants absorbed inorganic elements. It remained for Hoagland to demonstrate through use of the alga *Nitella* that such absorption could be effected only when "right metabolic conditions" prevailed. It remained to determine the essential facts governing the absorption of nutritive elements by the roots of plants. What were the factors basic, for example, to salt absorption by the roots of a given plant? By experimental procedure he found that, when excised, barley roots from experimentally grown plants were "the most active salt-accumulating system so far [1936] investigated."

Finally, Hoagland studied the effect of reversing the external concentration gradient on ion entry and the effect of inhibitory agents on accumulation of ions. This enabled him to confirm the conclusion he and his associates had reached nearly twenty years earlier, namely, that ion accumulation comes about through a metabolically linked process. His interest in ion accumulation and absorption was lifelong. Yet this did not lessen his grasp of the importance of other aspects of plant nutrition as a whole. Important as was the culture medium, Hoagland was fully convinced as to the importance of research on the physiology and control of such growth factors as light, temperature, and humidity. In his mind's eye, he pictured the day when "the development of a quantitative plant physiology in relation to mineral nutrition" would enable the experimenter to "do exactly the same thing twice." While such a condition might be experimentally attainable, he realized the necessity of a variety of experimental methods because of the complexity of the total environment to which the plant is subject throughout its natural life. He was interested in revealing those principles, ascertained under controlled laboratory conditions, that would help the farmer solve his field problems; yet, he was aware of the limitations of such a procedure.

Hoagland's consistent respect for the objective viewpoint in his research and his ability to interpret ascertained fact won for him widely deserved respect and honor. In 1934 he was elected a member of the National Academy of Sciences. His closest scientific affiliation, the American Society of Plant Physiology, conferred upon him in 1930 The Stephen Hale Award in recognition of his exceptional research. The high esteem in which he was held by plant physiologists at home and abroad was signalized by his appointment as president of the Section of Plant Physiology at the VIIth International Botanical Congress. He was a member of the Botanical Society of America; the Western Society of Soil Science; the Western Society of Naturalists; the American Association for the Advancement of Science, the Pacific Division, of which he was president in 1941. In 1940 he was awarded the 1,000 dollar prize by the American Association for the Advancement of Science at its Philadelphia meeting. In 1942 he was invited by Harvard University to present the John M. Prather lectures, subsequently published in book form.

In 1920, at the age of thirty-six, Dr. Hoagland married Jessie A. Smiley. She died in 1933, leaving Dr. Hoagland with the care of his three boys, who survived him on his death in September, 1949.

Arnon, D. A. 1950. Dennis Robert Hoagland 1884–1949. *Plant Physiol.* 25: 5–16.
Arnon, D. A. 1950. *Soil Sci.* 69: 1–5.
Arnon, D. A. 1950. *Plant Soil* 2: 129–144.
Kelley, W. P. 1956. *Nat. Acad. Sci. Biog. Mem.* 29: 123–143, with portrait and bibliography.

Herman Theodor Holm

1854–1932

Herman Theodor Holm was born in Copenhagen, Denmark, February 3, 1854. He was educated at the University of Copenhagen and graduated in 1880. He studied under Prof. Eugene Warming, one of the most eminent European botanists of his day. In 1882 Holm was invited to join the North Polar Expedition and was appointed botanist and zoologist under Admiral Garda. For nearly two years the expedition was icebound in Greenland, a fortunate incident for the young botanist, since it afforded him the opportunity to study the flora of West Greenland and to make important contributions to our knowledge of altitudinal and circumpolar plant life.

At the age of thirty-four, Holm migrated to America and arrived in New York on April 12, 1888. Shortly thereafter he applied for United States citizenship. Soon after his arrival, he was appointed assistant botanist in the United States National Museum, which position he occupied for five years. He was then appointed assistant pathologist.

Holm held this position until 1897, when he resigned, but he continued active, as evidenced by the continued and voluminous output of worthy contributions during the years of his retirement. Especially notable and authoritative were his papers on the taxonomy and geographic range of the sedges (Cyperaceae) and the grasses (Gramineae). Other important contributions were his Claytonia gronov: a Morphological and Anatomical Study"; his paper entitled: "Commelinaceae: Morphological and Anatomical Studies of the Vegetative Organs of some North-and-Central-American Species"; "Some new anatomical characters for certain Gramineae"; "The vegetation of the Rocky Mountains in Colorado," and many other papers of like importance but too numerous to list here.

As a plant anatomist, Professor Holm had few rivals, and his extensive and scholarly acquaintance with germanic and romance languages enabled him to render invaluable service as reviewer and translator. For years he lived a more or less secluded life on his farm at Clinton, Maryland, where he could and did work at will on problems of his beloved botany. Increasingly conscious of the infirmities of advancing years, he was finally persuaded to give up his hermitage and accept an offer of a research professorship in the department of botany at the Catholic University of America, where he passed away on December 26, 1932.

WOODS, A. F. 1933. Herman Theodor Holm. *Science* n.s. 77: 183–184.

Marshall Avery Howe
1867–1936

Marshall Avery Howe was born on June 6, 1867 in Newfane, Vermont, and passed away at his home in Pleasantville, New York, December 24, 1936, while he was director of the New York Botanical Garden. He was the son of Marshall Otis and Gertrude Isabelle (Dexter) Howe, both of English origin and early Vermont lineage. His father and mother were mutually endowed as to tastes and intellectual interests; both were interested in botany and were natural-born students, inclined to read the more serious literature. With such a parental background it is not surprising that Marshall Avery Howe very early showed a marked inclination to study, and it is not unlikely that he received considerable encouragement from both his father and mother. His early education was in the public school.

Before he had completed his college-preparatory studies, he taught school and thus earned some of the money necessary to his support as a student in Glenwood Classical Institute of West Brattleboro, Vermont. On graduation from the institute, he entered the University of Vermont, where he met Abel J. Grout, who was to become his lifelong friend. He no doubt exerted some in-

fluence on Marshall and had a part in directing him toward a special study of the Hepaticae. Grout's chief interest was in the
mosses, and it is known that the two men worked side by side, the
one on his mosses, the other on liverworts. Howe graduated from
the University of Vermont in 1890, when he received his Ph. B.

On leaving the University he was engaged as a teacher by the
Brattleboro, Vermont, high school. He remained there somewhat
less than a year, when he was called to the University of California
as instructor in cryptogamic botany. For this appointment he was
indebted to Prof. Edward Lee Greene, then head of the department of botany. For some reason not clearly known, Howe was
not entirely happy during the early part of his instructorship, but
he became reconciled to it about the time (1895) when Professor
Greene accepted the headship of the department of botany at the
Catholic University of America. Howe accepted a fellowship at
Columbia University, calling for him to move to New York at the
end of the academic year 1895–1896.

Under Greene's influence Howe manifested a renewed interest
in the Hepaticae and was induced to publish a few of his earliest
notes and papers in *Pittonia* and *Erythea,* journals in which
Greene had more than a casual interest. While in California, Howe
had made an important collection of the liverworts of that state.
This he took with him to Columbia where it was his intention to
continue his study of them and there to complete the requirements
for the Ph.D. degree. His most important contribution to our
knowledge of the Hepaticae was his "The Hepaticae and Antho-
cerotes of California," a monumental work based on five years of
collecting and most thorough study. This monograph is, throughout, eloquent of the scholarship and thoroughness of his research
and of his characteristic excellence of portrayal and description.

Howe next devoted himself seriously to an equally searching
study of the Algae. His interest in the liverworts, however, continued, and his reputation as an authority on whatever pertained
to hepaticology never lessened. It is possible, however, that he will
be longest remembered as an algologist. His most extensive contribution as such was the outcome of his study of the marine algae of
the West Indies. Not only did he add much to the then current
knowledge of the West Indian algal flora, but he helped to clear
away the confusion that had long characterized the alleged infor-

mation pertaining to it. It was in Howe's research on the West Indian marine algae that we find him at his best as a phycologist.

Howe received his Ph. D. from Columbia University in 1898, and, from that time until 1901, he served as curator of the university's herbarium. About this time the New York Botanical Garden, yet in its infancy, appointed Marshall Avery Howe as a member of its scientific staff, and, in 1906, he was promoted to the position of curator of the garden. In 1923, he became assistant director, and, in 1935, he was made director, succeeding E. D. Merril, who had resigned. This position he held until his death in 1936.

Merely to outline Dr. Howe's extraordinarily productive service to the New York Botanical Garden between 1901 and 1936 will suffice to show the magnitude of his contribution as collector, taxonomist, morphologist, curator, horticulturist, editor, and administrator. In any and all of these capacities, he served with eminent distinction and without at any time losing sight of the many-faceted objectives of the Garden. His eminence in research was recognized by his Alma Mater, the University of Vermont, when he was awarded the honorary D. Sc. degree in 1919. He was elected in 1923 to membership in the National Academy of Sciences. He was a member and served as president of the New York Academy of Sciences, a member of the Botanical Society of America, of which he was vice president in 1913. In 1936 he was elected president of the Torrey Botanical Club.

On June 8, 1909, Marshall Avery Howe and Edith Morton Packard of Stratford, Connecticut, were married. To this union were born a daughter, Gertrude Dexter and a son, Prentiss Mellon Howe.

BARNHART, J. H. 1937. Marshall Avery Howe. *Science* n.s. 85: 91–92.
GROUT, A. J. 1937. Marshall Avery Howe 1867–1936. *Bryologist* 40, No. 2: 33–36, with portrait.
SETCHELL, W. A. 1938. Biographical Memoir of Marshall Avery Howe 1867–1936. *Nat. Acad. Sci. Biog. Mem.* 19: 243–269, with portrait and bibliography by John Hendley Barnhart.
STOUT, A. B. 1937. *J. N.Y. Botan. Gard.* 38: 25–31.

Thomas Jefferson Howell
1842–1912

Thomas Jefferson Howell, son of Benjamin, a physician, and Elizabeth (Matthews) Howell, was born on October 9, 1842, in Pisgah, Cooper County, Missouri. Reputedly he had descended from Howel, King of South Wales. His early American ancestor, John Howell, was a native of Wales who came to America about 1650. Thomas Howell's father, Dr. Benjamin Howell, and family migrated to Oregon by ox team in 1850 and settled on a United States land grant near Portland. The boy Thomas' schooling did not exceed a total of six months. His father, however, being a physician, had received a better-than-average education, and it is probable that Thomas may have profited from it though the evidence of such advantage seems scant indeed.

By occupation Thomas Howell was a farmer and livestock husbandman. At heart he yearned for the woods and fields and an acquaintance with the plant life he found there. His interest in the plant life of the countryside near Portland, Oregon, gave him no rest. Being a natural-born woodsman and perfectly at home in the midst of the Oregon wilderness, he had, by 1877, built up a considerable herbarium. For several years specimens from his herbarium were made up in sets and sent to established herbarium centers in the United States and Europe. This resulted in the disclosure that, of the plants he had collected and thus distributed, more than fifty were new to science.

Howell's success as a collector greatly stimulated his interest in further and more extended excursions into the Oregon wilderness. A favorite region proved to be the then but little known Siskiyou Mountains of south-western Oregon and northern California. There he discovered an exceedingly interesting species of spruce peculiar to the region. Specimens from it, sent to Sereno Watson, confirmed Howell's discovery of a new species of *Picea*, which Watson forthwith, and apparently without justification other than pure fancy, named *Picea breweriana*, in honor of W. H. Brewer, who had nothing to do with either its discovery or identification.

By 1881 Howell had carried on his work to a point where it seemed desirable to publish a list of all the phanerogams of Washington, Oregon, and Idaho. By 1887 this had grown to "A Catalogue of the Known Plants (Phaenogamia and Pteridophyta) of Oregon, Washington, and Idaho," comprising 2,152 species and more than two hundred and twenty varieties. There still remained to be published something more than a catalogue of the known plants of the Pacific Northwest; so, Howell undertook the herculean labor of preparing and publishing a descriptive text. He commenced the preparation of the manuscript in 1897, and in 1903 he saw the completion of his "Flora of Northwest America." He, being a man of limited material resources, was unable to employ adequately qualified editorial aid. He therefore undertook and learned the art of typesetting. His very limited schooling made the task so difficult that it was necessary to seek instruction in composition. All of his pages of type were set by hand, and, little by little, these blocks of type were carried from his home in the village of Clackamas to Portland, where they were run off on a power press. Howell was of pioneer stock and was, himself, a pioneer in the field of learning. His knowledge of spelling and of the English language was so limited that much of the text of his "Flora" was not altogether his own composition. Although thus handicapped, he had a good understanding of the requirements of such a text. His sense of organization enabled him to appraise the work of others who had labored in the same field of research and to produce a flora of genuine merit and usefulness. For nearly half a century his remained the one most complete account of the flora of the Pacific Northwest.

Howell remained single until fifty years of age, when he married Effie (Hudson) McIlwane, a widow. He passed away in December, 1912, at Portland, Oregon.

SARGENT, C. S. 1898. *The Silva of North America*, Vol. 12. Houghton Mifflin Company, New York.
SMITH, H. H. 1913. Thomas Jefferson Howell. *Botan. Gaz.* 55: 458–460, with portrait.

Harry Baker Humphrey*
1873–1955

Born August 4, 1873, in a log cabin on a homestead farm near the Minnesota frontier settlement of East Granite Falls, Harry was the first of the 5 children of John Wadsworth Humphrey and Adeline Regester Humphrey, descendants of respected early American colonists.

In 1877 the family moved to Oregon but 5 years later returned to farming in Minnesota near Elk River. Harry's first interest in plant life was awakened by his teacher in the nearby country school. At 18, encouraged by his mother, he decided that he must have further education even though the farm needed him. To get across the Mississippi to high school he built a row boat. Lumberjacks broke the lock and sent the boat downstream. Another boat was built only to be carried away in a log jam. Not to be stopped, he built a third. Doing a man's work on the home farm much of the time and rowing or skating over the river to his classes, Harry succeeded in graduating in 3 years from Elk River High School, president of his class.

Entering the University of Minnesota in 1895, he worked his way through, specializing in botany and modern languages. Through Dr. D. T. McDougal, renowned plant physiologist, he received an assistantship in botany at the University where he graduated with a B.S. degree in 1899. There followed 4 years of secondary school administration and teaching. In 1901 he married Olive Agatha Mealey of Minneapolis; she had been a fellow student in botany in the University. Through the years that followed, her judgment, understanding, and steadying influence were a great help to him and to their 6 children.

In 1903 he enrolled for graduate work in Leland Stanford Jr. University, where he became a part-time instructor and in 1907 received his Ph.D. degree. There D. H. Campbell and David Starr

* Adapted from a biography by Howard P. Barss (*Phytopathology*, Vol. 47, No. 5).

Jordan provided his chief inspiration. For 3 summers he taught marine biology at Hopkins Marine Biological Laboratory at Pacific Grove.

In 1908 Dr. Humphrey was appointed Professor of Botany and Plant Pathologist in the Experiment Station at the State College of Washington at Pullman. His successful work led to his promotion to Head of the Department of Botany and Vice Director of the Experiment Station in 1911. In the summer of 1912 he taught at the Marine Biological Laboratory at Friday Harbor on Puget Sound.

In 1913 he was appointed Pathologist in charge of cereal disease investigations in the Bureau of Plant Industry in the U.S. Department of Agriculture in Washington, D.C. Here he achieved the rank of Principal Pathologist in the Division of Cereal Crops and Diseases where he served until his automatic retirement in 1943, at the age of 70. He and his co-workers, in cooperation with State Agricultural Experiment Stations, carried out important basic research on diseases of cereal grains and made significant progress in their practical control, particularly by testing and breeding for resistance.

Those who knew him best emphasize the strong constructive influence Dr. Humphrey exerted throughout his personal relationships during his long career. Seeking nothing for himself but the chance to be of service, he was a constant source of sympathetic encouragement, inspiration, and sound advice. Time and again his helpful words and understanding letters to troubled or discouraged workers gave new energy and direction to their endeavors.

Dr. Humphrey's staunch and vigorous personality was marked by absolute integrity, devotion to duty, unselfishness, and great kindliness. He was a versatile scholar with exceptionally wide interests; an able, stimulating, exacting teacher; a considerate and conscientious administrator; a linguist of parts; and a scientist of inquiring mind who stressed both fundamental research and its practical applications. He loved Nature in all her aspects and was attracted to the best in art, music, and literature. Above all, he possessed a dynamic faith in young people and a deep affection for his fellow men regardless of race, creed, or station. A man of quiet dignity, uncompromising toward slothfulness or low standards in conduct or language, Dr. Humphrey was conscientiously thorough and precise in every undertaking. Withal, he had great zest for life and a keen sense of humor revealed by the sparkle in his eyes and his energetic chuckle. He often regaled friends with inimitable tales in French-Canadian or in Swedish dialect.

Dr. Humphrey's contribution to scientific literature numbered more than 50. His earliest works were concerned with algae, hepatics, and plant ecology. His later contributions, many with joint authorship, dealt mainly with cereal diseases, particularly the smuts and rusts. Although administrative work occupied much of his time, whenever possible he participated personally in the research he directed. In 1918 the important cooperative barberry eradication campaign in the North-Central States was initiated under his direction. Likewise, a nation-wide campaign for seed treatment against grain smuts was organized about that time. His studies with Woolman on the physiology of stinking smut in relation to infection and control and the studies of stripe rust of cereals (caused by *Puccinia glumarum*) conducted with C. W. Hungerford and A. G. Johnson are especially noteworthy. His effective cooperation with plant breeders in the Department of Agriculture and in State Experiment Stations was a great aid in their development of the disease-resistant lines of cereal grains, which have saved American agriculture from destructive losses. Dr. Humphrey extended helpful cooperation to his Canadian colleagues and was invited to address the Royal Society of Canada in Quebec in 1934.

Dr. Humphrey was a life member of the American Phytopathological Society, serving as Vice President (1926), President (1945), a Councilor for many years, and Editor-in-Chief of *Phytopathology,* the Society's official organ, from 1929 to 1943. During this period he was also Editor of Phytopathological Classics, for which his broad command of languages was a great asset. His 190-page translation from the French of Tillet's dissertation of 1755 on the smutting of wheat appeared in 1937 as No. 5 in this series. In his editorial work, his understanding and considerate helpfulness to inexperienced contributors and his patient insistence on correct and lucid English won high commendation for him and placed the Journal in the first rank among publications of its kind.

Besides the American Phytopathological Society, Dr. Humphrey was a member of Sigma Xi, A.A.A.S. (Fellow), American Academy of Arts and Sciences, Washington Academy of Sciences, Botanical Society of America, Botanical Society of Washington (President 1930), Biological Society of Washington, Minnesota Historical Society, Cosmos Club, Washington College of Music, and American Federation of Arts. He was also active in church work.

In 1951, Dr. Humphrey and his wife moved to Los Altos, California, not far from Stanford University where he had access to the library in connection with the work which occupied his last years. At the time of his passing, he was working on his biographies of North American botanists.

BARSS, H. P. 1957. Harry Baker Humphrey, 1873–1955. *Phytopathology* 47: 247–248.

James Ellis Humphrey
1861–1897

Born August 5, 1861, in Weymouth, Massachusetts, James Ellis Humphrey was the son of James and Susan (Cushing) Humphrey. He received his early education, in part, in Weymouth schools. To his father, however, he was indebted for his intelligent appreciation of and love for literature and for his marked facility in speech and writing. He graduated from high school at the age of sixteen and was that same year appointed master of the North Weymouth grammer school. Notwithstanding his youthfulness, his conduct of the stewardship reposed in him won for him the respect and confidence of his pupils.

Humphrey next was employed by a firm dealing in school and college supplies, a position that brought him in contact with those who awakened his interest in the pursuit of scientific lines of study. During a vacation of rest and study at the Martha's Vineyard Summer Institute, he became interested in marine and other algae. Returning to his home, he equipped for himself a laboratory, where he devoted his spare hours to the study of the algae he collected from the Weymouth River. This so interested him that he forthwith decided to cast his lot with the sciences by enrolling in the Lawrence Scientific School of Harvard University, where, in 1886, he received his B.S. degree.

During his undergraduate years, Humphrey devoted himself particularly to the study of botany, and on graduation he was offered the opportunity to serve as laboratory assistant in botany under Prof. G. L. Goodale. The following year he received an appointment as instructor in botany at Indiana University. In 1888 he returned to his native state, where he had accepted an offer as botanist in the Massachusetts Agricultural Experiment Station. Here he remained for four years, applying himself especially to research on parasitic fungi, notably those of pathological importance to horticultural crops. Here it was also that he conducted his monographic research on the Saprolegniaceae under the direction of the Harvard Faculty, and in 1892 he was awarded the degree of Doctor of Science.

That same year he spent three months in Jamaica, collecting plants. He then proceeded from Jamaica to Germany, where, at Bonn, he studied under the direction of Prof. Edward Strasburger, at that time one of the world's most eminent botanists. On returning to the United States, Humphrey obtained a fellowship at Johns Hopkins University and was subsequently appointed to the position of lecturer in botany and, in 1897, to associate professor. In June of that year, he and several Johns Hopkins University students sailed to Jamaica to work in the university's marine laboratory, located there for that summer. It was there that Professor Humphrey's brilliant career in botanical teaching and research was suddenly ended by fatal illness. Thus was terminated the career of a botanist of much promise.

Notable among Humphrey's contributions were: "Comparative Morphology of the Fungi," "The Saprolegniaceae of the United States," "On Monilia fructigena," "Botanical Micro-technique" (from the German by Zimmermann), "Development of the seed in the Scitamineae," "The Rotting of Lettuce," "Nucleolen and Centrosomen," and several shorter papers, reports, etc.

As indicated by the nature and quality of his published research, Dr. Humphrey arrived on the botanical scene at a time when the importance of cytology was becoming more and more keenly realized. He, himself, foresaw this fact, and as a result of his vision his translation and ultimate publication of Zimmerman's "Botanical Microtechnique" was a contribution of no little importance.

ANON. 1897–1898. *Johns Hopkins Univ. Circ.* No. 17. Pp. 17–19.
ANON. 1898. *Wood's Hole Marine Biol. Lab. Lectures.* Pp. 341–343.
ANON. 1897–98. *Nature* 57: 60.
ANON. 1897. *Am. Nat.* 31: 920–922.

Thomas Potts James
1803–1882

Thomas Potts James, the son of Dr. Isaac and Henrietta (Potts) James, was born at Radnor, Pennsylvania, the first of September, 1803. His parents came from families that had gained considerable prominence in early American colonial history. David James, a paternal ancestor, had migrated to America from Wales prior to 1682 and purchased a large tract of land from William Penn. On the maternal side the grandfather of Thomas James served in the Continental Army and was promoted to the rank of colonel. As a civilian he had an active part in the early and formative years of his country's history. The first few years of Isaac James's married life were spent in Radnor, but, in order that he might be assured of better facilities for the education of his children, he moved his family to Burlington, New Jersey.

Because of financial reverses, his plans for the education of his children were foiled, and his two sons, Thomas and John, undertook to pay for their education. They studied pharmacy, and, as young men, established a wholesale drug business in Philadelphia. This they carried on for more than thirty years. Thomas studied medicine but did not finish the requirements for graduation. His interest in botany was awakened while he was still young, and it is known that he had some knowledge of the flowering plants of his native environment before he became interested in the mosses and liverworts.

At forty-eight he married Isabella Bachelder of Cambridge, Massachusetts, a friend of Asa Gray's and a lady who had a natural interest in botany. She was, therefore, able to help her husband in his botanical research. Thomas James was successful in disposing of his interest in the drug business, and in 1866 he moved to Cambridge, where, through the rest of his life, he had free access to the laboratory and herbarium facilities of Harvard University and was able to devote his time and energy to his study of the bryophytes.

Among James's earliest published results was the section on mosses and liverworts in Darlington's *Flora Cestrica* (1853). In 1856 there appeared in "Proceedings of the Academy of Natural Sciences of Philadelphia," Vol. VII, "An Enumeration of the Mosses Detected in the United States not Comprised in the Manual of Asa Gray, M.D." Eleven years later appeared his list of mosses as a part of Rothrock's "Sketch of the Flora of Alaska" (contained in "Smithsonian Report for 1867"). In 1871 he published a catalogue of western mosses in Volume V of the "Report of the Geological Exploration of the Fortieth Parallel"; and, in 1878, Vol. VI, of the "Report of the Geographical Surveys West of the One Hundredth Meridian in Charge of Lt. George M. Wheeler." These contributions to the knowledge of American mosses were of superior excellence.

His unremitting devotion to his research made such exacting demands on his health that he sought rest in Europe. There he met W. P. Schimper, the leading European authority on mosses, and, in London, he renewed his acquaintance with Joseph Hooker. After five months' rest, James undertook with Lesquereux the preparation of a "Manual of North American Mosses." This he failed to finish before his death, but he left it in such order that it could be and was completed and published in 1884. It remains to this day a classic on the mosses of America.

James was a fellow of the American Association for the Advancement of Science and of the American Academy of Arts and Sciences. For a quarter century he served as secretary of the Pennsylvania Horticultural Society and was its treasurer for twenty-seven years. He was a founder of the American Pomological Society and an active member of the American Philosophical Society, the American Pharmaceutical Society, and the Boston Society of Natural History. It is fitting here to quote what Léo Lesquereux wrote in a letter to J. T. Rothrock:

I came to this country in 1848, and it was only a little after my arrival here that he [James] began sending me his mosses for determination. Our connection continued until his death. I received a letter from him but a few days before this. When I was obliged to abandon the use of the microscope, he worked constantly upon sketches of all the interesting or doubtful American species and prepared for the descriptive part of which I took charge. He had, moreover to give much time to the examination of collections of mosses sent for determination from various parts of the continent, those of E. Hall from Oregon, Macoon in Canada, Wolff and others from Illinois, so that his work and influence in the Bryology of North America have been very great, though his publications are limited to a few catalogues or Memoirs.

Thomas Potts James died on February 22, 1882, survived by Mrs. James and four children.

Gozzaldi, M. I. J. 1903. Thomas Potts James. *Bryologist,* Sept.
Gray, A. 1882. *Am. J. Sci.* 3rd Ser. 23: 330–331.
Gray, A. 1882. *Proc. Am. Acad. Sci.* 17 n.s. 9: 405–406.
Rothrock, J. T. 1883. *Proc. Am. Philos. Soc.* 20: 293–297.

Willis Linn Jepson

1867–1946

Willis Linn Jepson, son of William Lemon and Martha Ann (Potts) Jepson, was born August 19, 1867 at Little Oak, near Vacaville, California. His ancestry was Scottish-English, and his parents were California pioneers who settled in the Vaca Valley, northeast of San Francisco Bay. He was a "native son" who, according to one of his biographers, "never quite forgave the march of progress for its inroads on the pristine landscape that was early California." His college preparatory education was acquired in California, as was also the major part of his university experience. He was graduated from the University of California in 1889 and was awarded the Ph.B. degree.

In 1890 Jepson was appointed assistant in botany, and was thus given the opportunity to devote long hours to taxonomic botany under the direction of E. L. Greene, a pioneer worker in systematic botany and founder of the university's department of botany. For three years (1895–1898) Jepson served the university as instructor in botany and carried on his postgraduate research with Professor Greene, Marshall Avery Howe, Dr. Setchell, and J. C. Merriam. There were also Atkinson and Rowlee of Cornell and Robinson of Harvard. In 1905 he was busy at Kew Gardens, London, where he had access to the all but priceless herbaria of that great botanical center. In 1906 he enjoyed a like privilege extended to him in Berlin. In 1899, having met the requirements for the doctorate in botany, he was awarded the Ph.D. degree by the University of California. Thereupon he was appointed assistant professor of botany and successively associate professor in 1911, professor in 1918, and professor emeritus in 1937. Here was a good example of an American-born, American-bred, and American-educated botanist—a man eminent in research as he was in teaching, who contributed creditably to North American botany and earned the plaudits of those who for generations to come will enjoy the fruits of his labor.

In addition to his years of teaching and research, Jepson indulged his taste for botanical exploration. He acquainted himself with many mountain and desert areas in California during the more than forty years of his devotion to botany. During this time he enjoyed botanical expeditions to Alaska and the Bering Sea, to Syria and Palestine.

From 1893 to 1900, and in 1922 he was editor of the botanical journal "Erythea." From 1915 to 1934 he was editor of the journal of the California Botanical Society. In 1905 he was a delegate to the International Agricultural Congress at Liege, Belgium, and in 1930 and 1935 to the International Botanical Congress, first at Cambridge, England, and then at Amsterdam.

Jepson's reputation as a botanist may be said to rest chiefly on his "Flora of Middle-Western California" (1901); "Silva of California" (1910); "Manual of the Flowering Plants of California" (1923–1925); and his monumental "Flora of California" (1909–1943). His name has been memorialized in that of the genus *Jepsonia*, a member of the family Saxifragraceae, dedicated to the memory of Jepson by the botanist John Kunkel Small.

Jepson was never married and was therefore free to devote his full attention to California botany. He passed away at his home November 7, 1946.

CONSTANCE, L. 1947. *Science* n.s. 105: 614.

Duncan Starr Johnson

1867–1937

Duncan Starr Johnson was born at Cromwell, Connecticut, on July 21, 1867. He was the son of Edward Tracy and Lucy Emma (Starr) Johnson. Very little is recorded as to his college-preparatory education, though it is a matter of record that he was granted the Bachelor of Science degree on his graduation from Wesleyan University, Connecticut, in 1892. The same university, forty years later, granted him the honorary degree of Doctor of Science. Soon after his graduation from Wesleyan, he spent a brief period as a student at Yale and then entered Johns Hopkins University in 1893. There he received invaluable training as a graduate student under J. P. Lotsy and James Ellis Humphrey, the one a specialist and authority in morphology, the other a man of much promise as a cytologist, fresh from the influence of the great German botanist, Strasburger. The untimely passing of Professor Humphrey, in 1897, left Johnson, his one and only graduate student, without a teacher. That year he completed his requirements for the doctorate and was granted his Ph.D. degree.

Thereafter, excepting certain summer intervals of work in other laboratories, Johnson spent the rest of his life in the service of Johns Hopkins University. His first appointment there was as assistant in botany; then he was promoted to the rank of associate. In 1901, he became associate professor and served as such until 1906, when he became professor of botany. In 1901 he spent a few months in the laboratory of von Goebel of Munich. In 1913, Johnson was appointed director of the newly created Johns Hopkins botanical garden, for the organizing and planting of which he became wholly responsible.

Dr. Johnson's botanical activities were many and varied, and in all of them he was eminently successful. Not all of them can be adequately represented in a sketch of this brevity. Altogether, he conducted seven summer expeditions to Jamaica. On these expeditions he was accompanied by other botanists and by such of his students as found it possible to go. From 1896 to 1900 he was in charge of botany at the Cold Spring Harbor Biological Laboratory on Long Island. Two years later and until 1911, he was placed in charge of cryptogamic botany in the same laboratory. From 1914 to 1923 he was vice president of the Harpswell Laboratory on Casco Bay, Maine, and of the Mount Desert, Maine, Laboratory from 1924 until he was claimed by death in 1937. He was deeply interested in field and seaside laboratories, where plant life in relation to natural environment could be studied on the spot.

During the United States' participation in World War I, Dr. Johnson had an active part in the regional leadership of a nation-wide project of cereal-smut control under the auspices of the U.S. Department af Agriculture in cooperation with the several states concerned. In the summer of 1935, he lectured at the Mountain Lake laboratory of the University of Virginia. In 1930, he toured Europe extensively, visiting several botanical gardens. While abroad he participated actively in the fifth International Botanical Congress, at Cambridge. Five years later he attended the sixth Congress, at Amsterdam.

Dr. Johnson's first published paper was on the crystallization of cellulose. He early became primarily interested in plant morphology and remained so throughout the rest of his life. His first contributions as a morphologist related to the development of the sporocarps of two water ferns, *Marsilia* and *Pilularia*. These two papers at once cast the die of one of America's outstanding botanists, a fact later to be fully confirmed by a remarkable series of articles, first on the Piperales (ten papers), followed by authoritative contributions to our knowledge of the relation of plants to tide levels; papers on plant migration, and a study of factors affecting the development of the flowers of the giant cactus (*Carnegiea*). In his study of *Marsilia* and *Pilularia* he was the first to work out the development of the sporocarp.

Commencing in 1900 his research on the developmental history of the Piperales, he discovered a kind of embryo-sac development in *Peperomia pellucida* in which sixteen free nuclei are formed first, half of which fuse and form a single nucleus—the endosperm nucleus. In this family he discovered that many genera were characterized by a marked proliferation of endosperm. Johnson's study of the Piperales led him to offer the generalization that "the sporophyte is perhaps everywhere nourished through the gametophyte and not by the sporophyte directly." His subsequent studies of different representatives of the order served only to convince him that Professor Hofmeister was right in maintaining that "the developmental history of the embryo sac and nucellus does not furnish a satisfactory . . . basis for classification." Dr. Johnson's marked ability as a teacher won for him the respect and gratitude of many an earnest student; for, as educator, as well as botanist, he attained stature for originality and leadership which placed him in the very forefront of those who developed the American school of botany.

In June, 1904, Dr. Johnson married Mary E. G. Lentz of Baltimore, Maryland. To this union were born two children, George Duncan and David Starr. He enjoyed membership in a number of scientific societies, chief among which were the American Association for the Advancement of Science, the Botanical Society of America, and the Société Botanique de Géneve. He was also a member of the National Research Council.

Dr. Johnson passed away in Baltimore on February 16, 1937 in his seventieth year.

ANON. 1937. Memorial adopted by the Division of Biology and Agriculture of the National Research Council on Apr. 24, 1937. *Science* n.s. 86: 29.
COKER, W. C. 1937. Obituary. Professor Duncan Starr Johnson. *Science* n.s. 86: 510–512.

Calvin Henry Kauffman

1869–1931

Calvin Henry Kauffman was born March 10, 1869, in Lebanon County, Pennsylvania. He was the son of John Henry and Mary Ann (Light) Kauffman. According to family records, his American paternal ancestor came to the New World from the German Palatinate and settled in Pennsylvania sometime in the eighteenth century. Calvin Henry was born on the family farm, and there he spent the years of his boyhood. He attended the country schools of the region, and the Palatinate College at Myrostown, Pennsylvania. At the close of his second year, he went to Cambridge, Massachusetts, where he enrolled at Harvard University and, in 1896, received his A.B. degree. As an undergraduate student he specialized in Greek and Latin. He later registered at the University of Wisconsin for postgraduate study. While at Harvard he married Elizabeth Catharine Wolff, daughter of Herman Wolff of Lebanon, Pennsylvania.

From 1896 to 1898, Kauffman served as principal of a preparatory school in Lebanon. From there he moved to Decatur, Indiana, where he had been appointed as teacher of science in a high school and in Bushnell (Ill.) Normal School. In addition to his postgraduate work at the University of Wisconsin, he spent some time in graduate study at Cornell University. At Wisconsin he became acquainted with Prof. Robert A. Harper who did much to cultivate Kauffman's interest in the fungi. At Cornell, he continued his mycological research and was a graduate assistant to Dr. G. F. Atkinson, who, in his own right, was a widely recognized authority on the fungi.

With this background of academic accomplishment and proved ability as a botanist and mycologist, he was well equipped for further advancement in his chosen botanical field. In 1904, he was offered an instructorship at the University of Michigan. His acceptance of the offer made possible his completion of the requirements for the doctorate, and, in 1907, he was awarded the Ph.D.

degree, for which he submitted as his thesis a dissertation entitled "A Contribution to the Physiology of the Saprolegniaceae with Special Reference to the Variations of the Sexual Organs."

The course of Dr. Kauffman's career was by this time clearly defined. As a teacher, he outlined and developed courses in cryptogamic botany and directed research in his chosen field of mycology. In 1911, he was promoted to the rank of assistant professor of botany and to associate professor in 1919. From 1912 to 1921, he served as curator of the cryptogamic herbarium and then as director of the university herbarium. During World War I (1917–1919) he was granted leave of absence from his university duties to serve as pathological inspector for the Federal Horticultural Board of the U.S. Department of Agriculture.

Among the many papers contributed by Kauffman, his more important ones were the "Agaricaceae of Michigan" (1918), "Monographic Studies on various genera of the Agaricaceae," a series of reports covering several years; published papers on the Thelephoraceae, the Polyporaceae, and the Phycomycetes. In addition to these he conducted field studies and published a series of reports covering his mycological observations in Michigan, Tennessee, Kentucky, Colorado, the Siskiyou and the Mt. Hood regions of Oregon, and the North Elba region of New York. He was a member of several scientific societies such as the Botanical Society of America, the American Phytopathological Society, the Torrey Botanical Club, American Association for the Advancement of Science, etc. He died without issue at Ann Arbor, Michigan, June 14, 1931.

ANON. 1931. Calvin Henry Kauffman. *Science* n.s. 74: 235.
MAINS, E. B. 1932. *Mycologia* 24: 265–267.
MAINS, E. B. 1932. *Phytopath.* 22: 221–275, with portrait and bibliography.

Karl Frederic Kellerman
1879–1934

Karl Frederic Kellerman, bacteriologist and plant pathologist, was born in Göttingen, Germany, on December 9, 1879, while his parents, Prof. and Mrs. William A. Kellerman, were in temporary residence to enable the father to pursue his postgraduate botanical studies at the University of Göttingen. On the return of the family to the United States in 1881, they moved to Lexington, Kentucky, resided there for one year, and then moved to Manhattan, Kansas, where Professor Kellerman had been appointed to a position in the State College of Agriculture and Mechanic Arts. Here the son Karl Frederic obtained a part of his elementary schooling. In 1891, he moved with his parents to Columbus, Ohio, where he completed his college-preparatory work and entered Ohio State University. At the end of his third year there, he registered at Cornell University where, in 1900, he received the Bachelor of Science degree.

Immediately thereafter Karl Kellerman was appointed instructor in botany at Cornell. In 1901, having been appointed to a position in the Bureau of Plant Industry, U.S. Department of Agriculture, he moved to Washington, D.C. From 1901 to 1904, he served as assistant physiologist. He was then advanced to the position of director of the laboratory of plant physiology. In 1906 he became director of the laboratory of soil bacteriology and water purification investigations. Here he served until 1914, when, in recognition of his abilities, he was advanced to the position of assistant chief of the Bureau of Plant Industry. In 1917, in further recognition of his genius for leadership and his outstanding research ability, he was selected to fill the newly created office of associate chief of the Bureau of Plant Industry. This position he held with distinction until 1933. He was then appointed chief in the division of plant-disease eradication and control in the Bureau of Entomology and Plant Quarantine, where he continued to serve until his death in August, 1934. The honorary degree of Doctor of Science was conferred upon him in 1923 by the State College of Kansas.

Early in Kellerman's career as a botanist, he developed methods of water purification. This accomplishment resulted in his appointment by the Secretary of Agriculture as a special assistant to the chief engineer of the Panama Canal to discover how to improve the water supply of the Canal Zone. He was a pioneer in the investigation of ways and means of the bacterial purification of water and sewage. Also, he did pioneer work in the investigation of nitrogen-fixing bacteria in soils. Credit is due Dr. Kellerman for his development of a synthetic medium that has since proved basic to much of the success realized in this field of bacteriological research. In 1911, he spent some time abroad in consultation with leading European bacteriologists. There he acquired important bacterial cultures, potentially valuable in future experimental studies.

Man of vision that he was, Dr. Kellerman early realized the necessity for a scientific journal devoted specifically to the publication of contributions to our knowledge of scientific agriculture. Therefore, in 1913, he advocated and brought into being the "Journal of Agricultural Research," and for ten years he served as chairman of its editorial committee.

In 1913 he was asked to organize and direct a cooperative campaign for the eradication of citrus canker, a plant disease that threatened to destroy the citrus industry in the Gulf States. This was the first time that a campaign of this kind had ever been undertaken in the United States. It was predicted by many that it would fail, but it was successfully conducted and is now generally accepted as one of the most, if not the most, notable achievement of its kind in the history of plant pathology. From 1914 to 1924, Kellerman was a member of the Federal horticultural board, and during that time played an important role in shaping a practicable policy of plant quarantine.

In 1917 Kellerman was designated by Pres. Woodrow Wilson to serve as a member of the National Research Council, and, from 1918 until his death (1924), he was a member of the division of biology and agriculture and the division of federal relations. His interest in and direction of citrus-canker control included also the national direction of barberry eradication for the control of stem rust of such cereal crops as wheat, oats, and barley—a project that has been carried on with vigor and the promise of ultimate success. Other plant diseases in which Kellerman was actively interested were the white-pine blister rust, the phoney disease of the peach, and the Dutch elm disease in the Eastern States. Notwithstanding the many demands placed upon Dr. Kellerman as administrator, he found time for research, as may be noted from the number and character of his many scientific papers, contributions to the "Journal of Agricultural Research," the "Journal of Applied Microscopy," "Science," "Journal of the American Society of Agronomy," "American Journal of Public Health," "Journal of the Washington Academy of Sciences," and a number of European journals.

Dr. Kellerman was richly endowed with those qualities essential to the success of one charged with administrative responsibilities. His training and experience in scientific research, combined with his vision and sound judgment, made of him a man of sure and unfailing worth in all matters of consultation. He was loyal, courageous, and patient in his defense of what to him seemed just and right. He was a fellow of the American Association for the Advancement of Science, a member of the United States Golf Association, the Washington Academy, the International Society of Soil Scientists, the American Society of Agronomy, the American Society of Naturalists, the Society of American Bacteriologists, the Biological Society of Washington, and the Cosmos Club. On August 17, 1905, Dr. Kellerman was married to Gertrude Hast, daughter of Mr. and Mrs. George Perry Hast, of Cumberland, Maryland. To this union was born a son, Karl Frederic Kellerman, Jr.

ANON. 1934. News Notes. *Torreya* 34: 125–126.
TAYLOR, W. A. 1934. Karl Frederic Kellerman. *Science* n.s. 80: 373–374.

William Ashbrook Kellerman
1850–1908

William Ashbrook Kellerman, son of Daniel Kemberling and Ivy (Ashbrook) Kellerman, was born in Ashville, Ohio, May 1, 1850. He was a descendant of Frederic Kellerman who came to America in 1760 and served in the Continental army in the Revolution. William Kellerman attended country school in his native Ohio. At the age of seventeen he was employed as a school teacher. This afforded him opportunity to prepare for a university career. In due course we find him registered at Cornell University, where, in 1874, he received his Bachelor of Science degree.

Immediately upon graduation from Cornell, he obtained employment as a teacher of the natural sciences in the Oshkosh, Wisconsin, Normal School. He held this position until 1879, when he sailed for Europe to attend the Universities of Göttingen and Zürich. From Zürich he obtained the Ph.D. in 1881. On returning to the United States he was appointed professor of botany and zoology at the Kentucky State College of Agriculture and Mechanic Arts in Lexington. From Lexington he moved to Manhattan, Kansas, as professor of botany and zoology in the State College of Agriculture.

He was soon devoting all of his time to botany and was designated botanist of the Kansas State Agricultural Experiment Station. As such he undertook an experimental study of the smuts of wheat and oats and with the help of a student assistant, proved the effectiveness of hot water as an agent in preventing loose smuts of wheat and oats. The results of these pioneer studies were published in 1889 as a bulletin entitled "Loose Smuts of Cereals."

In 1891, Dr. Kellerman went to Columbus, Ohio, as professor of botany at the Ohio State University. In 1893 he was appointed botanist to the Ohio State Geological Survey and was asked that same year to prepare, for the World's Fair in Chicago, an exhibit of the forestry of Ohio. This exhibit presented every tree indigenous to the state. In recognition of the excellence of this exhibit,

Kellerman was presented with a Columbian Exposition medal and diploma.

From 1904 to 1908, he made four yearly expeditions to Guatemala, where he made extensive collections of that part of Central America. It was during the 1907–1908 expedition that he became stricken with a fever from which he failed to recover. It is known that Dr. Kellerman had long hoped he might some day be authorized to establish a tropical school of botany. Realization of this dream came to him in the summer of 1907, when Ohio State University authorized the extension of its botanical field to include Guatemala. Kellerman prepared to leave for Guatemala in December of that year, as the school was to open on the nineteenth of that month and to close on the nineteenth of March, 1908. Most of the time he spent in Guatemala was devoted to collecting plants for herbaria, the most favored being those of Kansas State College and Ohio State University. One of the most important of the herbaria built by Dr. Kellerman was his own, which comprised 20,000 specimens of phanerogamic plants. His collection of parasitic fungi was, at the time, the most complete of its kind in the United States. Following his death these herbaria were sent to Palestine, there to form the nucleus of an herbarium for the Haifa Experiment Station.

Kellerman's *fungi exsiccati* for the State of Ohio presented an exceptionally good series. These were distributed among the more important European and American herbaria. At the time of his last illness he had already begun the distribution of his *fungi selecti Guatemalenses.* He discovered hundreds of new fungi, many of which were parasitic on cultivated and wild plants.

In 1885 Dr. Kellerman founded the "Journal of Mycology" and served as its editor and publisher until 1894, when it was transferred to the U.S. Department of Agriculture. From 1902 to the time of his death, he was again its editor and publisher. Thereafter it was taken over by the New York Botanical Garden and issued as "Mycologia." Kellerman also founded, in 1903, the "Mycological Bulletin." To the Journal of Mycology and other technical journals he contributed some three hundred papers. In addition to these papers, he was the author of several textbooks, notable among which were: "Elements of Botany" (1883); "Plant Analysis" (1884); "Analytical Flora of Kansas" (1888); "Ohio Forest Trees,

Identified by Leaves and Fruit" (1895); "Phytotheca" (1897); and "Elementary Botany and Spring Flora" (1898). Although eminent as a collector and taxonomist and as a specialist in other branches of plant science, Professor Kellerman was by nature and accomplishment preeminently the scholar and teacher. Many now engaged in botanical research can testify to his genius as a teacher and rare friend. As a token of respect to his botanical renown and his importance as a contributor to our knowledge of the plant sciences, a genus of the order Sphaeropsidales, belonging to the Fungi Imperfecti, and many other fungi have been named in his honor.

Dr. Kellerman was married in July, 1876, to Stella Victoria Dennis of Amanda, Ohio. She assisted her husband in the preparation of many of his published papers.

ANON. 1908. William Ashbrook Kellerman. *J. Mycol.* 14: 46–63, with publications.
WILLARD, J. T. 1909. *Trans. Kan. Acad.* 22: 46–47, with portrait.

Albert Kellogg
1813–1887

Albert Kellogg was born in Hartford, Connecticut on December 6, 1813. He was a son of Isaac and Aurilla Barney Kellogg and a descendant of Joseph Kellogg of Great Leighs, Essex, England, who migrated to Connecticut in 1651. From his youth, Kellogg was interested in nature and particularly in plant life. On completion of his preparatory schooling, he studied medicine, not in an accredited medical school but with a physician residing in Middletown, Connecticut. After this preparation, he became a student of medicine at the Medical College of South Carolina and subsequently at Transylvania University in Lexington, Kentucky, where he received his M.D. degree.

During his years in the South, Kellogg sought opportunities to travel and botanize wherever possible as well as to practice medicine. In 1845, he, looking for adventure, traveled extensively in the South and Southwest and, incidentally, became acquainted with John J. Audubon, the artist-naturalist whose work on American birds had won for him no little renown. Yielding to a desire to join the California gold rush of 1848–1849, Kellogg took ship via the Cape Horn route and eventually reached Sacramento, where he engaged in business. After a number of years in Sacramento, he moved to San Francisco and there resumed his practice of medicine.

Notwithstanding his interest in medicine, he was at heart a botanist and, as such, applied himself whenever possible to the observation and study of plants. It was he who first undertook a thorough and systematic study of the "big trees" (*Sequoia gigantea*) of the Sierra Nevada mountains. He was the first resident botanist in California. Here he found himself in the midst of a botanical paradise, in the presence of an unbelievably rich and remarkable flora that had long awaited the coming of an intelligently discriminating and appreciative student, such as Kellogg proved to be. He very soon undertook a painstaking study of S. *gigantea* (1852) but did not publish his results until 1855 ("Proc. Calif. Acad.," May, 1855), two years after the appearance of John Lindley's article on the "big tree" ("Gardeners' Chronicle," London). Kellogg's account is, even yet, valued for its comprehensiveness and accuracy.

In 1853, he and seven other men in San Francisco interested in natural science banded together and organized the California Academy of Sciences. In 1867, under the auspices of the U.S. Coast and Geodetic Survey, Kellogg was engaged as botanist and surgeon of the first expedition sent by the government to Bering Sea. This enabled him to study the coastal tree flora. In 1882, after thirty years of serious study, he organized and published a manual of 148 pages entitled "Forest Trees of California," the first scientific account of one of the most remarkable of the world's forest empires.

The tree flora of the West Coast, however, was not Kellogg's sole botanical interest. Nothing, seemingly, escaped his keenly observant eye, and, during his residence in California, he contributed to our knowledge of California botany some sixty-odd species and genera. He was a conscientious and scrupulously careful student. For nearly forty years he continued his labor of love and was a highly esteemed pioneer who, through his ministrations as a physician and his devotion to botany, won the love and praise of those who came to know him best. As a botanist he was memorialized by the genus *Kelloggia*, represented by a single species indigenous to the Sierra Nevada woodlands. Kellogg spent the last years of his life at Alameda near San Francisco Bay, where, unmarried, he passed away on March 31, 1887.

ANON. 1888. *Am. J. Sci.* 3rd Ser. 35: 261–262.
ANON. 1887–1888. Albert Kellogg. *Ann. Bot.* 1: 404.
ANON. 1889. *Proc. Calif. Acad.* 2nd Ser. 1.
GREEN, E. L. 1887–1889. *Pittonia* 1: 145–151.

Léo Lesquereux

1806–1889

Léo Lesquereux, renowned for his contribution to our knowledge of the mosses and of paleobotany, was born in Fleurier, Canton Neufchâtel, Switzerland, on November 18, 1806. It was his father's wish that Léo should be a manufacturer of watch springs, but because of the son's poor health, his mother thought he should study for the ministry. With this in mind he was sent to Neufchâtel to attend an academy that would prepare him for the university. It was his good fortune there to become acquainted with Arnold Guyot and August Agassiz, younger brother of Louis, the zoologist. Léo and the younger Agassiz became good friends, but it was to Guyot that Lesquereux became most intimately drawn.

The university career of Lesquereux suffered an interruption because of a paucity of funds with which to defray his tuition and incidental expenses. He therefore accepted a position as teacher of French in a young ladies' academy in Eisenach, Saxe-Weimar. There he became engaged to one of his pupils, Sophia, daughter of General von Wolffskeel and a lady of intellectual note. While a mere child she had won the affection of the poet Goethe, whose letters to her were long treasured by the family. At the end of four years in Eisenach, Lesquereux taught for a brief interval at Locle and was then appointed principal of an academy at La Chaux de Fonds.

At twenty-six he became virtually deaf, a condition believed to have resulted from an accident experienced when he was ten. This affliction compelled him to abandon teaching and to engage in a trade. He first tried his hand at engraving watch cases, but, finding this injurious to his health, he joined his father as a business partner. Even this was not wholly to his liking, so he devoted his leisure hours to the collection and study of mosses. Publication of the results of his research attracted the attention of the elder Agassiz, who then occupied the chair of professor of natural history at the Academy of Neufchâtel. On invitation from Agassiz he visited him, and they became fast friends for the rest of Agassiz's life.

The destruction of Switzerland's timber trees became a matter of serious concern to the Swiss government, and a gold medal was offered for the best treatise on the restoration and development of the nation's peat bogs. Lesquereux won the prize. In due season, he was invited to write a manual on peat, which was adopted as a text in the schools. The author was employed as director of operations in the government's peat bogs. His renown as an authority on bogs and their formation won for him, under the patronage of the King of Prussia, an opportunity to explore the peat bogs of a number of north European countries and thus to acquaint himself with the mosses and other plants of those countries.

Having become entirely deaf and finding himself without employment because of the revolution of 1847, he and his family took ship for America and landed at Boston in September, 1848. Here, on invitation of Agassiz, Lesquereux devoted three months to the botanical account of Agassiz's trip to Lake Superior. Later, he went to Columbus, Ohio, where he entered the laboratory of the already well-known bryologist, W. S. Sullivant; again he was permitted to resume his study of the mosses.

On recommendation of Sullivant, he made an exploratory trip into the southern Appalachians for the sole purpose of collecting not only the mosses but also other plants peculiar to the region. In this undertaking he was eminently successful and was able to realize an appreciable financial return through the sale of his specimens to botanical students. The results of this exploration and the work necessary to the preparation of specimens made it possible for him to contribute importantly to the "Musci Americani" by Sullivant and Lesquereux. Lesquereux availed himself of the advantages of Sullivant's library and laboratory in his preparation of mosses collected during the Wilkes's South Pacific Expedition and Whipple's Pacific Railroad Expedition.

It was Sullivant's intention to publish a full account of the North American mosses. He had already made an impressive collection when death overtook him. Asa Gray, aware of Sullivant's ambition, urged Lesquereux to complete the task. He labored long and effectively until 1869, when his eyesight became so impaired as to necessitate his asking for assistance. It was then that Prof. T. P. James of Cambridge, Massachusetts lent a skilled hand to the project. He did the necessary microscopic work until his death, and the task was not finished until 1884, when the "Manual of the Mosses of North America" was completed at last.

Lesquereux's interest in geology led him early into a serious study of paleobotany. By 1845 he had begun writing on the subject, and by 1850 his most valuable research on the origin and development of coal formations in Pennsylvania, Ohio, Illinois, Kentucky, and Arkansas was appearing in the geological survey reports of those states. It was Lesquereux who conceived the notion that his theory as to the formation of peat should rightly apply to the formation of coal. In this he was unquestionably right. Of special value are his contribution on the subject published in the "Rogers Report" of 1858.* and his catalogue of the fossil plants, named or described, as observed in the coal measures of North America. A further result of Lesquereux's tireless labor was his "coal flora" in the second geological survey of Pennsylvania.

During a long and fruitful life, Lesquereux published twelve important works on the natural history of North America. His final contribution was a treatise on "The Flora of the Dakota Group," published posthumously as Monograph No. 17 of the United States Geological Survey in 1891. Lesquereux died on October 25, 1889, soon after the death of his wife. Surviving the parents were three sons and a daughter.

* See Meisel, Max, 1926. A Bibliography of American History, Vol. 2, p. 627.

ANON. 1890. Obituary Notice of Leo Lesquereux. *Proc. Am. Philos. Soc.* 28: 65–70.
BARNES, C. R. 1890. Leo Lesquereux. *Botan. Gaz.* 15: 16–19.
LESLEY, J. P. 1895. Memoir Leo Lesquereux. *Nat. Acad. Sci. Biog. Mem.* 3: 189–212.
SARTON, G. 1942. *Isis* 34: 97–108, eight figures and portrait.
YOUMANS, W. J. 1896. Pioneers of Science in America. D. Appleton & Company, Inc., New York.

David Hunt Linder

1899–1946

David Hunt Linder, mycologist and curator of the Farlow Herbarium and Reference Library at Harvard University, was born in Brookline, Massachusetts on September 24, 1899. Most of his boyhood years, however, were spent in the rural community of Canton, Massachusetts, where he had opportunity to become acquainted with nature and to receive impressions that remained with him throughout his life. The influence of his parents was such as to inspire him with a growing interest in and a love for plants. It is said that his father, a chemist, was more devoted to botany and horticulture than to chemistry. The family home at Canton possessed such accessories as a greenhouse, a nursery, and gardens for vegetables and flowers. Moreover, there was sufficient acreage for growing trees and shrubs. Small wonder then that a boy of David's scientific curiosity, exposed as he was to such a botanical environment, should have become a botanist.

He and his brothers attended a country school near Canton. As to what they learned there we are not informed, but from there David went to Dedham, where he attended Noble and Greenough's School for boys. There he completed his college entrance requirements and entered Harvard College in 1917. He graduated in 1921 with an A.B. He had already become interested in mycology to a degree that, on completing his undergraduate course, he proceeded with his graduate studies on the fungi. He made due acknowledgment of his gratitude and indebtedness to his father and his great-uncle, Professor Farlow, both of whom had given him encouragement and guidance.

Linder received his M.A. from Harvard University in 1922, and, having received a Sheldon Traveling Fellowship, he went to South America where he spent some time in the tropical wilds of British and French Guiana. In 1926, he completed the requirements for the doctorate at Harvard and was offered an opportunity to join the Harvard expedition to Africa. The rigors of such a climate as he encountered there were almost too severe for him. On returning to the United States, he went direct to St. Louis, where he had received an appointment as instructor in the Shaw School of Botany. He also was to fill the position of mycologist at the Missouri Botanical Garden. Recognition of his qualifications was shown in his promotion from instructor to assistant professor of cryptogamic botany.

In 1931, Dr. Linder returned to Harvard University to accept a position as instructor in cryptogamic botany. In 1932, he accepted the acting curatorship of the Farlow Herbarium. In 1935, he attended the Amsterdam meeting of the International Botanical Congress. Sometime during the next four years he lost his wife, whom he had met as Elinor Alberts, while both he and she were staff members of the Missouri Botanical Garden, he as mycologist and she as orchidologist. When they later moved to Canton, Massachusetts, they made it the home of her orchid collection. Sometime between 1935 and 1939, Linder was married a second time. He had disposed of his Canton estate and made for himself and wife a home at Wakefield, Massachusetts.

As curator of the Farlow Herbarium, Linder devoted himself more zealously than ever to his official duties. In 1947 there were approximately 980,000 specimens in the cryptogamic herbarium cases. Of these about 200,000 were added during the period 1932–1947, nearly half of which accessions were fungi. In addition to the dried and preserved specimens of fungi, Linder kept on hand a collection of approximately five hundred fungi in culture, for exchange in case of need. In addition to the herbarium and related to it was the Farlow library, which, in 1932, numbered a total of 19,750 accessions. By July, 1946, this number had increased, thanks to Linder's active interest in it, to 37,208 items. It is known that he recognized the importance of monographic studies of the fungi. His ambition for such publication was in part realized before his death. In the initial number of "Farlowia," which appeared in 1943, we find the sort of journal he had hoped for and had unremittingly labored to realize.

Occupied as he was with administrative duties, Dr. Linder found time to contribute many important mycological papers, to participate in fungus forays, and to join botanical expeditions at home and abroad. A list of his principal publications will be found in "Mycologia" 39: 142–144, 1947. In less than twenty-five years he described, illustrated, and established a new family of fungi, sixteen new genera and one hundred and seventy new species or combinations. All this in addition to multitudinous editorial, administrative, and routine duties.

Dr. Linder passed away on November 10, 1946.

RUSDEN, P. L. 1947. David Hunt Linder. *Mycologia* 39: 133–144, with portrait.
WESTON, W. H. 1947. David Hunt Linder. *Farlowia* 3: 141–154, with portrait.

Charles Bernard Lipman
1883–1944

Charles Bernard Lipman was born in Moscow, Russia, August 17, 1883, the son of Michael Gregory and Ida (Birkhahn) Lipman. He was brought to the United States in 1889 and, on completing his college preparatory studies, entered Rutgers University where, in 1904, he received his B.S. and, in 1909, his M.S. degrees. That same year he was awarded the M.S. degree by the University of Wisconsin and thereafter moved to Berkeley, California, where he pursued his graduate studies and received his Ph.D. in 1910. Rutgers later conferred upon him the honorary degree of D.Sc.

As a Goewy Fellow at the University of California (1908–1909), he became interested in soil bacteriology and, in 1909, was appointed instructor in soil bacteriology. In 1910, he was promoted to assistant professor of soils and two years later became associate professor. In 1913, he was appointed professor of soil chemistry and bacteriology, which position he held until he became professor of plant nutrition (1921–1925). From 1925 to his death, he served as professor of plant physiology.

Dr. Lipman's early years at Berkeley brought him into intimate association with Prof. E. W. Hilgard, whose influence directed Lipman into the field of research on microorganisms and, more specifically, on those that carry on nitrogen fixation and nitrification in arid or semiarid soils. Another line of research of major interest to Dr. Lipman was the survival of bacteria in dry soil. He discovered that they could survive many years of desiccation. This led him to look further into the problem and to ascertain whether in geologically old sedimentary rock he might find bacteria. He succeeded in finding them in limited numbers, but he was unable to determine their age because of possible contamination by ground water. In like manner, he examined specimens of igneous rock. These he found wholly free of any living organisms.

Because of the element of uncertainty as to the longevity of survival of organisms in portions of the earth's geologic crust, Lipman resolved to study their occurrence and survival in old materials of one kind or another, such as old herbarium specimens, bottled soil samples, and bricks obtained from pre-Inca structures in Peru. These materials, while not of geologic antiquity, had long been reasonably free from outside contamination and therefore afforded proof that many bacteria were capable of surviving many years, even centuries, of desiccation.

Dr. Lipman's curiosity led him to the discovery of symbiosis between the blue-green algae and nitrogen-fixing bacteria. Incidentally, he discovered a new kind of sulfur-oxidizing bacterial organism, *Thiobacillus coprolyticus.*

Professor Lipman served for twenty-one years as dean of the graduate division of the University of California. As such he contributed richly as teacher and counselor to graduate students and to the maintenance of high ideals of scholarship. As an educator, he was at heart an internationalist and did much to broaden and liberalize the thinking of those who came within the sphere of his influence as a teacher. He was a member of the Educational Board of the John Simon Guggenheim Foundation, director of the Belgian-American Educational Foundation, president (1941–1942), California Chapter of the American-Scandinavian Foundation, fellow of the American Association for the Advancement of Science, member of the American Society of Plant Physiologists, the California Academy of Sciences, California Botanical Society, etc.

Dr. Lipman married Marion Amesbury Evans, May 25, 1925. One child, a daughter (Georgia Evans Lipman) was born to them. Death claimed the husband and father on October 22, 1944.

ANON, 1944. Notes. *Plant Physiol.* 19: 713.
REED, H. S. 1844. Charles Bernard Lipman. *Science* n.s. 100: 464–465.

Burton Edward Livingston
1875–1948

Burton Edward Livingston, eminent American plant physiologist, was born February 9, 1875, in Grand Rapids, Michigan, the son of Benjamin and Keziah (Lincoln) Livingston. His early and college-preparatory education was obtained in Grand Rapids. He entered the University of Michigan in 1894 and there was awarded the Bachelor of Science degree in 1898. At the University of Michigan it was his privilege to receive instruction under two eminent botanists, V. M. Spalding and F. C. Newcombe. Through the latter's influence, Livingston's choice leaned increasingly toward plant physiology, and, following a year's experience in Newcombe's laboratory, he was appointed his assistant in 1895 and served as such until 1898.

Livingston then obtained a job as teacher of sciences in the Freeport, Illinois, high school. During his year there he applied for fellowships at several universities. A number were offered, and he accepted one from the department of botany of the University of Chicago. Here he served as fellow and assistant in plant physiology from 1899 to 1905 and was one of an outstanding group of young men who, each in turn, served as laboratory assistant to Charles Reid Barnes, at that time head of the department of plant physiology. It was while he was at Chicago University that he completed the requirements for the Ph.D. degree (1902) and saw the publication of his book, "The Rôle of Diffusion and Osmotic Pressure in Plants" (1903). This important contribution won for him the respect of plant physiologists generally and is still regarded as an able summary of the literature on the subject.

Those of his friends who had longest known Livingston did not wonder how the young botanist could have won such distinction in the dawn of his scientific career, for, even in his grammar- and high-school days, he had learned something of the fundamentals of biology, chemistry, physics, and other branches of scientific learning. When he entered the University of Michigan as a freshman, he was allowed ten hours of university credit in botany as a reward for his diligence in making an herbarium and in recognition of the sum total of his knowledge of plants. When old enough to earn his own livelihood, he found employment as a laborer in a large greenhouse and nursery establishment at Short Hills, New Jersey. Here he learned much about plants and plant-culture requirements in hothouses, cold frames, and in the open, an experience that, while largely horticultural, was in line with Livingston's botanical education and, therefore, of intrinsic value to him.

From 1905 to 1908, years leading up to the Johns Hopkins era of Livingston's career as a plant physiologist, he held a number of appointments that can be more properly said to be years of preparation for what we now regard as the most important epoch of his life. For a part of the year 1905, he was in charge of fertility investigations in the then Bureau of Soils of the U.S. Department of Agriculture in Washington, D.C. The following year brought him an offer from the Carnegie Institution of Washington of staff membership in the department of botanical research. Accepting this offer, he went at once to Tucson, Arizona, where he engaged in research that brought out and perfected his porcelain atmometers. These he used in his study of evaporation under desert conditions.

Livingston's next move took the form of a touch-and-go series of visits to certain eastern United States institutions, most important of which was to the Missouri Botanic Garden, where he investigated the transpiration of greenhouse-grown cacti. In 1908, he went to Europe, where he profited from his contact with Professor Goebel of Munich. Then he visited Pfeffer's institute at Leipzig, where he spent a number of weeks. Other men included in this round of European botanists were Klebs of Heidelberg and Hall of the Rothamsted Station in England. He returned from Europe in time to attend the 1908–1909 meeting of the American Association for the Advancement of Science, scheduled to convene in Baltimore where he met for the first time Dr. Duncan Starr Johnson and visited his botanical garden at Homewood, the new location for Johns Hopkins University. In estimating the impact of contacts made during his wanderyears, it is certain that they were important stages in his preparation for the years to come.

Following the Baltimore meetings, he returned to the desert laboratory at Tucson. In 1909, he was asked to accept the chair of plant physiology at Johns Hopkins University. In 1913, he was appointed director of the Laboratory of Plant Physiology, which position he filled with distinction until 1940, the year of his retirement. In 1932, he became responsible for forest ecology, which was added to his department.

Livingston and his several students made many contributions to our knowledge of botanical science and to that of plant physiology in particular. Altogether they published approximately three hundred papers during Livingston's years at Johns Hopkins. Important also were his contributions as an inventor of instruments designed to measure the physiologic importance of certain dynamic factors within and peculiar to the environment of the plants under consideration. His improved porous cups, cylinders, spheres, etc., made possible the more accurate measurement of evaporation rates and the determination of the effects of the humidity of the atmosphere and the effect of sunlight on the relation of water to plants. Autoirrigators enabled the experimenter to control the amount of soil moisture under conditions of pot culture. These and other pieces of apparatus were made in quantity and found their way to many parts of the world. Thus did they contribute to the extension of the influence of Johns Hopkins on research in many an institution beyond the United States.

Livingston's skill as an editor was widely recognized. In addition to his book "The Role of Diffusion and Osmotic Pressure in Plants," he published, with Forrest Shreve as coauthor, a book on

"The Distribution of Vegetation in the United States as Related to Climatic Conditions" (1921) and, in 1918, edited an English translation of Palladin's "Plant Physiology," a work that had appeared in three editions in three years. Journals to which Livingston contributed were "The American Scholar," Physiological Researches," 'Plant Physiology," and Botanical Abstracts."

In addition to his inventive genius and his contributions as a teacher and research worker, Livingston had an undying interest in the American Association for the Advancement of Science. He was named permanent secretary of that organization in 1920, a post in which he served with devotion and distinction for three successive terms until 1931. During the period 1931–1934 he served capably as general secretary. While in this office, he was primarily responsible for many of the association's successful projects, such as the Annual Science Exhibition, the Association Prize, and the Secretaries' and Academy Conferences. Throughout his affiliation with the society he devoted his time and energy selflessly to its promotion and improvement. Few have devoted themselves more wholeheartedly to this cause than did Livingston.

He was also active in the affairs of the American Society of Plant Physiologists. After participating for many years in the activities of this organization as a contributor of scientific articles and as an active member, he was elected president in 1934. During his year in office, many changes were effected in methods of handling the society's business, changes that tended toward increased democracy of action.

Dr. Livingston was twice married, first to Grace Johnson in 1905 and secondly to Marguerite A. Brennan MacPhillips in 1922. He died February 8, 1948, at the age of seventy-three, lacking one day.

ANON. 1945. Felicitations on 70th birthday of Burton Edward Livingston. Notes. *Plant Physiol.* 20: 316, portrait, 20: 170.
ANON. 1947. Stephen Hales Award. *Plant Physiol.* 22: 201–202.
SHREVE, J. W. 1948. *Soil Science* 66: 1–3.
SHULL, C. A. 1948. *Science* n.s. 107: 558–560.
SHULL, C. A. 1948. *Plant Physiol.* 23, No. 2, Supplement: iii–vii.

Curtis Gates Lloyd
1859–1926

Curtis Gates Lloyd was born July 17, 1859, at Florence, Kentucky. He was the son of Nelson Marvin and Sophia (Webster) Lloyd. He received his schooling in the private schools of Florence and Crittendon, Kentucky, and served an apprenticeship to a Cincinnati pharmacist in 1879. From 1880 to 1886, he was employed as bookkeeper for a publishing house. In 1886, he became a partner with his brothers, John Uri and Nelson Ashly Lloyd, in a Cincinnati firm of manufacturing chemists and wholesale druggists. From boyhood, however, Curtis Lloyd had maintained a lively interest in and enthusiasm for botany. He continued his business relationship with his brothers until July, 1918, when he sold his financial interest to them.

Once liberated from commerce, he devoted both time and energy solely to botany and to mycology in particular. That he might the more fully acquaint himself with what had been accomplished elsewhere, he visited the museums of Paris, Berlin, London, Upsala, Geneva, and other European centers of scientific interest. There he studied the mycological collections and became acquainted with European authorities. He already had made an important collection of his own and, through a world-wide correspondence, had been able to build up an exceptionally fine herbarium. This he housed in the Lloyd Museum, an adjunct of the Lloyd Library, founded in Cincinnati by the Lloyd brothers and assured of perpetuity by an endowment made by Curtis Gates Lloyd. Following his death in November, 1926, his mycological collection was, by action of his trustees, offered to the Smithsonian Institution, where it remains a monument to his industry and scholarship.

Lloyd's sustained interest in mycology inspired him to publish a periodical, "Mycological Notes," which he sent gratis to a worldwide list of institutions and individuals interested in mycology. In addition to this periodical, he published a number of monographs and circulars. In recognition of his scholarship and scientific attainments, he was awarded an honorary D. Sc. degree by the University of Cincinnati. To stimulate interest in wild life and its conservation, he purchased two unspoiled tracts of land near Ithaca, New York and one near Florence, Kentucky and made of them three wildlife reservations, the permanence of which has been assured by acts of perpetuity.

Lloyd was a member of the American Association for the Advancement of Science, La Société Botanique de France, La Société Mycologique de France, and the Cuvier Club. He remained single throughout life and died in Cincinnati, November 11, 1926.

FITZPATRICK, H. M. 1927. Curtis Gates Lloyd. *Mycologia* 19: 153–159.
NEEDHAM, J. G. 1926. *Science* n.s. 64: 569–570.
SIMONS, C. M. 1951. Curtis Gates Lloyd, Mycologist. *Nat. Eclectic Med. Quart.* 43(1): 13–16; 43(2): 11–14.

Francis Ernest Lloyd
1868–1947

Francis Ernest Lloyd was born October 4, 1868, in Manchester, England. He was the son of Welsh parents, Edward and Leah (Pierce) Lloyd. At an early age he, with his parents, came to the United States and settled in Philadelphia. After acquiring a limited preparatory education, Lloyd spent some time at Lafayette College and then completed his undergraduate studies at Princeton in 1891, where he received his A.B. and, in 1895, his A.M. degrees. Later (1933) he was awarded the honorary D. Sc. degree by the University of Wales (Aberystwyth) and Masaryk University (1938). In 1898 and 1901 he engaged in graduate study at the universities of Munich and Bonn, respectively.

Lloyd's teaching experience began at Williams College (Mass.), where he spent a year (1891–1892) as instructor in botany. From 1892 to 1897, he served as professor at Pacific University in Oregon. In 1897, he was appointed adjunct professor at Teachers' College, Columbia, where he served until 1906. From Columbia University Lloyd moved to Tucson, Arizona, where he was engaged by the Carnegie Desert Laboratory as an investigator until 1907. Then he was employed as cytologist by the Arizona Agricultural Experiment Station. In 1908, he was appointed director of investigations for the Continental-Mexican Rubber Company and as special expert for the United States Rubber Company. His next appointment was that of professor of botany at the Alabama Polytechnic Institute (1908–1912). In 1912, he was offered the position of professor of botany at McGill University (Montreal), where he served from 1912 to 1934, when he retired as professor emeritus. At McGill he found opportunity for research.

Lloyd was a botanist of broad concept, unwilling to confine himself solely to the academic approach; nor was he a narrow mechanist. He was familiar with botany in applied lines of research, notably in that of rubber production from the desert plant, guayule (*Parthenium argentatum*). The results of his research were published in his "Guayule: A Rubber Plant of the Chihuahuan Desert" (1911), an important contribution in that it presented for the first time the methods of culture essential to the successful production of this plant. A supplement to the book was published in 1932 and a revised edition was issued in 1942. Although Lloyd had retired from active life in 1934, he continued a consultant on rubber production from guayule and, for more than twenty years, on *Hevea*. Lloyd's zeal in and for research found satisfaction during his years at McGill, where he thoroughly studied the reproduction of the green alga *Spirogyra* and the peculiar functioning of carnivorous plants, for example, *Utricularia*. He was a keen observer, and his imagination enabled him to interpret accurately what he had seen.

Early in his botanical career (1902) Lloyd published his "Comparative Embryology of the Rubiaceae," the most important of his morphological studies. Other significant contributions were his book entitled the "Physiology of Stomata" (1908), a positive and convincing account based on experimentation showing that stomata are not adapted to control transpiration. Settled at Carmel-by-the-Sea, he devoted himself to the completion of his monumental work, "The Carnivorous Plants." His spirit of inquiry had led him into many interesting parts of the world, not for gold nor for selfish ends, but always to add to his store of knowledge and the enrichment of his gift as a botanist and teacher.

Professor Lloyd was a member of the Botanical Society of America, the Society of Plant Physiology, the Torrey Botanical Club, fellow of the Royal Society of Canada, fellow of the Linnaean Society of London, corresponding member of the Czechoslovakian Botanical Society, and corresponding member, Centro de Sciencias, Letras, e Artes, Campinas of Brazil.

It was while Lloyd was at Columbia that he became acquainted with Mary Elizabeth Hart, a teacher in her own right. This acquaintance culminated in their marriage, May 18, 1903. Professor Lloyd passed away at Carmel, California, October 10, 1947. He was survived by his wife and their two sons.

SCARTH, G. W. 1948. Francis Ernest Lloyd. *Trans. Roy. Soc. Canada.* 3 ser. 42: 99–102.
SCARTH, G. W. 1938. Francis Lloyd, an appreciation. *Plant Physiol.* 13: 878–880, portrait p. 669.
SCARTH, G. W. 1947. *J. N.Y. Botan. Gard.* 48: 292.
SCARTH, G. W. and MEMORIAL COMMITTEE. 1948. In Memorium Francis Ernest Lloyd. *Plant Physiol.* 23: 1–4.

Daniel Trembly MacDougal
1865–1958

In the year 1903, a botanist still filled with youthful enthusiasm and energy elected to come to the small, sun-baked adobe pueblo of Tucson, Arizona to help found a new biological laboratory. Three years later he was appointed its first director, a position held with distinction until his retirement in 1933. Daniel Trembly Mac-Dougal had been born thirty-eight years before, on March 16, 1865, in Liberty, Indiana, to Alexander and Amanda MacDougal. Here he grew to early manhood on the farm his grandparents had homesteaded on their arrival from Scotland.

Young Daniel graduated from high school in 1880, soon after his seventeenth birthday. His education at this point was interrupted briefly by the necessity to earn money to continue his schooling, and he did not receive his first degree until 1890, a B.S. from DePauw University. This was followed the next year by a M.S. degree from Purdue and then, in 1894, by the M.A. from his Alma Mater. Finally, after studies in Germany at Leipzig and Tübingen in 1895 and 1896 and visits to the famous botanical laboratories of England, Holland, and Germany, Purdue University awarded him the Ph.D. degree in 1897. MacDougal's doctoral thesis, initiated while at Leipsig, on "The Curvature of Roots" so impressed the Purdue faculty that he was awarded one of the only three doctor's degrees ever granted "in absentia" by that institution.

Although primarily a plant physiologist, MacDougal had an interest in the whole field of botany. He spent the summers of 1891–1892 collecting for the U.S. Department of Agriculture in Idaho and Arizona. By 1893, however, he was appointed instructor in plant physiology at the University of Minnesota. Two years later he was promoted to the rank of assistant professor, a title he held until he left in 1899 to become assistant director of the New York Botanical Garden. For the next few years and until he was named its director in 1906, MacDougal was active in helping establish the Carnegie Desert Laboratory at Tucson, Arizona. During the next twenty-seven years, until his retirement in 1933, Dr. MacDougal was a leader among the scientists in this growing southwestern university town and throughout the Southwest. He pioneered during this period as the foremost American student of desert ecology and physiology. Working in a land noted for its extremes of high temperature and drought, he contributed importantly to the knowledge of the desert environment and the ability of desert vegetation to withstand and even flourish under extremely adverse conditions. The MacDougal dendrograph, an instrument that he invented and perfected to measure rate of tree growth as indicated by changes in tree-trunk diameter, was probably the contribution for which he became most widely known. Of equal or greater scientific value, however, were his studies of weather cycles and the cyclic growth response of trees to this weather pattern.

Early in his career at the Desert Laboratory he recognized the need of additional facilities for studying arid climate-plant relationships. Carmel, California, also appealed to him as a desirable summer home location where he and his family could escape the Tucson summer heat. As a consequence, he founded the Coastal Laboratory at Carmel in 1909 to serve primarily as a summer research center for visiting scientists. During the next twelve years, work at the laboratory increased in importance and scope and absorbed increasing amounts of Dr. MacDougal's time. He finally moved to the adjacent Carmel Highlands in 1921 and continued to carry on his research primarily there and in the Sonoran Desert of Arizona and Mexico. On his retirement in 1933, Dr. MacDougal moved permanently to Carmel but continued his activity and interest in things botanical almost to the end of his long life. As a resident of Carmel he participated actively in community affairs, devoting much time to school activities and to the Monterey County Society for the Prevention of Cruelty to Animals.

The place occupied by MacDougal in the world of science and in the opinion of fellow scientists is indicated by the scientific societies in which he was active and that honored him in various ways. In addition to membership in organizations such as the American Philosophical Society, the Botanical Society of America, and the American Society of Plant Physiology, he held high offices in a number of others. In 1950, he was named honorary president of the International Botanical Congress in Stockholm and again in 1954, when the Congress reconvened in Paris. The New York Botanical Garden awarded him the Certificate of Distinguished Service in 1946, the only such certificate ever awarded by that institution.

Although his contributions to the field of botany resulted primarily from researches in southwestern United States and Mexico, their importance brought him international acclaim. In addition to the recognition awarded him by the International Botanical Congresses, the Botanical Society of Edinburgh elected him to honorary membership. He was a corresponding member of the Czechoslovak Botanical Society and a member of the Société d'Acclimatation de France and the Hollandsche Maatschappe d. Wetenschappen.

Dr. MacDougal was an energetic worker and a prolific writer. The available record shows six books in plant physiology and 138 published papers between 1884 and 1938, with the probability that the list of papers is not complete. His books included "Experimental Plant Physiology" (1895), "Living Plants and Their Properties: A Collection of Essays" (1898), "A Practical Textbook of Plant Physiology" (1901), "Elementary Plant Physiology" (1902), "Green Leaf: The Major Activities of Plants in Sunlight" (1930), and "Tree Growth" (1938).

His writings, while in the main dealing with plant physiology, were not restricted to this field. Many of his earlier articles dealt with evolution and genetics. Coming, as he did, to the Southwest at a time when it still represented, in large part, an unexplored frontier, he traveled extensively and published on the geography, ecology, and flora of the regions he visited. This interest in desert regions was not restricted to those of North America. A trip to northern Africa in 1912 resulted in the publication of three papers on the deserts and plant life of that area. The observations recorded in these papers are in part botanical, in part geographical, and in part an account of the living and traveling conditions encountered.

On January 24, 1893, Daniel T. MacDougal and Louise Fisher were married. He was twenty-eight at the time and just beginning his teaching career at Minnesota. One child, Alice, was born of this union.

McDougal was a man with a great zest for life and, as a consequence, he was a stimulating companion. His constant energy, actively probing mind, and refreshing sense of humor made it a pleasure to be associated with him in the field or office. He was equally at home in the Cosmos Club of Washington, the Old Pueblo Club of Tucson, or roughing it in the wilds of Mexico. An accomplished cook, few could excel him in his ability along this line over an open campfire.

An excellent informal picture of McDougal and his relations with his fellow man may be had by reading "Campfires in Desert and Lava" (Charles Scribner's Sons, New York, 1908). The dedication in the front of the book illustrates succinctly the esteem in which he was held.

To Daniel Trembly MacDougal, Ph.D., Etc. All-around botanist, zoologist, sportsman and good fellow, who built for us a chain of camp-fires from Tucson to Pinacate, on the greatest desert trip imaginable, this volume is dedicated forever.

ANON. 1949. MacDougal, Daniel Trembly: 1865–Indiana Authors and their Books: 1816–1916. Wabash College, Crawfordsville, Indiana. (Citing information from De Pauw University's *Alumnal Record*, 1920.)

CARNEGIE INSTITUTION OF WASHINGTON. 1923. Biography: Daniel Trembly MacDougal. Processed. Washington, D.C., March 29.

LONG, ESMOND R. 1958. Daniel Trembly MacDougal (1865-1958) *Am. Philos. Soc. Yearbook* (1958): 131–135.

Conway MacMillan

1867–1929

Conway MacMillan was born in Hillsdale, Michigan, August 26, 1867. Where he obtained his elementary and college-preparatory schooling seems not to be a matter of published record, but it is known that at some time in his youth he moved to Lincoln, Nebraska, where he matriculated as a student of classical studies and graduated in 1885 with an A.B. degree. In the following year he was awarded the M.A. degree and was appointed assistant geologist by the Board of Regents of the University of Nebraska. During that same year he accompanied Prof. S. E. Hicks on a scientific excursion into the Badlands of South Dakota. He remained at the University of Nebraska until early 1887, when we find him in the biological laboratory of Johns Hopkins University, where he served as instructor in botany. Later, in 1887, he received an appointment as entomologist at the Nebraska Agricultural Experiment Station and published, in February, 1888, a preliminary bulletin on injurious insects.

The University of Minnesota, then in quest of a man for the headship of its recently constituted department of botany, appointed MacMillan as instructor, which position he occupied for the period 1887–1891. Incidentally, he was at Harvard for a season from 1887 to 1888. From 1891 to 1893, he served as assistant professor of botany at Minnesota, and in 1893 he became professor of botany and state botanist of the Minnesota Geological Survey and Natural History Survey.

MacMillan was especially gifted as a teacher. During the comparatively brief period of his service as botanist and teacher at the University of Minnesota, he attracted, little realizing how he did, a considerable group of enthusiastic students who were later to make themselves known in the fields of research and teaching.

In the waning years of the past century, years in which he labored to build a new department worthy the distinction of an important state and its university, university professors' salaries were not flattering; it was, therefore, not uncommon for them to seek more remunerative fields. MacMillan continued his service as professor of botany until 1906. From 1901 to 1906, he was director of the Minnesota Seaside Station, established by him as a marine laboratory for the study of marine plant and animal life. In 1906, he resigned to engage in the advertising business in Philadelphia. He passed away on June 5, 1929.

Distinctive among MacMillan's published works were his "Metaspermae of the Minnesota Valley," "Minnesota Botanical Studies, I–VII," and "Minnesota Plant Life." The last, an ecological treatise long regarded as a work of more than ordinary importance and readability, became available at a time when plant ecology was young and in need of trustworthy guidance.

John Macoun

1832–1920

John Macoun, Canadian botanist, was born April 17, 1832, in Maralin, County Down, Ireland. He was self-educated until ready for college. Very soon after his arrival in Canada, he began his study of botany and soon thereafter became recognized as an authority on Canadian plant life. He attended college at Syracuse University (New York) and there earned his M.A. degree. In January, 1862, he married Ellen Terrill of Brighton, Ontario. From 1868 to 1879 he was professor of botany and geology at Albert University, Belleville, Ontario. Following that epoch of his career, he became professor emeritus on the faculty of the same university. In 1872 he was selected to serve as botanist on Sir Sandford Fleming's Expedition. This expedition extended across western Canada to the Pacific Ocean and was primarily concerned with seeking out a suitable route for the Canadian Pacific Railway. The party divided at Edmonton, Alberta; a part of it, including Macoun, headed northwestward for the Peace River country and thence westward across the mountains to the coast of what is now British Columbia.

Again, in 1875, he crossed the mountains from the west to the Peace River. It was during this crossing that he and a companion paddled in a dugout down the river a distance of 700 perilous miles and continued their journey eastward by way of the Athabasca River, numerous lakes, and other waterways to arrive at Winnipeg and, finally, Ontario. The distance covered by him in this trip alone was approximately 8,000 miles. An account of his experiences and the results he obtained from the expedition were published in the Railway Report for 1877. It was a notable chronicle, one that aroused much interest in Canada and was influential in bringing about the settlement of the Canadian northwest prairies. This time he took particular note of the potential agricultural capacities of these territories, particularly for wheat production. His predictions have since been well borne out.

In 1882, Macoun was made botanist to the Geological Survey of Canada. Three years later he was promoted in rank to assistant director and naturalist to the survey and was retained as such until claimed by death in Ottawa on the eighteenth of July, 1920. He resigned from Albert College and established his residence in Ottawa.

Macoun was a charter member of the Royal Society of Canada. He was a fellow of the Linnean Society of Canada, a member and one time president of the Ottawa Field Naturalists' Club, a director of the Canadian Forestry Association, and botanist to the

Ethnological and Natural History Society of Canada. He published numerous catalogues of Canadian plants and birds, "Manitoba and the Great North West" (1882), and "The Forests of Canada and their Distribution" (1895). His autobiography was published posthumously in 1922 by the Ottawa Field Naturalists' Club.

ANON. 1888. Bryological Names. *Bull. Torrey Club* 15: 185.
MacKay, A. H. 1922. *Proc. & Trans. Royal Soc. Canad.* 3rd Ser. 16: vii–x, with portrait.
Macoun, J. 1922. *Autobiography.* Ottawa Field Naturalists' Club.

Albert Mann

1853–1935

Albert Mann, botanist and diatomist, was born at Hoboken, New Jersey, on June 30, 1853. He was the son of Albert and Lydia Helen (Everett) Mann. His higher education was acquired at Wesleyan University, Middletown, Connecticut, where he was graduated in 1879. In due course he received from the same university his M.A. and D.Sc. degrees. In 1880, he entered Drew Theological Seminary with the intent of preparing for the ministry. On October 6 of that same year, he was married to Jennie F. Yard of Trenton, New Jersey, who bore him a son, Albert.

For a period of twelve years (1880–1892), Dr. Mann was active in the ministry in Philadelphia and in Vernon, Bloomfield, and Newark, New Jersey. It was in Philadelphia that he met Charles H. Kain, the diatomist, who first interested Dr. Mann in this field of botanical research. It was while he was pastor of St. Luke's Methodist Episcopal Church at Newark, New Jersey, that he wrote his first botanical paper, entitled "A List of Diatomaceae from a Deep-Sea Dredging in the Atlantic Ocean off Delaware Bay by the United States Fish Commission Steamer Albatross."

This paper was published in 1893 in the *Proceedings of the National Museum*, Volume 16.

In 1892, Dr. Mann retired from the ministry and went abroad to study at the University of Munich, where, in 1894, he received the Ph.D. degree. He returned to the United States and was offered the position of professor of botany at Ohio Wesleyan University. This he occupied until 1900. From 1900 to 1905 he served as collaborator of the University of Munich and as a research botanist in the Smithsonian Institution. During this five year interval, he devoted his spare hours to such research as was necessary to the preparation of his "Report on the Diatoms of the Albatross Voyages in the Pacific Ocean" (1888–1904). This monograph was published in 1907. In 1905 he was appointed scientific specialist in the U.S. Department of Agriculture and served in that capacity for fourteen years. In the early years of that period he served also as professor of botany in George Washington University.

Dr. Mann had long hoped that some day there might be established in Washington a laboratory devoted solely to research on diatoms. He lived to see the realization of this dream, for, in 1919, such a laboratory was established, and he, as an associate of the Carnegie Institution, was placed in charge of it. The laboratory was located in the Smithsonian Institution, where it soon became well known to students and research specialists interested in the Diatomaceae. Here also he found more leisure to devote to his own research and to the preparation of papers and reports relating to the same. Chief among these was his taxonomic study of the marine diatoms of the Philippine Islands, which appeared in published form in 1925. In addition to his more important papers, were many shorter ones, all of them contributing to our knowledge of the Diatomaceae.

Dr. Mann was a fellow of the American Association for the Advancement of Science and a member of several other scientific societies. He died at his home in Middletown, Connecticut, on February 1, 1935.

HAGELSTEIN, R. 1935. Albert Mann. *Science* n.s. 81: 308–309.

Brother Marie-Victorin
1885–1944

Brother Marie-Victorin, eminent Canadian botanist and educator, was born at Kingsey Falls, Quebec, on April 3, 1885, and died July 15, 1944. He was then in his sixtieth year, and, had he completed that year, he would have finished a quarter century of service as a university teacher. Brother Marie-Victorin's ancestors were from Brittany, and he, Joseph-Louis Conrad Kirouac, was the only son of Cyrille and Philomene (Luneau) Kirouac. While a small child, he went with his parents to live in the city of Quebec, where, in the course of time, his father established a lucrative feed-and-grain business. Conrad's early education was obtained at St. Sauveur, where he attended the Christian Brothers' school. Later, he spent two years at the Commercial Academy in Quebec City, and he was graduated in 1901 at the head of his class. He then entered the Christian Brothers' Novitiate of Mont-de-la-Salle in Montreal, at that time in Maisonneuve Park, later to become, under Brother Marie-Victorin's leadership, the Montreal Botanical Garden. After serving for brief terms as a teacher in St. Jerome College and St. Leo's Academy in Westmount, Montreal, he became established in 1904 in Longueuil College, where he enjoyed teaching for several years and where he continued to reside until his death.

During the years of his early manhood, he suffered from a prolonged illness and spent many months in the Laurentian Mountains, where he slowly recuperated. While there, he improved the opportunity to become acquainted with the plant life of the Laurentians. By 1907 he was contributing botanical articles to such journals as the "Naturaliste canadienne," the "Ottawa Naturalist," the "Bryologist," the "Revue trimestrielle canadienne," etc. Then came what was, up to that time, his most important contribution, his *Flore du Témiscouta*, a work of 125 pages published in 1916. Four years later the University of Montreal was reorganized, and Brother Marie-Victorin was named head of its department of botany. Thereafter there was renewed interest in research and publication.

The newly appointed professor of botany conceived the plan of producing a series of contributions, with the result that by the time of his death more than fifty issues had been published. But his work was not limited to the duties of a teacher or to those of a contributing taxonomist. Brother Marie-Victorin was deeply interested in phytogeography and ecology. Opportunity to travel came his way in 1929, and he visited countries in Europe, South Africa, and western Asia. He returned to Montreal with a wealth of notes and photographic records and an enriched professional outlook. Already he had envisioned a greater botany for his country.

Immediately on his return from his long trip of many months abroad, he opened a campaign looking to the establishment of a botanical garden. Success crowned his efforts, and in 1932 the Montreal Botanical Garden became an assured fact. By 1939 it had grown measurably, and the Montreal Botanical Institute had moved into the large building that had been erected to house the administrative and technical activities of both the garden and institute. Here, Brother Marie-Victorin labored as botanist, as dreamer, as realizing builder and educator. Here he conceived the plan of doing something for the youth of Quebec, and there came into being an organization known as the Young Naturalists' Clubs. Connected with the botanical garden there was also the Awakening School, where provision was made for the instruction of little children eager to learn the elemental facts of natural history and of botany in particular. Here was the founder of the Montreal Botanical Garden in the realization of his dream.

But this was not all. In 1935 was published his monumental "Flore Laurentienne," the most important published contribution of his busy life, comprising 916 pages and 324 carefully executed illustrations done by Brother Alexandre, one of several collaborators who had labored to bring out this crowning achievement. On the initiative of Brother Marie-Victorin, several botanical expeditions were made in the interest of both the garden and the institute. These expeditions added much to the knowledge of the regional botany of the Province. One of these expeditions was that of 1924–1928, along the north shore of the Gulf of the St. Lawrence and of Anticosti Island. On the eve of his death, Brother Marie-Victorin was about to finish his report of this expedition. When finally published it will appear under the title "Recherches Floristiques sur l'Anticosti-Minganie."

Even under the handicap of failing health, Brother Marie-Victorin did not cease to labor as botanical explorer and contributor. Finding the Canadian winters increasingly difficult, he sought the comforts of life in Cuba. During his several winters there, he explored the island from one end to the other and published the results of his investigations in two volumes entitled "Itinéraires botaniques dans l'île de Cuba."

Brother Marie-Victorin was a member of the Royal Society of Canada, the Société botanique de France, the Linnaean Society of London, the American Association for the Advancement of Science, and several other scientific societies. He was everywhere recognized for his scholarship and his eminence as a botanist. He was loved and respected as a teacher by all those who came within the sphere of his influence.

AUDET, L. P. 1942. *Le Frère Marie-Victorin Éducatein, ses idées pédagogiques.* Les Éditions de l'Érable, Quebec.
DANSEREAU, P. 1945. Brother Marie-Victorin. *Am. Midl. Nat.* 33: iii–viii.
KUCYNIAK, J. 1946. Frère Marie-Victorin. *Rhodora* 48: 265–272.
LLOYD, F. E., and J. BRUNEL. 1944. *Science* n.s. 100: 487–488.
ROUSEAU, J. 1945. *Proc. & Trans. Roy. Soc. Canad.* 39, 3rd Ser. 93–96.

Humphry Marshall
1723–1801

Any treatise on the history of American botany certainly would name John Bartram as America's first pioneer explorer of the plant life of the North American continent. But, important as was his station in this virgin field of the unknown, he found himself sharing honors with his cousin Humphry Marshall. From humble beginnings, Marshall rose to recognition, both at home and abroad, as an authority in a branch of scientific learning that was as uncertain of recognition and of such questionable authenticity as botany.

In the commonly accepted sense of the word, Marshall's education was most rudimentary. He reports that his schooling ended in his twelfth year, and such learning as he acquired thereafter was the result of his natural interests, prompted by his own initiative. His first vocation was agriculture. Later, he learned the stone mason's trade, an accomplishment that later stood him in good stead as builder of his own house, a substantial stone residence that still testifies to the skill and integrity of its builder. At the age of twenty-six he took a wife in the person of Sarah, the daughter of Joseph Pennock. It was then that he seems to have resolved to devote himself earnestly to acquiring learning. He showed special interest in astronomy and the natural sciences. More and more important to him became an abiding devotion to botany, which, according to Dr. William Darlington, in "Memorials of John Bartram and Humphry Marshall" may have been awakened and supported through the happy and fruitful contact he enjoyed with his distinguished cousin, John Bartram, and the latter's botanical garden.

It is altogether probable that Humphry Marshall's taste for Horticulture and Botany may have been awakened and promoted by a familiar intercourse with his cousin, John Bartram, and by the attraction of that cousin's interesting *garden*. Enjoying such privileges, he would at once catch the spirit, and profit by the skill and experience of his enthusiastic relative.

It was his good fortune at the age of forty-five, and in the full prime of his life, to receive a patrimony, a large part of his deceased father's estate in Pennsylvania. He continued to reside there until 1774, when he moved to what is now known at Marshalltown, Pennsylvania. Here, in 1773, he had laid out and planted the beginning of what was to become another celebrated botanical garden. Few, indeed, of the botanists of our day realize and appreciate what these men and their contemporaries contributed to the knowledge and enthusiasm experienced by subsequent generations of young men and women, some of whom were, like their precursors, to become the botanists of another day, sworn to do their bit in extending ever more and more the horizon of man's knowledge of the vegetable kingdom.

Humphry Marshall's most ambitious work, and certainly the most important was his "Arbustum Americanum: The American Grove or an Alphabetical Catalogue of Forest Trees and Shrubs, Natives of the American United States," a duodecimo volume of approximately two hundred pages and said to be the earliest of botanical treatises to be published in the Western Hemisphere. This work was of the utmost importance to botanists and horticulturists seeking to acquaint themselves with the forest flora of the New World.

American men of science of the latter part of the eighteenth century were becoming more and more aware of the fact that there was among them an unpretentious man of the soil, a farmer, who was yet more than a farmer, a botanist, and yet even more than a botanist—one who was a moral force among men, a prodigious worker in the realm of beauty and culture. As a man of science, he was honored on January 20, 1786, by election to the American Philosophical Society. From the inscription on his diploma we learn:

The American Philosophical Society, held at Philadelphia, for promoting useful knowledge, desirous of advancing the interest of the Society, by associating to themselves men of distinguished eminence, and by conferring marks of their esteem upon persons of literary merit [had] elected Mr. Humphry Marshall of Chester County, a member of the said Philosophical Society, [thereby] granting unto him all the rights of fellowship, with all the liberties and privileges thereunto belonging.

ANON. 1884. *Early Proc. Am. Philos. Soc.*
ANON. 1913. *Bull. Chester Co. Hist. Soc.*, Sept. 27.
DARLINGTON, W. 1849. *Memorials of John Bartram and Humphry Marshall.* Lindsay & Blakiston, Philadelphia.
HARSHBERGER, J. S. 1899. *The Botanists of Philadelphia and Their Work.* T. C. Davis & Sons, Philadelphia.
HAZARD, S., ed. 1828. *Hazard's Register of Pennsylvania 1.*

Elmer Drew Merrill
1876–1956

Elmer Drew Merrill was born October 15, 1876, in a small village near Auburn, Maine. He was surrounded by and constantly exposed to the Maine countryside and the Maine woods, and his interest in things botanical stems back to this early beginning. Rather surprisingly, perhaps, his interest in nature survived a boyhood of milking cows, clearing rocks and ever more rocks from the fields, and planting, weeding, hoeing, and harvesting potatoes.

Many botanists develop a love of plants and nature from early boyhood associations. Most, however, follow these early leanings with moderate to intensive formal education in their chosen field. Merrill's formal education in botany, however, consisted of no more than two one-semester courses taken while he was an undergraduate at the State College at Orono (later the University of Maine). As a freshman, he registered at first for a course in engineering but decided by the end of the first year that he did not possess the necessary mathematical aptitude for this field. As a sophomore, therefore, he registered as a general science student without, as he says, any very definite idea of what work this course of study might fit him for.

As a student he worked to help pay his expenses, serving as assistant in the botanical laboratory. Here he developed a close working relationship with Prof. F. L. Harvey, an enthusiastic botanist who appears to have been the one individual more than all others who was responsible for diverting to botany Merrill's general biological interests.

In June, 1898, he graduated with a B.S. degree and returned in September of the same year to serve as assistant in natural science at the generous salary of 250 dollars for nine months of work. The following spring, in the "forlorn hope" of receiving an appointment, he took a United States Civil Service examination for the position of assistant agrostologist in the Department of Agriculture. The examination was successfully passed, and he was offered, and accepted, an appointment in Washington, D.C., at 1,200 dollars per annum. The work there, in a sense, constituted a postgraduate course that laid a firm foundation for much of his later research. He was fortunate to be employed as assistant to F. Lamson Scribner, at that time the country's leading grass taxonomist. During the next three years, he became thoroughly grounded in the fundamentals of taxonomic work including collecting (in Idaho, Montana, and Wyoming), identifying, preserving, mounting, and describing the specimens with which he worked.

Three years later, on February 22, 1902, Merrill left New York en route for the Philippine Islands to serve as botanist in the newly organized Bureau of Agriculture in Manila. For most of the next twenty-two years, he remained in the archipelago, collecting and classifying the vegetation. He quite literally had to build from the ground up, as earlier herbaria had been burned or otherwise destroyed. The few books that had at one time been available had been either burned or stolen. Yet, by the time he left the islands twenty-two years later, he had explored and collected in all parts of the Polynesian archipelago and parts of Java, Borneo, and the Malay Peninsula, as well as in parts of southern and eastern China. During this time he developed a herbarium of 270,000 mounted specimens and named roughly 4,000 species of plants. The major results of this phase of his life were assembled and published in 1945 under the title "Plant Life of the Pacific World." The scope of this work indicates the breadth of his interest, a breadth that had been shown earlier by his publications in floristics, plant nomenclature, plant geography, and botanical bibliography.

It was an early hope of Merrill's to write a flora of the Philippine archipelago, and in 1912 he published "Flora of Manila." This was written as a teaching aid for use in the university, but his personal services were also solicited, and teaching eighteen to thirty-six hours a week on a half-time basis was added to his other responsibilities. The time available for his botanical work was further curtailed in 1919, when he was appointed director of the Bureau of Science. His added activities during this period appear to have led him to abandon hope of completing his projected flora. He did, however, assemble the results of his studies into the four-volume, 2,136-page, "Enumeration of Philippine Flowering Plants," which was published during the period 1923–1926.

Early in his assignment to the Philippines, he became interested in weeds, their origin and manner of dispersal in historical time. This interest was perhaps first stimulated by the discovery that the plants endemic to the islands were often better known than the weedy introductions. He retained this interest throughout his life, carrying it so far as to make a detailed study of the plants collected by Cook in his South Pacific voyages, as a means of determining the time of introduction of the many exotics that were common in the archipelago, both as weeds and as crop plants.

Those who knew Merrill personally speak of him in terms that indicate tolerance of the ideas of others, though an intolerance of shoddy thinking or ill-founded conclusions. His last book, "The Botany of Cook's Voyages," also attests to this critical, though withal kindly, attitude. Other characteristics attributed to him were "quickness of perception, unfailing patience and courtesy, great store of common sense, promptness in taking action, approachableness, and consideration for others" (Robbins, 1958, P. 285). His scholarliness and industry are indicated by the herbaria he built and the books and scientific publications he wrote.

In addition to his various books, Merrill published more than five hundred scientific papers. The administrative duties alone with which he was charged from 1919 to 1946 would have been adequate as a full-time load for most men. Merrill's interest in his scientific studies, however, never relaxed as is indicated by the continued flow of publications that appeared under his name down through the years.

The honors awarded Merrill and the scientific organizations of which he was a member indicate his activity and the great esteem in which he was held by other scientists.

He was awarded honorary degrees of Doctor of Science from the University of Maine in 1926 and from Harvard University in 1936, Doctor of Letters from the University of California in 1936 and from Yale University in 1951. In 1939 he was given the old medal of the French Ministry of Agriculture and a diploma from the Société Nationale d'Acclimatation. In the same year the Linnaean Society, of London, of which he was a Foreign Member, decorated him with its medal, and in 1950 he was awarded the Geoffrey St. Hilaire medal and made a Commander in the Netherlands Order of Oranje Nassau. He was an honorary member of the Deutsche Botanische Gesellschaft, an honorary member of the Netherlands Botanical Society, and a member of the National Academy of Sciences and of the American Philosophical Society. He served as official U. S. delegate to the

Fifth Pacific Science Congress in Vancouver in 1933, as President of the Botanical Society of America in 1934, as President of the Section of Taxonomy and Nomenclature of the Sixth International Botanical Congress in Amsterdam in 1936 and of the Seventh in Stockholm in 1950, as Acting President of the American Association for the Advancement of Science in 1931, and as President of the New England Botanical Club, 1937–1939, the American Society of Plant Taxonomists, 1946, and the International Union of Biological Sciences, 1935. He held membership in many scientific societies, including: American Academy of Arts and Sciences (fellow), Philadelphia Academy of Natural Sciences, Académie des Sciences de l'Institut de France (correspondent), Torrey Botanical Club, Sigma Xi, Phi Beta Kappa, Alpha Zeta, Phi Kappa Sigma, Royal Horticultural Society of London, Edinburgh Botanical Society, Royal Society of Edinburgh, Universidad Nacional de la Plata (Académico Honorário), Malayan Branch of the Royal Asiatic Society, Muséum National d'Histoire Naturelle of Paris (correspondent), Nederlandse Botanische Vereniging, Kon. Nederlands Aardrijkskundig Genootschap, Naturhistorisches Museum of Vienna (correspondent), Svenska Ventenskaps Akademien, Institut Genevois, Société Botanique de France, Japanese Botanical Society, Peking Society of Natural History, and Royal Agricultural and Horticultural Society of India. In 1936, he was official guest of Harvard University at its Tercentenary Celebration. For a number of years he was a member of the Latin American Committee of Selection of the John Simon Guggenheim Foundation. He served at various times as a member of the board of directors or as trustee of a number of institutions and societies, such as the Escuela Agricola Panamericana in Honduras, the Gorgas Memorial Institute, the New York Horticultural Society, and the Board of Managers of the New York Botanical Garden. (Robbins, 1958)

Although plant taxonomy and distribution and a variety of other scientific fields including geology, climatology, and comparative philology constituted Merrill's lifelong, all-absorbing interests, his activities were dictated to a considerable extent by his family responsibilities. In May 1907, he married Mary Augusta Sperry. Although they were married in Manila, the couple spent the next year in Washington, D.C., New England, at Kew and the British Museum, Leiden, Berlin, Geneva, and Florence. A primary objective at each of these locations was examination of type specimens of Philippine plants. Between 1909 and 1914, three children, a daughter and two sons, were born to the Merrills. The loss of the last of these at an age of less than two months convinced the couple that Manila was not a desirable place to rear a family. As a consequence Mrs. Merrill and the two remaining children were left in Washington, D.C. at the termination of a short trip there in 1915, and Merrill returned to the islands alone. Except for a period in 1920–1921, he did not see his family again for eight years. His youngest daughter, born in Washington in 1916, was not seen by her father until she was five years old.

Family ties and other considerations finally overcame a strong attachment for the Philippines and its plant problems, and he left the Islands in 1923 to accept the position of dean of the College of Agriculture at the University of California. Within a year he was appointed director of the Agricultural Experiment Station in addition to his duties as dean of the college.

Merrill remained at California for six years, a period that saw many changes under his leadership. Research and instruction standards were raised, a Ph.D. degree was made a basic requirement for most positions, and junior members without advanced degrees were encouraged to continue their education. These were only a few of the changes for which he was responsible during the rather short period that he served as dean of the college, and it was with extreme regret that he was released in December, 1929. He had, however, been offered the directorship of the New York Botanic Garden and felt that he could not refuse.

He remained as director of the garden until 1935, serving as a highly capable administrator while continuing his botanical work. This scientific research and writing apparently always served as a kind of safety valve from the burdens of administration. Where most men would have turned to a variety of avocations for this release, Merrill fell back on his absorbing interest in botany, a fact that was responsible in no small measure for his lifelong high level of production.

An unexpected opportunity came in 1935 with an offer to serve as professor of botany and administrator of botanical collections at Harvard University. Merrill realized that the responsibilities of this position were to be largely administrative, but he must have felt that the contribution he might be able to make in thus furthering the cause of systematic botany was one that he could not conscientiously bypass. He, therefore, accepted the offer and began another, and the last, of his major periods of service to his profession. One year after his appointment the position of Arnold professor of botany and, in 1937, that of director of the Arnold Arboretum was offered him. In these capacities he served until July, 1946, when at the beginning of his seventieth year he requested retirement from administrative work. He remained as Arnold professor for an additional two years before becoming Arnold professor emeritus. For several years after this, he continued his botanical work as vigorously as his failing health would permit. He was possessed to the end with an unremitting drive to accomplish and to produce, a characteristic handed down by his Maine forebears and which typified his whole life and made it so peculiarly fruitful.

EWAN, JOSEPH. 1956. E. D. Merrill. *J. Wash. Acad. Sci.* 46(8): 267–268.

MERRILL, E. D. 1953. Autobiographical: Early Years, the Philippines, California. *Asa Gray Bull.* n.s. 2(4): 335–370.

ROBBINS, WILLIAM J. 1958. Elmer Drew Merrill. *Nat. Acad. Sci. Biog. Mem.* 32: 273–333.

ROLLINS, REED C. 1956. Elmer Drew Merrill, Administrator and Botanist. *Science* n.s. 123(3202): 831–832.

SCHULTES, R. E. 1957. Elmer Drew Merrill—An Appreciation. *Taxon* 6: 89–101.

André Michaux

1746–1802

Born at Satory, Versailles, France, a royal domain that had long been managed by his ancestors, it was intended that André Michaux should be assigned to the responsibility of managing a farm belonging to the royal estate. As a consequence and quite by intention, his interest in agriculture was encouraged while he was yet a mere cadet in pursuit of a knowledge of the classics. At the age of twenty-three he married Cécile Claye, comely daughter of a wealthy farmer near Beauce. Eleven months following this happy union, death claimed Cécile, shortly after the birth of their son, François André.

In his despondency, the grief-stricken father applied himself with absorbing zeal to a study of the sciences. At this time it was his good fortune to have as a teacher of botany the celebrated Bernard de Jussieu, a privilege that helped shape his career as a botanist. He traveled extensively in England and in Auvergne and the Pyrenées of his own France, where he studied and collected the plants of special interest to him. Later, we find him in Persia on a dual mission—botanical and political. In 1785 his government asked him to go to North America, where he was to make an intensive study of the trees and shrubs and to conduct such experiments as might be necessary to determine their fitness for transport to France.

He and his son landed in New York where they established residence for a year, and he made botanical field studies and collections with the idea of establishing a botanical garden there. Having discovered that conditions farther south were better suited to such a project, he went to Charleston, South Carolina, where, in 1785, he purchased a plantation not far from the city. There he inaugurated the enterprise that was to do so much to enable him to accomplish his objective. This same year he explored the mountains of the Carolinas and a year later made an exacting exploration of the swamps and sloughs of Florida. In 1789, he was in the Bahamas and then in the Appalachians—this time in search of ginseng and other plants of possible commercial worth. Then came the French Revolution and, with it, his resources from the home government were discontinued, notwithstanding the fact that he had joined the Republican cause.

In 1792, Michaux undertook a journey into the wilderness of Canada, penetrating as far as Hudson Bay. He left Charleston in April, resolved to journey overland as far as Quebec. According to his manuscript journal, he stopped first in New York; thence he went to New Haven; then, on June 14, he arrived in Albany, New York. He next proceeded to Lake Champlain where he spent several days in botanical exploration of both shores of the lake. On June 30, he arrived in Montreal and by mid-July he was in Quebec. Since it was now late in the growing season, he tarried but a few days for, according to his planned itinerary, he had yet to traverse many hundreds of miles, much of which was a wilderness of lakes and rivers and unexplored terrain.

From Quebec, Michaux and his party continued down the St. Lawrence to Tadoussac at the mouth of the Saguenay, thence up the Saguenay to Chicoutimi, then but a little village not far from Lake St. John. There he found a vast body of fresh water, catch basin of numerous streams, one of which, the Mistassini, is a river navigable for canoes for a distance of about 120 miles. Another 30 miles and the explorer and his guides found themselves in Lake Mistassini and past the northern limit of merchantable pine, spruce, and related trees. Michaux made accurate note of the position of the divide and observed a marked difference in the height and vigor of the arboreal vegetation on either side of the watershed. Certain of the tree species, common south of the divide, were no longer to be found to the north and west. He observed that between the Mistassini Lake region and Hudson Bay lay a vast plain peopled with stunted trees and shrubs.

On the way down the Rupert River, leading from Lake Mistassini to Hudson Bay, Michaux was obliged to terminate his journey. His Indian guides refused to go all the way to the Bay because they believed it dangerous to proceed farther north so late in the season. Reversing the course of their journey, therefore, we find Michaux returning to Philadelphia by the route he had followed in June and arriving there on December 8. He had been gone from Charleston eight months, three months of which had been spent in going from Quebec to the Mistassini Lakes.

The published works of Michaux are few in number. Principal among them is his "Histoire des Chênes d'Amérique," published in Paris in 1801. Another and monumental work, done in Latin, was his "Flora Boreali-Americana, Sistens Characteres Plantarum quas in America Septentrionali collegit et Detexit Andreas Michaux."

André Michaux was an outspoken man, taciturn, but withal friendly and generous, ready to help the unfortunate, particularly those of his own country who had met with misfortune in America. His marked simplicity and love of independence made him a bit queer in comparison with more conventional men, but this singularity did not spring from any intention or desire to be different. He took little part in casual conversation because he spoke of and listened to matters of useful and practical interest. His contribution to our knowledge of American plant life made for him a place of imperishable distinction as an American botanist.

COULTER, J. M., ed. 1883. Some North American Botanists iii André Michaux. *Botan. Gaz.* 8: 181–183.

DELAUZE, J. P. F. 1804. Notice Historique sur André Michaux. *Annales du Museum National d'Histoire Natural* 3.

SARGENT, C. S. 1889. *Proc. Am. Philos. Soc.* 26: 2–7, with Journal of André Michaux (in French) 1785–1796. Pp. 7–145.

François André Michaux
1770–1855

François André Michaux, like his father, was a native of France. Consequently there might be a question as to the legitimacy of our claiming him as an American botanist. But, as was true of Michaux the elder, the most important segment of the son's career as a botanist was American, quantitatively and qualitatively. It therefore seems only proper to identify him as an American botanist.

François André Michaux was born August 16, 1770, at Satory, the same royal domain that was the birthplace of his father, André Michaux. Concerning the son's early life, there seems available but little information. He was the only child of his father, his mother, Cécile (Claye) Michaux, having died eleven months after her marriage. The young François, therefore, never knew her. We have no information as to where he may have received any training in the sciences, particularly in botany. We do know that he traveled extensively with his father and that he, therefore, must have profited immeasurably from such association. It is a matter of record that he rendered valuable aid to his father. It is also known that he helped the elder Michaux in arranging and classifying the materials that went into the preparation of his "History of the North American Oaks" and his "Flora Boreali Americana."

While assisting his father, François was studying medicine with the intention of returning to the United States, there to practice as a physician. But circumstances ruled otherwise. Both he and his father longed for the rigors of the unexplored wilderness. Both were animated with a zeal to serve in some such capacity as might redound to the benefit of their country.

François André, inspired on his own account to accomplish something worthy the name and spirit of his father, was fired with a desire to realize the objective that both he and his father had hoped to achieve within his father's lifetime. In 1801, while the elder Michaux was engaged in an expedition to Madagascar, François André sought and was given a commission to the United States. Deeply grateful for the opportunity afforded him, the younger Michaux set out for Charlestown whence he forwarded from the nursery established there by his father in 1787 the remnant of trees and shrubs intended for shipment to France. Immediately thereafter he went to New York for a like purpose.

With the advent of the spring of 1802, Michaux made botanical excursions into New Jersey and along the "banks of North River." These herborizations enabled him to enlarge his acquaintance with certain American oaks and to determine accurately the characters peculiar to the black oak (*Quercus tinctoria*).

The young botanist went next to Philadelphia, where he became acquainted with such notable worthies as the Rev. Dr. Collins, Benjamin S. Barton, William Bartram, and others. He was deeply interested in botanical gardens, particularly those of William Bartram and William Hamilton, in which an effort had been made to include every tree and shrub capable of enduring the rigors of the Philadelphia climate.

Michaux next visited the states of Kentucky and Tennessee. His itinerary led him from Philadelphia westward by way of Lancaster and Shippensburgh, through the Alleghanies to Pittsburgh. This much of the way had been covered variously by stagecoach, horseback, and on foot. Leaving Pittsburgh on July 14, he walked to Wheeling, West Virginia. There he bought a canoe, descended the Ohio, and in three days was in Marietta, Ohio. Continuing his descent of the river he landed at Limestone (now Maysville) and journeyed overland to Lexington, Kentucky, and thence to Nashville, Tennessee, where he lingered a month, botanizing and acquainting himself with the local flora. He then set out upon his return to Charleston, by way of Knoxville, where he spent several days exploring in the vicinity of the falls of Roaring River. Subsequently, his route led him over the Tennessee-Carolina state line into North Carolina. This part of his journey was more mountainous and difficult but botanically more rewarding. In the course of events, he reached Morgantown and, after a total of three and a half months, was again in Charleston, having covered some 1,800 miles. An account of his explorations was published in 1804 under the title "Voyage a l'ouest des Montes Allegheny," etc. A year later appeared his "Naturalization des Arbres forestiers de l'Amérique du Nord." Both of these works were published subsequent to his return to France.

Michaux's expert knowledge of the soils of his native land and of its natural capacity for reforestation with certain of the North American trees induced him to try to increase the number of forest trees in France. This he proposed to do by collecting seed and young trees in America to ship to France for distribution among the national nurseries of that country. In 1806, Michaux again embarked at Bordeaux on a ship bound for Charleston. On the way across the Atlantic, the vessel was captured by a British man-of-war. Michaux was taken on board and transported to the Bermudas, where he was finally released and allowed to set sail for the United States. Arriving at some point in Maine, he set out upon a botanical cruise that took him a total of approximately 2,000 miles from Maine through all of the Atlantic States to Georgia and over diversion trails into the interior. The scope of his observations was seemingly unlimited, and the facts gleamed by him were of great value and interest to the American people, as well as the people of France. Michaux remained in the United States almost three years, during which time he was busy preparing a memoir of his explorations, a splendid contribution to our then meagre knowledge of American trees and shrubs. Incidentally, he formed a number of acquaintances that would have been precious to any botanist but must have been more so to him, a man keenly sensitive to the worth of professional contacts.

During the two years following Michaux's return to France, he was engaged in writing his monumental work "Histoire des Arbres forestiers de l'Amerique Septentrionali." In publishing this magnificent contribution, the author planned to combine the purely botanical and the ethnobotanical, and he was eminently successful. Although as botanist he may not have attained the renown of his distinguished father, his achievement was none the less distinctive and meritorious.

ANON. 1849. *J. Franklin Inst.* July.

DURAND, E. 1857. *Am. J. Sci.* 2nd Ser. 24: 161–177.

DURAND, E. 1860. Biographical Memoir of the late François André Michaux. *Trans. Am. Philos. Soc.* 11: 17.

Edwin Cyrus Miller
1878–1948

Edwin Cyrus Miller, plant physiologist, son of Benjamin F. and Mary (Brandt) Miller, was born December 16, 1878, on a farm near the village of Baltimore, Ohio. There he obtained his early schooling and later attended college at Lebanon, Ohio, where, in 1904, he received the B.S. degree. In 1906, he obtained the A.B. degree from the National Normal University. He then attended Yale University, where he was awarded the Ph.D. degree in 1910. In the autumn of that year he accepted an instructorship in botany at the College of Agriculture at Manhattan, Kansas. He was promoted to the rank of assistant professor, then to associate professor, and subsequently to professor of plant physiology. In addition to teaching and research, he became a member of the Kansas Agricultural Experiment Station staff in 1911, which position he held until 1919, when he became plant physiologist in the Experiment Station, a position he held until he retired from active service. He served for two years as acting head of the department of botany and plant pathology, during which time he demonstrated his fitness for the assumption of such responsibility.

Dr. Miller's ability as a teacher and his interest in his students were outstanding, and his devotion to teaching was maintained throughout his career. Interested as he was in the techniques and results of teaching, he realized fully the importance of research as an accompaniment to successful teaching. He realized the difficulty of the teacher's task as a source of enthusiasm and inspiration, without the dynamism afforded by research. His research was confined largely to scholarly studies on the water relations of plants and the chemical aspects of plant behavior.

In selecting a doctoral problem, he showed what was to be characteristic of him, seeking the basic phenomena of plant behavior. He was led directly to a fundamental study of the chemical changes involved in the germination of fatty seed, for example, of *Helianthus annuus*, the common sunflower. This and his study of

the origin of chloroplasts in the cotyledons of the sunflower, projects initiated while at Yale, were completed at Kansas State College.

Other research by Dr. Miller included a comparative study of
the water requirements of maize and sorghum, a study of the daily
variation of water and dry matter, and their relative transpiration.
Later in his career at Kansas State, he conducted a technical study
of the winter-wheat plant at consecutive stages of its development.
This period proved to be the most extensive of his research under-
takings. Altogether Dr. Miller was author or coauthor of twenty-
four technical papers. He was a fellow of the American Academy
for the Advancement of Science and a member of the American
Society of Plant Physiologists, of Sigma Chi, Phi Beta Kappa, Phi
Kappa Phi, Alpha Zeta, Gamma Sigma Delta, and Farm House
Fraternity.

ANON. 1945. Edwin Cyrus Miller on retirement. Notes. *Plant Physiol.* 20: 692.
ANON. 1946. E. C. Miller. *Plant Physiol.* 21: 243–245, portrait p. 115.
ANON. 1949. Notes. *Plant Physiol.* 24: 775.

Charles Frederick Millspaugh
1854–1923

Charles Frederick Millspaugh, son of John Hill and Marion
(Cornell) Millspaugh, was born in Ithaca, New York, June 20,
1854. His father was an artist, and his mother was a sister of Ezra
Cornell, Quaker and founder of Cornell University. In his boyhood
Charles Frederick's interests centered chiefly in athletics and natural history. It was his good fortune while yet a boy to become acquainted with the great naturalist and teacher, Louis Agassiz, a
contact that became an important factor in shaping Millspaugh's
destiny. Having completed his college-preparatory schooling, he
entered Cornell University in 1871, but, because of lack of funds in

his second year, he was obliged to curtail his studies and seek outside employment. He next resumed his college work at the New York Homeopathic College and Hospital and was graduated there in 1881 with the M.D. degree.

For the next ten years he practiced medicine in Binghampton and Waverly, New York. It was during this time that he became particularly interested in plant life and especially in such plants as were of accepted importance in medicine. This study led to his monumental, two-volume work entitled "American Medicinal Plants" (1887), a compendium of information, illustrated by nearly two hundred plates, the work of the author's own artistic skill. This botanical masterpiece attracted much attention, and Millspaugh was called to accept the headship of botany at West Virginia University in 1891. In 1892, his "Preliminary Catalogue of the Flora of West Virginia" ("Ann. Rep. W. Va. Agr. Exp. Sta.") appeared.

He was appointed curator of botany at the Field Museum of Natural History in Chicago in 1894, a position he retained for the rest of his life. He devoted many years of his curatorship to the development of the herbarium, which, by the time of his death, had become one of the most important of its kind anywhere. The great care with which its contents had been catalogued added much to its accessibility and usefulness. During the years of his curatorship, he carried on his studies on the American Euphorbiaceae, a project he had started while at West Virginia University.

Opportunity for travel enabled him to explore the plant life of Mexico, Yucatan, the West Indies and Bahamas, Cuba, Haiti, Jamaica, and Brazil. These botanical travels were followed by the publication of numerous papers, chief among which were his "Flora of Yucatan" (1895), "Plantae Insulae Amanasensis" and "Plantae Utowanae" (1900), "Flora of St. Croix" (1902), "Flora of the Sand Keys of Florida" (1907), "Flora of the Alacran-Reef" (1916), and Flora of Santa Catalina Island" (1923).

Professor Millspaugh won enviable renown as a lecturer, in recognition of which he retained for several years a professional lectureship at the University of Chicago. As curator of a museum he was able to envision the educational function of such an institution —to reveal the varirelatedness of plant life to the life, labor, and welfare of man and to combine artistic and mechanical skills with scientific knowledge. Thus did the Field Museum of Natural History become, educationally, a unique institution.

Millspaugh was a member of the Illinois Academy of Science, the Torrey Botanical Club, and a fellow of the American Academy of Arts and Sciences. He was twice married, first to Mary Louisa Spaulding of Waverly, New York on September 19, 1877, who passed away in 1907; second to Clara Isobel Mitchell (1910), the daughter of Albert J. Mitchell of Chicago, Illinois. Dr. Millspaugh died in Chicago, September 15, 1923, survived by his wife and a son.

SHERIFF, E. E. 1924. *Botan. Gaz.* 77: 228–230, with portrait.

David Myers Mottier
1864–1940

David Myers Mottier, son of John David and Lydia (Myers) Mottier, was born in Patriot, Indiana, September 4, 1864. He married Antoinette J. Snyder of Switzerland County, Indiana, August 31, 1893.

Little has been recorded concerning Mottier's early schooling. It is known that he attended Indiana University from which he received his A.B. in 1891; a year later he was awarded his Master of Arts degree. It was during his years at this university that he was a student of David Starr Jordan, Douglas Houghton Campbell, and John Merle Coulter, a group of men remarkable as teachers and outstanding in their respective fields of research.

Mottier completed his postgraduate studies at the University of Bonn, where he pursued his botanical work under Eduard Strasburger, then at the zenith of his renown as a botanist. Mottier received his Ph.D. in 1897. The following year he continued his research at the University of Leipzig and at the Naples Biological

Station. Excepting for his few years spent in European schools, virtually all of Dr. Mottiers botanical experience was at Indiana University, where he was appointed instructor of botany in 1891. Two years later he was promoted to an associate professorship, which position he held until his retirement in 1937. He died on March 25, 1940.

Dr. Mottier devoted himself to his profession with unswerving fidelity. He was a gifted teacher and an investigator of marked enthusiasm and soundness. He had high respect for the thoroughness and general excellence of the teaching and laboratory technique he had observed at Bonn and Leipzig. He was well grounded in the traditions of those universities and was not slow to admit and adapt certain of them to his own teaching and research. He was an exacting judge of the quality and worth of work done by his graduate students. As a direct result of his strict adherence to these high standards, the average excellence of the botanists who had been his students was high. He was just as careful and exacting in his own research as he was in that required of his students; in fact, he was a perfectionist, a quality plainly observable in the surpassing beauty and accuracy of his cytological preparations and drawings.

Mottier became widely known through his published research and botanical textbooks. He was especially well known because of his work on cell-division phenomena, sporogenesis, and the embryology of the ferns and their allies and seed plants. Chief among his contributions to our knowledge of botany were: "Polyembryony of certain Polypodiaceae and Osmundaceae," "Chondriosomes and the Primordia of Chloroplasts and Leucoplasts," "The Behavior of Certain Fern Prothallia Under Prolonged Cultivation," "Textbook of Botany for College Students," and numerous other important contributions.

Anon. 1941. Necrology. *Ind. Acad. Sci. Pub.* 50: 7–8.
Cleland, R. E. 1940. David M. Mottier. *Science* n.s. 91: 423-424.

Gotthilf Heinrich Ernst Mühlenberg
1753–1815

Gotthilf Heinrich Ernst Mühlenberg was the son of Heinrich Melchior Mühlenberg, the champion of Lutheranism in North America. He received his formal education in the schools of Philadelphia and at Halle, Germany, where he was prepared for the ministry. Returning from Halle to his native Pennsylvania, he served his church until 1780. To escape capture by the British, he sought refuge in the country. While in hiding he devoted himself seriously to the study of the plant life of his surroundings. Thus began his career as a botanist. On his ultimate return to Philadelphia, he continued his botanical studies and devoted much time to consideration of the pharmaceutical properties of plants. In due course he commenced to correspond with European botanists and devoted serious attention to a systematic study of the plants in and about Lancaster, Pennsylvania. By 1791 he had collected more than a thousand plants within a radius of three miles of Lancaster. He was one of the first American botanists to make a special study of native and introduced grasses.

A born naturalist, Mühlenberg observed and made note of the animal life encountered in his ramblings, as well as the mineralogy and meteorology. His earliest botanical papers appeared in 1791 with his "Index Flora Lancastriensis" comprising 454 genera and more than a thousand species of native and cultivated plants.

Prompted by a spirit of unselfishness, Mühlenberg conceived the idea of a cooperative project, to be participated in by all American botanists, whereby they would jointly write a flora of North America. This would do away with the individual publication of numerous conflicting papers. But his proposal and attempt to interest others in such a cooperative effort got little encouragement. Finally, in 1809, he and twenty-eight correspondents completed a "Catalogue of the Known and Naturalized Plants of North America," a monumental achievement. It was published in 1813. Listed were more than 1,500 phanerogamic plants and ferns and an added 727 species of algae, fungi, lichens, liverworts, and mosses.

Mühlenberg's account of the plants of the Lancaster region and of such North American plants as he had observed and had added to his herbarium was left in manuscript. A part pertaining to grasses was published posthumously in 1817. Not a little of the information on grasses left by him was incorporated in the published work of less scrupulous contributors, without courtesy of credit due Mühlenberg. A genus belonging to the Gramineae (Mühlenbergia) was named after him, and many are the plant species that do honor to their discoverer.

Gotthilf H. E. Mühlenberg married, in 1774, Mary Catharine Hall of Philadelphia by whom he had four sons and four daughters. His death occurred May 23, 1815.

ANON. 1894. Sketch of Gotthilf Heinrich Ernst Mühlenberg. *Pop. Sci. Monthly* 45: 689–698.
BECK, H. H. 1938. Henry E. Muhlenberg. *Castanea* 3: 41–53.
HARSHBERGER, J. W. 1899. *The Botanists of Philadelphia and Their Works*. T. C. Davis & Sons, Philadelphia.
YOUMANS, W. J. 1896. Pioneers of Science in America. D. Appleton & Company, Inc., New York.

Frederick Charles Newcombe

1858–1927

Frederick Charles Newcombe, plant physiologist, was born on May 11, 1858, in Flint, Michigan. He was the son of Thomas and Eliza (Gayton) Newcombe. It is probable that his elementary and college-preparatory schooling was obtained in Flint, though careful search of the records gave no information concerning his boyhood or as to what his early interests were. His professional career got off to a late start, for he was already thirty-two years old when he was appointed instructor in botany at the University of Michigan (1890–1892). His advancement from this time on was rapid, for he became assistant professor of botany (1893–1897), junior professor (1897–1903), and professor (1905–1923). He retired in 1923.

Newcombe's botanical interest centered chiefly in plant physiology, and his first bit of published research ("Spore Dissemination in *Equisetum*") appeared in the "Botanical Gazette" of 1888. He received his B.S. degree from the University of Michigan in 1890 and later went to Europe to pursue his graduate studies in plant physiology under Pfeffer of the University of Leipzig, where, in 1893, he was awarded the Ph.D. degree. On completion of his studies at Leipzig, he returned to the University of Michigan to accept appointment as assistant professor of botany.

Although physically somewhat frail, Professor Newcombe was a man of tremendous enthusiasm and indefatigable mental energy. He appeared upon the botanical scene at a time when the professional standards as affecting university men were not high. He had little sympathy for those who were content with continuing at the dead level of teaching without the inspiration of research and the vitalizing spark of new ideas born of laboratory and field experimentation and reasoning.

Newcombe entered actively into the work of those botanical organizations that sought to awaken young men and women to an interest in plant science by bringing them into more frequent contact with the older botanists. It was he who founded the Botanical Journal Club of the University of Michigan and had an important part in organizing the Michigan Academy of Science, of which he was elected president in 1903–1904. Dr. Newcombe was an active participant in the affairs of the Botanists of the Central States, an organization that ultimately became merged with the Botanical Society of America. Throughout his career as a botanist he took a continuing interest in the American Association for the Advancement of Science and in the affairs of the Botanical Society of America. He was secretary of Section G of the American Academy for the Advancement of Science in 1897 and president of the Botanical Society of America in 1917. For several years he recommended, and finally brought about the founding of the "American Journal of Botany," the technical journal of the Botanical Society of America.

Outstanding among Newcombe's contributions to the University of Michigan was the part he played in bringing about the establishment of the Botanical Garden, now known as the Nichols Arboretum of the Department of Landscape Design.

On June 25, 1884, Dr. Newcombe married Susan Eastman of Flint, Michigan. When he retired and was appointed professor emeritus, both he and Mrs. Newcombe were in poor health. They went to Honolulu in the hope of improved strength and vigor. Their hopes were not realized; instead, at the end of two years, Mrs. Newcombe passed away, and the professor's death followed shortly after, on October 1, 1927.

BARTLETT, H. H. 1929. Obituary. Frederick Charles Newcombe. *Mich. Acad. Sci. 31st Ann. Rept.* 78–80.
BROWN, E. D. W. B. 1927. Hawaii's Tribute to Dr. Newcombe. *Science* n.s. **66**: 499–500.
POLLOCK, J. B., and H. H. BARTLETT. 1928. *Am. J. Botany* 15: 1–5.

George Elwood Nichols
1882–1939

George Elwood Nichols, bryologist and ecologist, was born April 12, 1882, in Southington, Connecticut, a son of Rev. and Mrs. George E. Nichols. After completing his college-preparatory schooling by graduation from Hillhouse High School, he became a student at Yale, where he received his A.B. in 1904 and the Ph.D. in 1909. Dr. Nichols was a familiar figure on the Yale campus from the beginning of his postgraduate years until near the close of his active life. His employment with the university began with his appointment as assistant in botany, and continued as instructor in the same department. Thereafter, he was appointed assistant professor (1915–1924). From 1924 to 1926 he served as associate professor. In 1926 he was appointed Eaton professor of botany, head of the department, and director of the Marsh Botanical Garden.

Early in Professor Nichols's career as a botanist, he was a member of the teaching staff of the Michigan Biological Station of the

University, where he was in charge of courses dealing with the taxonomy of the algae and mosses. Here his outstanding ability as a teacher was soon recognized, and, through his students, he became widely known. At Yale he came in contact with the eminent hepaticologist Alexander W. Evans. Thereafter his interest in bryology broadened, and he was invited to assume, with Dr. Evans, the joint authorship of "The Bryophytes of Connecticut," a work of more than casual importance, published in 1908 by the Connecticut State Geological and Natural History Survey. Its importance lay in the fact that it was the most comprehensive work of its kind on the taxonomy of the mosses and liverworts of the Northeastern States.

During World War II, Dr. Nichols served as botanical advisor to the American Red Cross on matters pertaining to *Sphagnum* and its use for surgical dressings. His published work on the subject was of more than temporary importance. His field studies and collecting in Nova Scotia and particularly those relating to Cape Breton Island resulted in his "The Bryophytes of Nova Scotia with Special Reference to the Bryophytes of Cape Breton." From 1922 to 1938 a series of pioneer studies on the bryophytes of Michigan were published in the *Bryologist*.

Dr. Nichols won honor and distinction not only as a bryologist but as a plant ecologist. In 1910, he was a student at the University of Chicago, where it was his privilege to receive training under Henry Chandler Cowles. This brief association did much to determine Dr. Nichols's ultimate leadership in ecology. Outstanding among his contributions to the ecology of the Northeast is his monograph entitled: "The Vegetation of Northern Cape Breton Island, Nova Scotia" ("Trans. Conn. Acad. Arts and Sci." 1918).

Lutz, H. J. 1939. Obituary. George Elwood Nichols. *Am. J. Sci.* 237: 609–610.
Olmsted, C. E. 1941. *Ecology* 22: 235–236.
Steere, W. C. 1939. *Bryologist* 42: 137–142, with portrait and publications of interest to bryologists.

Thomas Nuttall

1786–1859

Thomas Nuttall was born in Settel, Yorkshire, England, in the year 1786. At the age of twenty-two he emigrated to the United States, where he settled in Philadelphia. Here, the day after his arrival, he collected a species of *Smilax*. Unable to identify it, he was directed to consult Prof. Benjamin Smith Barton, who at once became interested in the young Englishman and gave him instruction in the elements of botany. Barton's interest in him led Nuttall to decide upon botany as a career. Being an apt and enthusiastic pupil, he advanced rapidly and indulged his taste for exploratory trips that led him deeper and deeper into the wooded wilderness along the Atlantic Coast of Virginia and North Carolina.

In 1809, it was his good fortune to meet John Bradbury, the Scottish naturalist, who was on the eve of undertaking a natural-history excursion into the then Far West. The upshot of this meeting was an agreement whereby Nuttall was to join Bradbury as his traveling companion. One objective of the excursion was the collection of whatsoever might be of natural-history interest. The party proceeded westward to St. Louis, Missouri, and thence northward across the Kansas and Platte rivers. In the spring of 1910, it was pursuing its way up the Missouri River into little-known parts of the Dakota territory. The trip was fraught with severe hardship and with danger of attack by Indians. Early in 1811, our excursionists returned to Philadelphia. But Nuttall's love of search for the unknown gave him no rest. He next began exploration of various sections of the United States east of the Mississippi, from the south shores of the Great Lakes to the Everglades of Florida.

In due course he was elected to membership in the Linnaean Society of London, then to membership in the American Philosophical Society, and the Academy of Natural Sciences in Philadelphia. In 1818, Nuttall published, in Philadelphia, his master-piece, a two-volume work entitled: "Genera of the North American Plants."

In the autumn of that same year, he set out for the wilds of Arkansas, a region that had never been explored by a scientist. This fact spurred Nuttall's determination to make this excursion, an adventure marked with incessant hardship and toil. All went fairly well until the tenth month (Oct.) when he was compelled by illness to halt. By December, he had so far recovered as to be able to resume his way to New Orleans. By early spring, he was again in Philadelphia, having completed a round trip of more than 5,000 miles. In the course of his search for plants, he had observed and collected a prodigious number of specimens, many of which represented new genera as well as new species. In 1821 he published his "Journal of Travels into the Arkansas Territory."

That same year he was offered a professorship in natural history by Harvard College and, at the same time, was appointed curator of the botanical garden. While at Harvard, he had leisure for work peculiarly his own, and it was not long until he published his "Introduction to Systematic and Physiological Botany." He was offered an opportunity to join the Wyeth Expedition to the Pacific Coast. By this time he had become deeply interested in ornithology and, in 1832, published his "Manual of the Ornithology of the United States and Canada." This book and a single paper entitled "Remarks and Inquiries Concerning the Birds of Massachusetts" established his reputation as an ornithologist. In 1842, Nuttall inherited an estate in England under the will of an uncle stipulating that his nephew should spend nine months per year as a resident of the estate. Nuttall accepted the suggestion and, with the exception of a short sojourn in the United States, spent the rest of his days in his native country, where, on September 10, 1859, he died.

Elias Durand said of him immediately following his death:

No other explorer of the botany of North America has personally made more discoveries; no writer on American plants, except perhaps Prof. Asa Gray, has described more new genera and species.

ALDEN, R. H., and J. D. IFFT. 1943. Early Naturalists in the Far West. *Calif. Acad. Sci. Occ. Papers* 20: 42–46.

DURAND, E. 1859–1861. Biographical Notice of the late Thomas Nuttall. *Proc. Am. Philos. Soc.* 7: 297–315.

PENNELL, F. W. 1936. Travels and Scientific Collections of Thomas Nuttall. *Bartonia* 18: 1–51.

YOUMANS, W. J. 1895. Thomas Nuttall. *Pop. Sci. Monthly* 46: 689–696.

YOUMANS, W. J. 1896. *Pioneers of Science in America.* D. Appleton & Company, Inc., New York.

Stephen Thayer Olney
1812–1878

Stephen Thayer Olney, botanist and merchant, was born on February 15, 1812, in Providence, Rhode Island. He was the son of Stephen and Polly (Thayer) Olney, descended from Thomas Olney, a colonist who came as one of the earliest settlers in Providence, where he was ordained in 1668 as minister of the First Baptist Church in that colony. Stephen T. Olney, the subject of this sketch, was educated in Providence. He then entered the counting house of Isaac B. Cooke & Company. Later, he and Jesse Metcalf combined to establish the Wauskuck Company, which developed into a lucrative business in the manufacture and sale of woolen goods. Olney thus became wealthy, but his prosperity did not win him away from his love of botany, which was to become his major interest, leading him to become one of the best known botanists of his era.

Olney corresponded with all the leading botanists of the time and spared no effort or means to inform himself. Most of his time and labor was devoted to an exhaustive study of the carices. His work on the genus *Carex* was characterized by the most searching study of specific characters and lucidity of description. His exsiccatae, issued in 1871–1872, bear convincing evidence of his intelligence and discriminatory power. His herbarium, which he later bequeathed to Brown University, shows how intensively and with what care he considered each species. Unpublished notes bearing on his classification of species and varieties are sufficient proof of the accuracy of his analyses. Even though at times he might have been tempted to set up new species, his spirit of conservatism prevented him from doing so.

Among Olney's more important published papers are the following: "Catalogue of Plants" (1845), "Rhode Island Plants" (1846), "Carices Nord" (1868), "Carices Boreali Americanae" (1870), "Algae Rhodiacae" (1871), "Carices" in Watson's "Botany of King's Report on Exploration of the 40th Parallel" (1871), "Cyperaceae" in Hayden's Report for 1871–1872, and "Carices" in Gray's Report on Oregon plants of E. Hall (1871–1872).

In addition to his herbarium, Olney bequeathed to Brown University a professorship of botany, in grateful recognition of which the university honored him with a Master of Arts degree. He remained a lifelong bachelor and died at Providence, Rhode Island on July 27, 1878.

GRAY, A. 1879. Stephen T. Olney. *Am. J. Sci.* 3rd Ser. 17: 179–180.

James Bertram Overton
1869–1937

James Bertram Overton was born at Richmond, Michigan, on October 23, 1869. Little has been recorded concerning his early education and even less of his aptitudes. On completing his college entrance requirements, he enrolled at the University of Michigan, where he was graduated in 1894. He then obtained employment as a teacher in the Black River Falls, Wisconsin, high school. Following this experience, he was for three years senior master of mathematics at St. John's Military Academy at Delafield, Wisconsin. Convinced of the desirability of more education, Overton entered the University of Chicago in 1898 to engage in graduate study. There he was awarded the Ph.D. degree in 1901 and obtained appointment as professor of biology at Illinois College, where he served two years and where he was awarded the honorary degree of D.Sc. in 1930.

In 1903–1904, having been appointed by the Carnegie Institution of Washington, he spent a year in Bonn as research assistant in Strasburger's laboratory. Returning to the United States, Overton entered upon his career as botanist and plant physiologist at the University of Wisconsin. He was first appointed instructor; then, in 1907, he was promoted to the position of assistant professor and in 1912 to associate professor of plant physiology. Three years later he was advanced in rank to professor of plant physiology.

Overton's contributions in the field of botanical research include "Histologische Beiträge zur Vererbungsfrage," von Eduard Strasburger, C. E. Allen, Kuchi Miyake under J. B. Overton, 1905; "The Hydrostatic-Pneumatic System of Certain Trees"; "Movements of Liquids and Gases," by Dr. D. T. MacDougal, J. B. Overton, and Gilbert M. Smith, 1929; "The Organization of the Nuclei in the Root Tips of *Podophyllum Pellatum*," 1921; "Parthenogenesis in *Thalictrum Purpurascens*" (Ph.D. thesis, Univ. Chicago, 1902); "A Textbook of General Botany," by Gilbert M. Smith, J. B. Overton, E. M. Gilbert, R. H. Denniston, G. S. Bryan, and C. E. Allen, 1924.

In conjunction with D. T. MacDougal and G. M. Smith, Overton undertook a study of the structure and history of the long-lived cells of certain cacti. This bit of research was done in part at the Carmel (Calif.) and Tucson (Ariz.) laboratories of the Carnegie Institution of Washington, D.C.

Dr. Overton died on March 18, 1937.

Anon. 1937. Obituary. *Plant Physiol.* 12: 561–562.
Allen, C. E. 1937. James Bertram Overton. *Science* n.s. 85: 350–351.

Louis Hermann Pammel
1862–1931

Louis Hermann Pammel, botanist and conservationist, was born April 19, 1862, in Las Crosse, Wisconsin. His parents, Louis C. and Sophie (Freise) Pammel, were born in Germany and came to America to settle in Wisconsin in 1857. In his youth he attended country school. What he learned there was supplemented by a course at business college and by private instruction in mathematics, languages, and other subjects necessary to college entrance. In 1881, at nineteen, he entered the University of Wisconsin, where he pursued a four-year course in agriculture and was graduated in 1885.

Instead of continuing his study of agriculture, Pammel chose a career in one of the professions and became a student of medicine in Hahnemann Medical College in Philadelphia. He remained there for but two months, when he moved to Cambridge, Massachusetts, where he served as private assistant to Professor Farlow, then professor of cryptogamic botany at Harvard University. Later, he accepted an offer to act as assistant in the Shaw School of Botany, Washington University, St. Louis, Missouri, where he served upwards of three years. In January, 1889, he was offered a professorship. That same year he was awarded his M.S. by the University of Wisconsin and the Ph.D. degree in 1899 by Washington University. On June 29, 1887, he married Augusta M. Emmel, the daughter of Peter and Caroline Emmel of Chicago, by whom he had one son and five daughters. His acceptance of a professorship of botany at Iowa State College found him the sole member of his departmental staff. As a contributing botanist, his major interest was in the field of taxonomy. The large herbarium of nearly 200,000 sheets was in considerable measure the fruit of his own labor as a collector.

As a contributor to our knowledge of plant life, Pammel's more important published works were a two-volume account of "The Grasses of Iowa" (1903), "A Manual of Poisonous Plants" (1910),

"Weeds of the Farm and Garden" (1911), "Weed Flora of Iowa" (1913, revised, 1926), numerous bulletins, and popular articles for the press.

Important as were his contributions to research and teaching, Pammel is best known to the people of Iowa as a conservationist. He was the author of the Iowa conservation bill and was the first chairman of the State's conservation board. His active interest in conservation resulted in the acquisition of thirty-six state parks and in the assignment of authority over the lakes to the conservation board. Dr. Pammel was a member of several scientific societies. He died on March 23, 1931, while en route homeward from California, where he and Mrs. Pammel had spent the winter of 1930–1931.

GILMAN, J. C. 1932. Louis Hermann Pammel. *Phytopath.* 22: 669–674, with portrait and bibliography of works compiled by C. M. King.
PAMMEL, L. H. Autobiographical notes left with Department of Botany, Iowa State College.

Charles Christopher Parry
1823–1890

Charles Christopher Parry, botanist and physician, was born August 28, 1823, in Admington, Gloucestershire, England. He was the son of Joseph and Eliza (Elliott) Parry of a clerical lineage in the Established Church. When he was nine years old, the family moved from England to Washington County, New York. While yet a boy he showed marked interest in plants and promise as a scholar. His elementary schooling completed, he enrolled at Union College, where in 1842, he obtained his A.B. and subsequently entered Columbia College as a student of medicine, where, in 1846, he was granted the M.D. degree.

It was his good fortune here to become acquainted with John Torrey, whose influence as teacher and botanist undoubtedly helped to shape Parry's scientific career. On completing his course in medicine, Parry moved to Davenport, Iowa, where he went into medical practice. All around him was the virgin, unbroken prairie with its unspoiled wealth of native vegetation. His strong natural desire to acquaint himself with his botanical surroundings led him year by year away from his practice of medicine and ever deeper into what promised to become complete absorption in his growing devotion to botany and related branches of scientific study.

In 1848, he became a member of David Dale Owen's staff in the geological survey of Iowa, Minnesota, and Wisconsin. In 1849, he was appointed botanist to the United States and Mexican border survey. These two surveys afforded him an unbroken opportunity of nearly three years' devotion to botany and geology. For nearly forty years thereafter, he spent his summers in the botanical exploration of the Pacific and inter-mountain states and territories, either on his own account or as a botanist for some scientific survey or like enterprise.

It was Parry who discovered the Colorado blue spruce (*Picea pungens* Engl.) (*P. parryana* Sarg.). Two Rocky Mountain summits, Gray Peak and Torrey Peak, were named by him, the one in honor of Asa Gray, the other of John Torrey. In 1874, he sought out and followed the ancient trail taken by John C. Frémont across southern Utah, where he made new finds that added to his fame as a botanical explorer. As the years passed, he visited California repeatedly, devoting much time to his study of the chaparral. His thoroughness and conscientious attitude toward whatever he undertook led him repeatedly to England, where, at Kew Gardens, he could make the necessary comparisons of his western species with type specimens before publishing his descriptive notes.

It was Parry's good fortune to become acquainted with such eminent botanists as Edward Lee Greene and George Engelmann. With the former he explored botanically the mountains of Colorado, and with Engelmann he made a circuitous excursion of the extensive forests of the Pacific Coast. With John Gill Lemmon he explored the western Mohave Desert, the San Joaquin Valley, and the summits and canyons of the San Bernardino Mountains. His kindly and tolerant personality won for him the confidence and friendship of many who, in one way or another, were helpful in furthering his botanical interest and progress. Many were the plants named in his honor. Notable among these were the lily (*Lilium parryi*), the lotebush (*Zizyphus parryi*), the Ensenada buckeye (*Aesculus parryi*), and the Parry piñon pine (*Pinus parryana*).

In 1853 Charles Christopher Parry married Sarah M. Dabzell. Death claimed her in 1858, and, in 1859, he married a second time, choosing as his wife Emily R. Preston, a widow, who survived him. He died at his home in Davenport, Iowa, February 20, 1890, in his sixty-seventh year.

BRITTON, N. L. 1890. Charles Christopher Parry. *Bull. Torrey Club* 17: 74–75.
COULTER, J. M. 1890. *Botan. Gaz.* 15: 66–68.
KNOWLTON, F. H. 1892–1894. *Bull. Philos. Soc. Washington* 12: 497–499.
PRESTON, C. H. 1897. Sketch. Charles Christopher Parry. *Proc. Davenport Acad. Nat. Sci.* 6: 35–45. List of publications by Mrs. C. C. Parry, 46–52.

Charles Horton Peck

1833–1917

Charles Horton Peck was born March 30, 1833, at Sand Lake, Rensselaer County, New York. He was the son of Joel B. and Pamelia (Horton) Peck and a descendant of Henry Peck, who came to America from England and settled in New Haven, Connecticut, in 1638. The boy Charles obtained his early schooling at Sand Lake, where he attended a primitive village school built of logs. When eighteen years old, he enrolled at the Albany State Normal School, where he was a member of a voluntary class in botany. Here his interest in the subject was greatly stimulated, and he was so deeply impressed that it required only a chain of related circumstances to determine and shape the course of his life work.

He was graduated from the state normal school in 1852. Thereafter Peck returned to his father's farm, where he spent his spare time collecting and becoming acquainted with the plants of his locality. At Sand Lake Collegiate Institute, he prepared for college, and, in 1855, he became a student at Union college, where he graduated with high honors in 1859. He was thereupon appointed to a position in the Sand Lake Collegiate Institute to teach Latin, Greek, mathematics, and botany for a term of three years, and then, in the Classical Institute of Albany, he taught mathematics and the classics for four years.

Here he became acquainted with the Hon. G. W. Clinton, who was himself a botanist and much interested in improving the state herbarium and in extending a knowledge of the natural history of the state through its natural history museum. This acquaintance with Clinton led, in 1867, to Peck's appointment to the staff of the New York State Cabinet of Natural History. For nearly half a century Peck served his state as its botanist. As such he devoted much time to exploratory work and was thus able to enrich the state herbarium, to study the distribution of most of the groups of plants of which there were representatives in New York State, and to publish notes on their taxonomy and distribution.

Peck is best known for his painstaking and thorough work on the fleshy fungi on which he labored as a pioneer mycologist. The more than forty annual reports of the state botanist contain his descriptions of approximately 2,500 new species belonging to numerous groups of fungi, including the Agaricaceae, the Boletaceae, and the Hydnaceae, all of which were synoptically studied. Although Peck was a self-educated botanist, his keen, analytical mind and superior observational powers, combined with and aided by his clarity of exposition, enabled him to produce an amazing amount of highly dependable and, therefore, valuable work. His mycological studies are probably the most important of their kind yet contributed by any North American student of the fungi.

On April 10, 1861, he married Mary C. Sliter. Her death, in February, 1912, was followed shortly afterwards by his own failing health and his resignation in 1913. He passed away in 1917 in his eighty-fifth year.

ANON. 1917. *J. N.Y. Botan. Gard.*, Oct.
ATKINSON, G. F. 1918. Charles Horton Peck. *Botan. Gaz.* 65: 103–108.
BESSEY, C. E. 1914. A Notable Botanical Career. *Science* n.s. 40: 48.

Charles Vancouver Piper

1867–1926

Charles Vancouver Piper, botanist and agronomist, was born June 16, 1867, in Victoria, British Columbia, the son of Andrew William and Minna (Hausman) Piper. In his early childhood he moved with his parents to what was then Washington Territory, where he received his elementary and college-preparatory education. In 1885, he was graduated from the University of Washington with the degree of Bachelor of Science. In 1892, he received from the same institution his Master of Science degree.

Between 1885 and 1892, Piper helped his father in business, but found time also to devote to his beloved botanizing up and down the Puget Sound watershed and the rugged slopes of Mount Ranier. In 1893, he was appointed professor of botany and zoology at Washington State College, the young college of agriculture and mechanic arts at Pullman, Washington, where he remained as head of his department until 1903. In 1897, he married Laura Maude Hungate of Pullman and, in 1900, found time to prepare for and receive his M.S. degree from Harvard University.

Piper worked with persistent will and industry and, while at Pullman, did much to enrich the college herbarium and to build up a collection of insect and zoological specimens. He was an exacting and inspiring teacher and did much to develop student interest in biology. He and his assistants carried on, whenever possible, their exploratory work and spent long hours classifying the plants brought in by their collecting. In due time they were able to compile and publish the results of their labor in such works as "The Flora of the Palouse Region" (1901, Piper and Beattie), "Flora of Southeastern Washington and Adjacent Idaho" (1914, Piper and Beattie), and "Flora of the Northwest Coast" (1915, Piper and Beattie), In 1906, Piper alone published his "Flora of Washington," his botanical masterpiece and a work that filled a keenly felt need. Piper was a perfectionist. Everything he touched bore the imprint of his scholarly exactness.

In 1903, he was called to the Bureau of Plant Industry of the U.S. Department of Agriculture, where he became the administrative head of the Office of Forage Crop Investigations. Piper, the agronomist, was still the perfectionist. He worked at high pressure. His habits of industry and enthusiasm inspired his student associates with like zeal and ambition. He possessed the rare gift of mentally grasping and evaluating a project in its every aspect. If one of his colleagues offered for his consideration and criticism a project involving research, he would so take issue with it as to compel its proposer to defend it. This usually resulted in a thorough presentation of the problem and the plan for its investigation. If, after such a test, Piper was convinced, he would do his utmost to remove every obstacle in the way of its solution.

In 1911, Piper was asked by the War Department to go to the Philippines and there investigate the forage-plant resources of the islands. He conducted his mission with such distinction that he was asked to make a similar study in the Panama Canal region. Although he collected widely and contributed importantly to numerous herbariums, he was no laboratory or herbarium recluse. He was by nature and long experience a field botanist. Yet, he left behind him at Washington State College an herbarium of which any of our larger universities might well be proud.

As a taxonomist, Piper was reasonably conservative, ready to accept another's judgment once he became convinced of its soundness. He understood and maintained that species were based and founded on human judgment and plant names were for man's convenience. He described and recorded more than a hundred species and varieties of plants, and the genus *Piperia* was named in his honor by Rydberg ("Bull. Torr. Club." 28:269, 1901). On Piper's death his personal herbarium, his works on systematic botany, reprints, notes, etc., were bequeathed to Washington State College. Any record of Piper's contributions to the science in which he labored would be incomplete were one to omit mention of his work on the soybean and his collaboration with R. A. Oakley on turf grasses for golf courses.

Piper was a member of the American Association for the Advancement of Science, the American Academy of Arts and Sciences, the Washington Academy of Sciences, the American Society of Agronomy, the Botanical Society of Washington, and the Biological Society of Washington. He passed away on February 11, 1926, survived by his wife.

BEATTIE, R. K. 1928. Charles Vancouver Piper. *Proc. Biol. Soc. Washington* (D.C.) 41.

OAKLEY, R. A. 1926. *Bull. Green Sect. U.S. Golf Assocn.* 6: 54–57.

PIETERS, A. J. 1926. *Science* n.s. 63: 248–249.

VINALL, H. N. 1926. *J. Am. Soc. Agron.* 18: 295–300.

Frederick Pursh

1774–1820

Frederick Pursh, born at Grossenhayn, Saxony, in 1774, obtained his schooling in Dresden* and in due course (1779) came to America, where he made his home in Philadelphia. Strangely enough, even the principal facts of his life have been carelessly stated, if not distorted. His name, for example, was originally Friedrich Traugott Pursch, and, according to a letter written by his brother and published in 1827, he was born at Grossenhayn, Saxony, where also it is known that he received his preparatory education. He early developed an interest in natural history and ultimately became renowned as a botanist, horticulturist, and explorer. At Dresden he proved to be an apt and diligent pupil, interested primarily in the natural sciences. His exceptional ability soon won for him the plaudits of his superiors, and he was given employment in the Royal Botanical Garden of Dresden, where, with unflagging zeal, he devoted himself to his botanical and horticultural studies until 1799. That year he embarked for America, where he had been asked to assume the management of a botanical garden near Baltimore. From 1802 to 1805, Pursh served as

---

* According to Mr. James, in the "Journal of a Botanical Excursion," Frederick Pursh was born at Tobolsk, Siberia. For this statement there apparently is neither authority nor confirmation. The data given by Pritzel ("Pritz. Thes. Bot. Lit." 1872, 254.) is more reliable and is here accepted.

director of the already renowned botanical garden of William
Hamilton near Philadelphia.

In America, it was Pursh's good fortune to meet and become
acquainted with the Rev. G. H. E. Mühlenberg, William Barton,
and Humphry Marshall. In 1807, he assumed charge of the botanical garden established near New York by Dr. David Hosack and
later sold to the State of New York.

Pursh's chief patron was Benjamin Smith Barton, an Episco-
palian rector and man of many interests, ranging from the collection of native simples to theology and medicine and from literature and the North American Indian to botany and earthquakes.
Evidently he was a man of wealth as well as diversity of enthusiasm, for he made it financially possible for Pursh to undertake
important and fairly extensive botanical excursions into the mountains and westward reaches of Maryland, Virginia, and the Carolinas. Later, he undertook an excursion into the mountains of
Pennsylvania and thence northward into the Finger Lake region
of New York to Oswego on Lake Ontario. He had planned to explore the botanical resources of New Hampshire but apparently
abandoned the idea. At any rate, his collection shows no specimens from that remote region, and the indications are that he
went from Oswego to Champlain. It is evident also that he visited
the foothills of the Green Mountains in the neighborhood of Rutland, Vermont. At Rutland he turned southward for New York
and Philadelphia.

One of his most ambitious projects was that of working up the
plants collected by the Lewis and Clark expedition. The plants of
this collection were described by Pursh in his two-volume "Flora
Americae Septentrionalis," in 1814, the first complete treatise on
the plants of North America north of Mexico. Here he refers to
119 plants, several of which, according to him, were new and were
described as such. What became of the plants that comprised the
collections nobody knew. Pursh presumably took some of them
with him to England and must have left them there in the custody
of the then vice president of the Linnaean Society, A. B. Lambert,
who assisted Pursh in working up the identification and classification of the plants collected. Several of Lewis's plants—type specimens, at that—found their way into Lambert's herbarium and
subsequently became identified as member specimens of a number

of herbaria. Several of them are in the herbarium of the Academy of Natural Sciences of Philadelphia.

After spending about twelve years in the United States, he set out for the West Indies and from there to England with his North American plant collections, intending to prepare the two-volume work referred to above. With his masterpiece completed, he left for Canada, where, according to Canadian authority, he spent the rest of his life, a total of twelve years, working on publishing a flora of Canada. He made several important botanical excursions, always, as was his custom, on foot and assembled important collections, especially from the Province of Quebec, but all of these were destroyed by fire. As a consequence, nothing was salvaged, and there is no record of the years of labor he had devoted to his Canadian project. In addition to "Flora Americae Septentrionalis," he has one other publication ("Hortus Oliviensis") to his credit.

His physical strength was much impaired by ill health, and, after a little more than a score of active years as a botanist, he died at the age of forty-six in Montreal, virtually destitute; nevertheless, he left a permanent imprint on North American plant science.

ANON. 1825. Frederick Pursh. *Am. J. Sci. Arts* 9: 269–274.
ANON. 1882–1883. *Botan. Gaz.* 7: 141–143.
EWAN, J. 1952. Frederick Pursh and His Botanical Associates. *Proc. Am. Philos. Soc.* 96: 599–628.
HARSHBERGER, J. W. 1899. *The Botanists of Philadelphia and Their Works.* T. C. Davis & Sons, Philadelphia.

Constantine Samuel Rafinesque

1783–1840

Constantine Samuel Rafinesque, described by his biographers and by himself as a traveler and botanist, was born in Constantinople on October 22, 1783. His father was a native of Marseilles, and his mother was a member of the German family of Schmaltz. While Constantine was still a baby, the family returned to Marseilles. Without discipline or system, he became an enthusiastic reader of books of travel and adventure. Here also he discovered his insatiable hunger for things botanical. In his own words he states:

> It was among the flowers and fruits of that delightful region that I first began to enjoy life, and I became a botanist. . . . Thus some accidents or early events have an influence on our fate through life, or unfold our inclinations.

When Rafinesque was only eleven years old, he was collecting plants and had begun to make an herbarium. Although he had not received systematic instruction in Latin, he nevertheless learned to read it with sufficient facility to enable him to understand many of the scientific works of his day. To earn a livelihood, he decided to follow the example of his father by becoming a merchant. Such a pursuit, he fancied, would enable him to travel. About this time, with the outbreak of the French Revolution, his father sent his money out of France and shipped his two sons to America, where Constantine became a merchant's clerk and, in his spare time, a student of botany.

In 1805, at the age of twenty-two, he received word of an opportunity to engage in business in Sicily. He accepted the offer and spent ten years there. It was there that he married Josephine Vaccaro, a Sicilian woman, by whom he became the father of two children, a son and daughter. While in Sicily he discovered the presence of *Scilla maritima* (Squills), a medicinal plant, and he conceived the idea of shipping it in quantity to England and Russia. This enterprise proved successful until his trade secret was discovered by the Sicilians, at which point they themselves took over and continued to carry on the traffic.

In 1815, Rafinesque again set sail for the United States, taking with him many manuscripts, numerous drawings, notebooks, and unpublished papers. After an ocean voyage of six months' duration, the ship foundered upon a rock just outside the harbor of New London, Connecticut. Rafinesque lost everything that he valued most—his books and manuscripts, his plant collections and notebooks—all that he possessed save some of his money. It was after this episode that his wife deserted him to live with the Sicilian actor, Giovanni Pizzalour.

Once again on the coveted American shore, Rafinesque traveled extensively through most of the Eastern states. Much of it he covered on foot, following the Ohio Valley as far as southern Indiana and collecting the plants of the region as he journeyed. He found his way to that settlement known as New Harmony on the Wabash River, where he tarried long enough to become acquainted with what was destined to become the center of American science, made famous by such men as David Owen, Thomas Gay, and Alexandre Lesueur.

After a while, Rafinesque became professor of natural history and modern languages at Transylvania University in Lexington, Kentucky; he was said to be the first teacher of natural science in what was then known as the West. Because of his eccentricities, he became unpopular with the president of the university, who, according to Rafinesque, "despised and hated the natural sciences."

Rafinesque had other interests than those that led him into the wilderness of natural science. He was an inventor, but, for one reason or another, he was never able to perfect his inventions. He was something of an ethnologist and was especially interested in the languages and tribal customs of the American Indians. From Kentucky he returned to Philadelphia and there published the "Atlantic Journal and Friend of Knowledge," and the "Annals of Nature," of which he was not only the publisher but the editor, and often he was the only contributor.

His apparent lack of a sense of humor and his overbearing disposition, combined with his attempted reformation of procedure in classifying and naming plants, won for him the scorn of the American botanists of his day. At that time in the history of American botany, any departure from Linnaean principles in matters of taxonomy was frowned upon as a species of heresy, notwithstanding the fact that the natural system of classification as conceived by Antoine Laurent de Jussieu had contributed everywhere to its author's renown as a botanist, save in America. Therefore, Rafinesque's acceptance of de Jussieu's system and his advocacy of it served only to add to the distrust and indignation of his American contemporaries. Any well-informed botanist of our day will admit that the writings of Rafinesque, insofar as they relate to the origin of species, make better sense now than they did a century ago, when, according to Dr. William Baldwin, "these botanists possessed independence enough to reject the wild effusions of a literary madman." On the other hand, Dr. George Brown Goode, the ichthyologist, several years later said: "Perhaps the time has not yet come when full justice can be done to the memory of Constantine Rafinesque, but his name seems yearly to grow more prominent in the history of American Zoology. . . . He lived a century too soon."

Rafinesque died in 1840, in Philadelphia, where he had spent his last years in wretched obscurity.

COULTER, J. M., ed. 1883. Some North American Botanists. C. S. Rafinesque. *Botan. Gaz.* 8: 149–152.
HICKS, G. H. 1895. Rafinesque. *Asa Gray Bull.* 4: 6–8.
JAFFE, B. 1944. *Men of Science in America.* Simon & Schuster, Inc., New York.
YOUMANS, W. J. 1896. *Pioneers of Science in America.* D. Appleton & Company, Inc., New York.

Henry William Ravenel

1814–1887

Henry William Ravenel was born in Berkeley, South Carolina, on May 19, 1814. He was a son of Dr. Henry and Catharine (Stevens) Ravenel and great-grandson of the French Huguenot emigrant, René Louis Ravenel. Henry William acquired his advanced schooling at South Carolina College, from which he was graduated in 1832. From 1832 to 1854, he resided on his plantation in Saint John's Parish, the affairs of which he himself attended to, but he found leisure to devote to certain intellectual pursuits, chief among which was botany. In 1853, he moved to Aiken, South Carolina, where he spent the remaining years of his busy life.

Dr. Ravenel was a born naturalist and an indefatigable collector and student of plants of every kind. In due course he was the possessor of a comprehensive herbarium of both cryptogamic and phanerogamic plants. He was particularly interested in the cryptogams and was regarded, both at home and abroad, as an authority on those of America. Because of impaired hearing, he mingled but little among people, attended but few meetings, and became less and less communicative. Even so, he accomplished much.

In 1849, he was deservedly honored by election to corresponding membership in the Philadelphia Academy of Natural Science, and, in 1884, he became a member of the Zoölogische Botanische Gesellschaft of Vienna, Austria. In view of the fact that he had spent most of his life as a botanist and, as such, had won renown on both sides of the Atlantic, the honorary LL.D degree, conferred upon him by the University of North Carolina in 1886, one year before his death, was in a sense an overdue acknowledgment of his scholarship and scientific leadership.

Dr. Ravenel was for many years in editorial charge of the agricultural department of one of South Carolina's most important newspapers, the "Weekly News and Courier," and at the time of his death, he was botanist of the South Carolina Department of Agriculture. It was never his ambition to seek a position of great honor, but, had it not been for his hearing affliction, he might easily have won his way to leadership in any of our better-known universities.

In 1869, he was appointed botanist by the United States government to accompany John Gamgee in an investigation of the possible cause or causes of a serious bovine malady, prevalent at the time in Texas. The belief had been current that the disease was caused by some toxic fungus that the cattle had eaten. The data collected by Ravenel and Gamgee failed to show any connection whatsoever between the malady and any cryptogamic growth resulting from any fungus that may accidentally or otherwise have been consumed by the cattle.

Quantitatively, Ravenel's written and published output was not extraordinary, but the quality of his contributions was of a high order of excellence. Following are his better-known works: "Fungi Carolini Exsiccati" (5 vols.); "Fungi Exsiccati Americani" (Ravenel and Cook, 8 vols.). This published literature on the fungi of Ravenel's native state and of the United States won for him a well-earned recognition from European mycologists. He and Dr.

M.A. Curtis of North Carolina were among the very few who knew specifically the fungi of the United States. During Ravenel's most productive years, it is probable that no other botanist possessed such an extensive knowledge of our cryptogamic flora. His herbarium was recognized as one of the richest not alone in America but also in Europe. Subsequent to his death, that portion of his herbarium comprising the fungi, lichens, mosses, and algae was purchased by the London Museum; the spermatophyte portion was acquired by Converse College, South Carolina.

Dr. Ravenel was married in 1835 to Elizabeth Gaillard Snowden, who died twenty years later, leaving her husband and five children, one of the number being a son. He married a second time, a Mary Huger Dawson, who survived her husband. Dr. Ravenel's days ended at Aiken, South Carolina on July 17, 1887.

ANON. 1887. *J. Mycol.* 3: 106–107.
FARLOW, W. G. 1887. *Botan. Gaz.* 12: 194–197.
GEE, W. 1918. South Carolina Botanists, Biography and Bibliography. *Bull. Univ. So. Carolina.* No. 72: 38–42.
LAMSON-SCRIBNER, F. 1893. *Bull. Torrey Club* 20: 324–325.
STEVENS, N. E. 1932. The Mycological Work of Henry W. Ravenel. *Isis* 18 No. 52: 133–149.

Wilfred William Robbins

1884–1952

Wilfred William Robbins, the son of Isham B. and Jennie Marie (Hussey) Robbins, was born May 11, 1884, at Mendon, Ohio. On completion of his college preparatory requirements, he registered at the University of Colorado, from which he obtained his B.A. in 1906. Three years later he was awarded the M.A. degree, and in 1917 the University of Chicago conferred upon him the Ph.D. degree. From 1908–1911, he served as instructor in biology at the University of Colorado and from 1911–1913 as instructor in botany and forestry at the Colorado College of Agriculture. From 1913–

1914, he was assistant professor of botany and was then elevated to the rank of professor of botany and appointed botanist of the Colorado Agricultural Experiment Station. These positions he held from 1914 to 1919, when he was appointed physiologist and pathologist for the Great Western Sugar Company. In 1922, he became associate professor of botany at the University of California, which position he held until 1929, when he became professor of botany and botanist in the Agricultural Experiment Station.

Dr. Robbins was a member of the Botanical Society of America, the American Society of Naturalists, the American Association for the Advancement of Science, Sigma Chi, Alpha Zeta, and Phi Sigma Epsilon. He was author or coauthor of "Botany of Crop Plants" (1914), "Textbook of General Botany" (1924), "Principles of Plant Growth" (1927), "Sex in the Plant World" (1933), "Plants Useful to Man" (1933), "Practical Problems in Botany" (1935), "Weeds of California" (1941), "Weed-Control: A Textbook and Manual" (1942, and edition, 1952), and "Botany: An Introduction to Plant Science" (1950).

Professor Robbins was twice married, first to Louise Falk, June 15, 1911, by whom there were two children, a son and a daughter. His second marriage occurred April 21, 1939, when he chose as his wife, Barbara Richards, who survived him without issue.

Benjamin Lincoln Robinson
1864–1935

Benjamin Lincoln Robinson was born November 8, 1864, in Bloomington, Illinois, the son of James Harvey and Latricia Maria (Drake) Robinson. He was a direct descendant of Rev. John Robinson, who led the Pilgrims out of England to Leyden in the Netherlands and whose son Isaac migrated to Plymouth, Massachusetts in 1630.

Benjamin Robinson received his schooling through private instruction until his tenth year. Thereafter he spent six years in the public schools of his native Bloomington. His preparation for college was obtained in the Illinois Normal School at Normal, where it was his privilege to study under an eminent teacher, Edward J. James, who later became the president of the University of Illinois.

Robinson entered upon his undergraduate studies in 1883 at Williams College. He had already developed a strong bent for botany, and finding Williams inadequately equipped for specialization in this science, he remained there but three months and then returned to Bloomington. There he prepared for Harvard and entered that college in the autumn of 1884. At Harvard he devoted himself to the sciences with special emphasis on botany under the direction of Professors Farlow and Goodale. He was graduated from Harvard in 1887 and subsequently married Margaret Louise Casson of Hennepin, Illinois, a woman of intellectual gifts and musical talent.

That summer Mr. and Mrs. Robinson went abroad where he found opportunity to study under the direction of Graf zu Solms-Laubach of the University of Strasburg. He chose botany as his major and selected zoology and mineralogy as minor fields of graduate study. In 1889, he had completed the requirements for the advanced degree and was awarded his Ph.D. diploma. The following year he returned to Harvard as Sereno Watson's assistant in the Gray Herbarium. The Robinsons had profited much through their contact with Germanic culture and scholarship. From 1891 to 1894, Dr. Robinson offered a course in scientific German.

On the death of Sereno Watson, Dr. Robinson was appointed curator of the herbarium, which position he held until his death in 1935. Soon after his appointment, reorganization made it necessary for the herbarium to become self-supporting. On assuming the responsibility placed upon him, Robinson found, very much to his personal distaste, that if the herbarium were to thrive and meet the demands placed upon it for its increased scientific and popular service, it would be necessary for him, as its curator, to assume the responsibility for soliciting funds for its financial support and security. At the termination of his curatorship, a service covering a span of thirty-eight years, he had by dint of unflagging loyalty and industry increased the endowment of the Asa Gray Herbarium from 18,155 dollars to 526,000 dollars. That fact in itself bears ample testimony to Dr. Robinson's stature as a man and botanist. His service as curator of a great herbarium was in itself a major contribution to North American botany. It was more than that; for, through such men as Liberty Hyde Bailey, Kingo Miyabe, and many others, the importance and influence of the Gray Herbarium and its curator have become world-wide.

Robinson's first undertaking of a strictly scientific nature as curator of the Gray Herbarium was the completion and editing of such papers as had been left unfinished by Messrs. Gray and Watson, contributions comprising parts of the "Synoptical Flora of North America." During the early years of his service as curator, the demand for a revised edition of Gray's "Manual of Botany" became increasingly urgent. Yielding to the many entreaties, Robinson, with the collaboration of his associate M. L. Fernald, completed the revision, and the new edition was issued in 1908.

Robinson was not a man of rugged physique; consequently, the number and extent of his botanical explorations were not remarkable. Such papers as came from his pen, therefore, were largely based on the collections made by other men who had referred to him the plants they had found in Mexico, the Galapagos Islands, Cuba, and, later, South America.

In 1895, Robinson and certain of his associates and their students at Harvard organized and established the New England Botanical Club, of which Robinson was the president from 1906 to 1908. He also was editor in chief of the Club's journal, "Rhodora," for the period 1899 to 1928.

During his later years Dr. Robinson devoted more attention to his study of the Eupatorieae, a tribe of the family Compositeae. Wherever he went, he examined herbarium specimens; some of them were of great antiquity and from distant lands, specimens that for a century or more had been reposing in dust-laden bundles in the herbaria of Britain, France, and Germany.

Although Dr. Robinson's duties as curator of the Asa Gray Herbarium included no teaching responsibilities, those graduate students whose botanical interest was in the field of taxonomy enjoyed and certainly profited from their contacts with the curator, whose exacting scholarship left him satisfied with nothing but the best.

Dr. Robinson was well known to most of the leading plant science men in centers of European scholarship. His wisdom in matters relating to botanical nomenclature won for him unquestioned recognition as an authority in that branch of botanical knowledge, and he enjoyed participating in the deliberations of international botanical congresses. Aside from being active in such meetings, he was a member of several scientific societies both at home and abroad, and he was everywhere recognized as a world figure in his favorite field of natural science.

FERNALD, M. L. 1937. Benjamin Lincoln Robinson. *Nat. Acad. Sci. Biog. Mem.* 17: 303–330, with portrait and bibliography compiled by Lily M. Perry.
FERNALD, M. L. 1935–1936. *Am. Acad. Arts Sci.* 71: 539–543.
MERRILL, E. D. 1935. *Science* n.s. 82: 142–143.
RENDLE, A. B. 1935. *J. Botany* 73: 300–301.
SPRAGUE, T. A. 1935. *Proc. Kew Bull. Misc. Inform. No. 10.* 577–578.

William Edwin Safford
1859–1926

William Edwin Safford was born in Chillicothe, Ohio, December 14, 1859. He was the son of William Harrison and Anna Maria Pocahontas (Creel) Safford and a descendant of Thomas Safford, who came to America from England some time prior to 1641. It is known that while yet a boy William had manifested an interest in his natural surroundings and that through the influence of his mother this liking for plants had grown. Very little is known of his early schooling. It is, however, known that he attended the public school and that during his boyhood he acquired, from his German-speaking schoolmates, a considerable knowledge of idiomatic German. This led him later into an exploration of other languages. His interest in the biological sciences was enhanced by the fact that he read aloud from the works of Darwin and Huxley to his maternal grandfather, a mentally vigorous man.

In his seventeenth year, William Safford entered the United States Naval Academy, where he completed a four-year course and was assigned in 1880 to the ship Powhatan for a cruise to the tropics. In 1883, he entered Yale for advanced work in botany. In 1885, he registered at Harvard for marine zoology. On completion of his work at Harvard, he went on a cruise around Cape Horn and into the South Pacific. It was during this cruise that his urge to study botany and ethnology manifested its liveliest vigor. On Safford's return from this cruise, he was detailed for two years as an instructor of languages at Annapolis. In 1891–1892, while off duty, he was in South America as Commissioner to Peru and Bolivia for the Columbian Expedition. Here he devoted his attention chiefly to ethnological research. Returning to the Navy in 1893, he served in the Spanish-American War and, subsequently for a year, as vice-governor of Guam, at that time temporarily under the flag of the United States. In 1902, he resigned from the Navy and accepted an appointment as assistant botanist in the U.S. Department of Agriculture. In 1915, he was promoted to the rank of economic botanist and served as such until his death in 1926.

In 1920, George Washington awarded him the Ph.D. degree. His interests were many, but it was not until 1902 that he was free to devote himself to writing. In "Plant World" (Sept. 1902–Dec. 1904) he published a series of papers, which, in subsequent book form, were republished in the "Chamorra Language of Guam," reprinted from the "American Anthropologist" (1903–1905). This was later issued as a volume entitled "The Useful Plants of the Island of Guam" (Contributions from the United States National Herbarium, Vol. IX, 1905). This last book, amounting to a handbook on the island of Guam, virtually established Safford's reputation as an ethnobotanist, and, from 1905 on to the close of his career, he published many contributions of ethnobotanical interest. Chief among these were the following: "An Aztec Narcotic *Lophophora Williamsii*" ("J. Hered." Vol. VI, 1915), "*Lignum Nephriticum*" ("Ann. Rep. Smiths. Inst.," 1915), "Food Plants and Textiles of Ancient America" ("Proc. 2nd Pan-Am Sci. Cong." Vol. I, 1917), "Narcotic Plants and Stimulants of the Ancient Americans" ("Ann. Rep. Smiths. Inst.," 1916), "Daturas of the Old World and New" (*Ibid.*, 1920), "Peyote, the Narcotic Mescal Button of the Indians" ("J. Am. Med. Assoc.," 1921), and "The Potato of Romance and Reality" ("J. Hered." XVI, 1925). In addition to his contributions to our knowledge of ethnobotany, Safford published some important papers of taxonomic interest relative to certain tropical plants and plant families. Notable among these were the *Dahlia*, the Cactaceae, and an important series on the family Annonaceae. On September 14, 1904, Safford was married to Clare Wade, the daughter of Decius S. Wade, the chief justice of Montana. On the fourteenth of March, 1924, Safford suffered a paralytic stroke from which he partly recovered. He continued his work until claimed by death on January 10, 1926.

BARNES, W. C. 1926. William E. Safford. *Science* n.s. 63: 418.
KEARNEY, T. H., and E. F. SMITH. 1926. William Edwin Safford, an appreciation. *J. Hered.* 17: 365–367.
PEATTIE, D. C. 1926. Dr. William Safford. *Am. Botany* 32.

Charles Sprague Sargent
1841–1927

Charles Sprague Sargent was born in Boston, Massachusetts on April 24, 1841, and died on March 22, 1927, at his home in Brookline, Massachusetts. He was the third of five children born to Ignatius and Henrietta (Gray) Sargent. His ancestry was English, and his first American ancestor was William Sargent, who came from England sometime prior to 1678. Charles Sprague Sargent was privately educated in Boston, Massachusetts, and graduated from Harvard in 1862. Shortly thereafter (1863) he enlisted in the Federal army as an aide-de-camp on the headquarters staff of the Department of the Gulf with the rank of second lieutenant. He was mustered out in August, 1865, with the rank of brevet major. Thereafter he engaged in extensive European travel and returned to the United States three years later, in the autumn of 1868. During those three years, he busied himself in matters of horticultural and agricultural interest.

On returning to the United States, Sargent engaged in the practical application of horticulture and a more serious study of botany. In 1872, he was appointed director of the Harvard Botanical Garden and was professor of horticulture during the interval 1872–1873. The Arnold Arboretum, then but recently established, was in need of a director. In November, 1873, the directorship was conferred upon Sargent and retained by him until he was incapacitated by his final and fatal illness. As director of the arboretum he continued as professor of horticulture until 1879, when he became professor of arboriculture, which position he held the rest of his life.

In 1879, opportunity came to him through appointment under government auspices to make a complete survey of the forests of the United States. What was most needed was information as to the geographic distribution of tree species and their commercial value. The completion of this survey required five years. It was so thoroughly done that when completed and published it amounted to a volume of 600 pages and appeared as Volume IX of the final reports of the "Tenth Census of the United States."

This work inspired the idea of a bureau of forestry as a functioning and potentially important part of the U.S. Department of Agriculture. It also resulted in Professor Sargent's being appointed by the National Academy of Sciences as chairman of a committee authorized to investigate the need of and report on the initiation of a policy pertaining to the forest lands of the United States. This was in 1896. First-hand information regarding our public forest lands was forthwith obtained by this committee. This resulted in legislation setting aside some twenty million acres in forest reservations, legislation that in process of enactment was assailed by strong opposition. The logical and persistent reasoning of Professor Sargent prevailed over the pressure for annulment, and the legislation was allowed to stand as enacted.

His interest in the nation's forest resources did not, however, end here. He strongly urged the creation of national parks and forest reserves. He also recommended the appropriation of money with which to purchase a remnant of the redwood forests of California. Thanks to his unflagging interest in this highly commendable phase of forest conservation, many millions of acres have been saved to posterity.

Sargent's most monumental contribution to botany was his "The Silva of North America," a fourteen-volume work on the trees of this continent, illustrated by 740 plates made from carefully and beautifully executed copper plates. A revised edition, accompanied by 783 illustrations, was published in 1922. Another of his major contributions to botany is his "Manual of the Trees of North America" (1905).

As a dendrologist, his chief contribution was the Arnold Arboretum. This in part he redeemed from a worn-out farm of less than 150 acres, later to be enlarged to 250 acres. Plans for it were drawn up by Dr. Sargent with the aid of the celebrated landscape artist, Frederick Law Olmstead, who at that time was engaged in the development of a system of parks for the city of Boston. As a vitally important department of the Arboretum and one that received the lifelong devotion of its director, we should not neglect to mention the library, which had its origin in 1873 with Sargent's own private collection of works on botany. This modest library has grown until it comprises more than thirty-seven thousand volumes and upwards of ten thousand reprints, pamphlets, etc., nearly all of it Dr. Sargent's donation to the Arboretum.* In addition he left a sizable herbarium, destined to become representative of the tree flora of the world. In his "Forest Flora of Japan" and in "Plantae Wilsonianae," he contributed much to our knowledge of the flora of Japan and China.

During the years of his professional career, Dr. Sargent was the recipient of many honors. He was a fellow of the American Academy of Arts and Sciences, a member of the National Academy of Sciences, the American Philosophical Society, the Société botanique de France, the Société centrale forestiere de Belgique, the Société national d'horticulture de France, the Deutsche dendrologische Gesellschaft, and numerous other similar organizations.

On November 26, 1873, at the age of thirty-two, Sargent married Mary Allen Robeson, a Boston lady of talent and intellectual tastes, who shared the ideals and aptitudes of her husband. To this union were born five children. Dr. Sargent died March 22, 1927, Mrs. Sargent having preceded him by eight years.

* A list of Dr. Sargent's publications will be found in "J. Arnold Arb." VIII, No. 2, pp. 78–86, 1927.

ANON. 1927. *J. Forestry* 25: 513–514.
ANON. 1941. The one-hundredth anniversary of the birth of Charles Sprague Sargent. *Arnoldia* 1: 29–32.
HENRY, A. 1926–1927. *Proc. Linn. Soc.* (London) 139: 96–98.
REHDER, A. 1927. *J. Arnold Arb.* 8: 69–86, with portrait and bibliography.
TRELEASE, W. 1929. *Nat. Acad. Sci. Biog. Mem.* 12: 247–270, with portrait and bibliography prepared by Dr. Alfred Rehder of Arnold Arboretum.

George William Scarth

1881–1951

George William Scarth, plant physiologist, was born in the Orkneys, Scotland, in 1881 and died on September 6, 1951. He obtained much of his early schooling at Kirkwall, in the Orkneys. His undergraduate years were spent at the University of Edinburgh. While there he was for a time an assistant to Bayley Balfour. His first published paper was on the grassland of Orkney. In due course he figured importantly on grazing committees in the Province of Quebec. His career as a botanist ultimately led to his being accepted as an authority on the physiology of the plant cell. It was while he was associated with F. E. Lloyd at McGill University that he was asked to organize and teach one of the earliest courses in cellular physiology. This he did, and the course was published, with Lloyd, under title of "An Elementary Course in General Physiology." Other papers published by Scarth while he was at McGill were "Colloidal Changes Associated with Protoplasmic Contraction," "The Mechanism of Accumulation of Dyes by Living Cells," and numerous other contributions during the period 1936–1944.

Scarth became an early member of the American Society of Plant Physiologists, was its vice president in 1937–1938, and for an extended period was a member of the Editorial Board of "Plant Physiology." By way of recognition of his scientific attainments and his contributions to our knowledge of plant physiology, he was made the twenty-second Charles Reid Barnes Life Member of the American Society of Plant Physiologists. In 1933, he was awarded the D.Sc. degree; in 1928, he had been elected to membership in the Royal Society of Canada and to the presidency of Section V (Biol. Sciences) in 1935–1936, choosing for his presidential address the title "The Yearly Cycle in the Physiology of Trees."

Dr. Scarth retired from McGill in 1946. Thereafter he devoted time and attention to lecturing and to the further improvement of equipment designed for the measurement of photosynthesis, respiration, and transpiration by way of the infrared total absorption method.

Dr. Scarth married, in 1920, Margaret Ramsey. To this union were born three children.

GIBBS, R. D. 1951. George William Scarth. In Celebration of His Seventieth Birthday May 29, 1951. *Plant Physiol.* 26(2): iii–iv.
GIBBS, R. D. 1952. George William Scarth. *Proc. & Trans. Roy. Soc. Canad.* 46 ser. 3: 99–100, with portrait.
LEAVITT, J. 1952. *Science* n.s. 115: 509.

John Henry Schaffner
1866–1939

John Henry Schaffner was born in Agosta, Ohio, on July 8, 1866. While he was a small boy, his parents moved to Kansas. There the boy grew to manhood, the boy who, from early childhood, was of an inquiring disposition, not at ease until his curiosity was satisfied. Little seems to have been recorded as to his early schooling. It is, however, known that he attended country school and thereafter high school. He then entered Baker University in Baldwin, Kansas, where it was his good fortune to meet Charles Sylvester Parmenter, a teacher of biology and geology, who did much to inspire and shape the determination of his botanical aspirant.

On graduation from Baker University, Schaffner was appointed to teach natural sciences in the Methodist College in Mitchell, South Dakota, where he served one year. In 1895, he resigned to register for graduate study at the University of Michigan, where he remained until 1897 and devoted his time and energy to research in cytology under the direction of Prof. Frederick C. Newcombe. It was while there that his first papers: "The Nature and Distribution of Attraction-Spheres and Centrosomes in Vegetable Cells" and "The embryo Sac of *Alisma plantago*" were published, both in the Botanical Gazette, with the approval of Dr. Spalding, then head of the department of botany, and of Dr. J. M. Coulter, then associate editor of the "Botanical Gazette."

We next find Schaffner pursuing his research in the University of Chicago, where he really commenced in earnest his intensive work as a botanist. He was there but a short time when he received an offer of an assistant professorship in botany from Ohio State University. This brought him into close association with Dr. William A. Kellerman, who was already an eminent figure in American botanical research and teaching.

Even before he went to Columbus, Schaffner had done outstanding research as a pioneer in the study of the microscopic structure and behavior of the plant cell. His research on chromosome behavior, in particular, was of commanding importance to those primarily interested in Mendelism. Early in his botanical career, he became attracted to the genus *Equisetum* and studied it thoroughly in its every botanical aspect. He devoted serious study to determinative evolution and published a series of papers on the subject; the last one came off the press shortly after his death.

Although Professor Schaffner's reputation as a botanist resulted largely from the unquestioned importance of his cytological research, he had not been idle in the field of taxonomic botany. His approach to the subject was phylogenetic, and here again he was a pioneer. His system of classification was based on morphologic facts, a system confirmed by a series of papers entitled: "The Classification of Plants." The first of this series appeared in 1905 and the last in 1922. In his "Phylogenetic Taxonomy of Plants," he stated that the science of botany had advanced to a point where it could be said that taxonomy was now established on an evolutionary basis. To properly discern and understand the subject, so as to cease reasoning from the particular to the general, "the botanist must certainly be familiar with the general characteristics of the whole plant kingdom, have a knowledge of life cycles, and also must be somewhat acquainted with paleontology and with ecological relations."

This broad and fundamentally important concept of taxonomy enabled him, and others after him, to grasp the rising and vitally interesting subject of genetics. It also led directly into a more considered and reasonable view of the nature and development of sex in plants. Schaffner's concept was the non-Mendelian in contrast to the Mendelian, and he was, through experimentation in sex reversals, to prove the correctness of the former, or non-Mendelian, concept. He showed that sexuality and sex were to be explained in terms of a balance of physiologic states rather than that of genes. The balance of genes apparently does not change, whereas that of physiologic states does.

Professor Schaffner's experience in European universities was limited. He had gone to Europe in August, 1907, in the hope of qualifying for his Ph.D. degree, but through an unfortunate turn of events over which he had no control, the fates ruled otherwise. On October 14, 1907, he had matriculated as a graduate student of botany at the University of Zürich, Switzerland. Two months later it was found necessary for him to cancel his registration and to return to Columbus, disappointed, but undaunted.

Schaffner was thrice married. The first Mrs. Schaffner (Miss Mabel Brockett) died in 1906. Sometime subsequent to April, 1907, Mrs. Mary Morton Sample became the second Mrs. Schaffner. She lived until September, 1914. In June, 1916, Schaffner married Cordelia Garber, by whom he had three children.

ANON. 1939. Notes. John Henry Schaffner. *Plant Physiol.* 14: 186–187.
WALLER, A. 1939. Professor Schaffner. *Castanea* 4: 64–66.
WALLER, A. 1939. *Science* n.s. 89: 427–428.
WALLER, A. 1939. *Ohio J. Sci.* 39: 207–210.

Lewis David de Schweinitz
1780–1834

Lewis David de Schweinitz was born at Bethlehem, Pennsylvania, February 13, 1780. Following in the footsteps of his ancestors, both maternal and paternal, he entered the institution of the Community of Nazareth, in 1787, with the intention of preparing for the clergy. It was there that he experienced his first impulse to study nature, plants in particular. This awakening of interest in what later became his passion for botany had its simple beginning in his inquisitive observation of a lichen lying on a table. From this time on his absorbing interest in and his knowledge of botany grew apace and with ever-abounding enthusiasm.

At the age of eighteen, in 1798, he went to Europe with his father. There, at Niesky in Upper Lusatia, he matriculated as a student of theology, where, on completing his theological studies, he found employment as a teacher. Throughout the time he was a student of theology, he devoted much time and labor to the study of the fungi. By 1805, he and his inspiring, botanically minded teacher, J. B. d'Albertini, together issued an ambitious conspectus, in which were listed the many fungi they had collected and identified. Up to the time of publication of this work, nothing to compare with this monumental contribution had been issued.

After an enormously beneficial sojourn of twelve years in Europe, he was appointed to serve his church (United Brethren) as general agent in the Southern States (U.S.). Before setting out on his return voyage, he married Louisa Amelia LeDoux, an estimable young lady, daughter of highly respected French ancestry. This was in 1812.

In 1816 his "Synopsis Fungorum Carolinae Superioris" appeared. That same year, on call to Herrnhut (Bavaria), de Schweinitz spent some time in England, France, and the Netherlands, where he established invaluable contacts with men of science, who later, through correspondence and exchange, were destined to aid him materially with contributions to his herbarium.

In 1821, he published a description of seventy-eight species of Hepaticae in the hope that he might thereby arouse a more general interest among American botanists in what seemed to him a neglected, if not forgotten, group of plants. Before the close of that year, he had completed for publication in "Silliman's Journal" his monograph on the genus *Viola*. Shortly thereafter, he was transferred from Salem, North Carolina, to Bethlehem, Pennsylvania, where his duties involved, among others, superintendancy of a school for women. There he was free to pursue his botanical studies and to recapture once more the joy that only a naturalist can find on searching the unknown of valley and hill and the mystery of the dark and hidden ravine. Here, on the beautiful banks of the Delaware River, he felt again the urge and vigor of his youth; he worked and studied and realized. Here he became the botanist of his dreams. Recognition of his ability and the soundness of his accomplishment came to him from abroad as well as from his contemporaries at home. In 1823, he was invited to examine and describe the plants of the Say collection, obtained during the Maj. Stephen H. Long expedition to the headwaters of the St. Peters (the Minnesota) River, a task that by previous arrangement had been assigned to Thomas Nuttall, who, at that time, enjoyed an enviable reputation as a botanist but who, because of an unavoidable absence from the country, was unable to carry out the assignment. Thus it fell to the lot of de Schweinitz.

The year 1824 witnessed the publication of his monograph on the North American carices, one of his more important and scholarly productions. But, as a botanist, he is best and most widely known as a student of the fungi. His crowning achievement is his well-known "Synopsis Fungorum in America Boreali Media Degentum," communicated to the American Philosophical Society of Philadelphia, April 15, 1831. In this work one finds recorded 3,098 species of North American fungi, of which total more than 1,200 were collected and identified by de Schweinitz himself.

On his death in 1834, de Schweinitz's herbarium embraced a collection of approximately twenty-three thousand species of plants, other than fungi and other cryptogamic plants that he had collected or received through exchange but had not incorporated. The collection became, by bequest, the property of the Academy of Natural Sciences of Philadelphia.

ANON. 1927. *Ind. Hist. Soc. Pub.* 8: 205–285.

BENEDICT, D. M. 1935. Lewis David de Schweinitz, the Mycologist. *Bartonia* 16: 12–14.

HARSHBERGER, J. W. 1899. *The Botanists of Philadelphia and Their Works.* T. C. Davis & Sons, Philadelphia.

JOHNSON, W. R. 1835. *Mem. Acad. Nat. Sci. Phil.* May 12.

PENNELL, F. 1934. The Botanist, Schweinitz, and his Herbarium. *Bartonia* 16: 1–8.

YOUMANS, W. J. 1896. *Pioneers of Science in America.* D. Appleton & Company, Inc., New York.

William Albert Setchell
1864–1943

William Albert Setchell, son of George Case and Mary Ann (Davis) Setchell, was born on April 15, 1864 in Norwich, Connecticut. There he received his preparatory schooling and spent the years of his youth. At nineteen he entered Yale University. On completing his undergraduate work there, he sought the opportunity to continue his studies at Harvard, where, with the help of Dr. William Gilson Farlow, he obtained a fellowship in botany. Although he had spent some time in the zoological laboratory under the direction of Prof. E. L. Mark, his main interest was in the algae, and it was his good fortune to study them under the guidance and inspiration of Dr. Farlow, who, at that time, was America's leading authority on cryptogamic botany.

Setchell devoted three years to graduate study at Harvard, years of inestimable value to him, for the work done there and the knowledge acquired did much to prepare him for his career in algological research. It was not remarkable that he, as a graduate student, should have devoted so much time and energy to the study of botany. Even as a boy at Norwich Free Academy, he showed a marked penchant for natural history, and it required but little encouragement to turn his taste for living things definitely toward plant life. He found Gray's "Lessons in Botany" more than casually interesting and had already collected and familiarized himself with much of the plant life in and near Norwich.

In a Mr. Case, deputy collector of internal revenue for the Norwich district, young Setchell found a sympathetic friend, and they together undertook the compiling of a descriptive list of all the plants within a 10-mile radius of Norwich. The results of their labor were published in 1883, the year of Setchell's matriculation as a freshman at Yale. At that time Yale was without a recognized department of botany. Fortunately, however, one man on the faculty "knew his ferns," Daniel Cady Eaton. Setchell had by chance collected a fern, *Asplenium montanum*, a new discovery, "far west of its hitherto known range." This aroused Professor Eaton's interest in his young disciple. Yale was without equipment or other facilities for special work in botany, but, nothing daunted, Setchell was generously given permission to avail himself of the professor's own private herbarium and library.

During his student years, it was not Setchell's privilege to study abroad, but, at Harvard, his master Dr. Farlow, fresh from the laboratories of DeBary, Müller, Bornet, and Thuret, gave his graduate students the full benefits of all he had acquired through his contact with these renowned authorities in their respective fields of plant science.

It was while Setchell was a student at Yale that he was introduced to the marine algae through his chance acquaintance with Isaac Holden, an amateur botanist of Bridgeport, Connecticut, who had done some collecting in the vicinity of his home. Later Setchell collected extensively with F. S. Collins. Later still, he found an able collaborator in the person of N. L. Gardner, who, as a graduate student under Setchell, was awarded his Ph.D. degree. In due course Gardner became a member of the botanical faculty and, as such, was privileged to collaborate with his former teacher in numerous important contributions to our knowledge of the marine algae.

It was in 1890, while Setchell was at Harvard, that he received his Ph.D. degree. From 1888–1891 he was Dr. Farlow's assistant. From 1890–1895 he was employed as instructor of marine botany at Woods Hole, Massachusetts, where it was his privilege to continue his collecting. In 1891, he joined the botanical faculty of Yale as an assistant and was subsequently promoted to the rank of assistant professor. In 1895, he resigned from his position at Yale to accept an offer to go to the University of California as professor of botany. There his opportunity unfolded, and his responsibility as chairman of his department and as botanist of the State Agricultural Experiment Station made of him an important figure in shaping the destiny of both the university and experiment station as factors in the ever-broadening field of the plant sciences.

Botanically speaking, in moving from New England to California, Dr. Setchell had gone to a region of unrivaled richness not only of land plants but also of algae. Here he found access to the immense and new field of the Pacific, where he could collect and study the marine flora not only of California but also of the far reaches of the South Pacific and of the shores of British Columbia and Alaska.

During his more than forty years' service at the University of California, Dr. Setchell was sole or joint author of 150 papers. Much of his work was of a taxonomic nature. Probably the most important of all his contributions to our knowledge of North American plant life were his "Algae of Northwestern America" (1903), and "The Marine Algae of the Pacific Coast of North America," Parts I, II, and III, (1919, 1920, 1925). All four of these papers were published in collaboration with N. L. Gardner. Other important contributions were his reports on his investigation of the factors affecting the distribution of the Laminariaceae, and his proof of the role of the coralline algae in reef-formation.

Dr. Setchell traveled widely. He never failed to observe and study the plant life of every region he visited. Wherever he went he collected algae and thus built up a great first-hand knowledge of the major part of the Pacific marine area.

Dr. Setchell married, in 1920, Mrs. Clara B. Caldwell of Providence, Rhode Island. During the twelve years immediately following their marriage, they traveled extensively and visited many of the more important islands of the South Seas. They visited also Australia and New Zealand. Mrs. Setchell entered wholeheartedly into the spirit and purpose of these excursions and contributed much to the volume and worth of their joint botanical labors.

Dr. Setchell died on April 5, 1943.

CAMPBELL, D. H. 1945. William Albert Setchell. *Nat. Acad. Sci. Biog. Mem.* 23: 127–147, with portrait and bibliography compiled by T. H. Goodspeed and Lee Bonar.

DROUET, F. 1943. *Am. Midl. Nat.* 30: 529–532.

GOODSPEED, T. H. 1936. *William Albert Setchell, a biographical sketch.* University of California Press, Berkeley, Calif.

LIPMAN, C. B. 1943. *Science* n.s. 97: 458.

John Lewis Sheldon

1865–1947

John Lewis Sheldon was born at Voluntown, Connecticut, November 10, 1865, and died at his home in Morgantown, West Virginia, January 15, 1947. He received his college-preparatory schooling in Connecticut, where he was subsequently to become a public-school teacher from 1885 to 1890. During the years 1892–1894, he was employed as an instructor at the Mt. Hermon School. Some time later he received the B.S. and B.Pd. degrees at Ohio Northern University. In 1895, he returned to Connecticut, where, until 1898, he again taught in the public schools. He then served from 1899 to 1900 as a teacher at a state normal school in Nebraska. From 1900 to 1903 he was employed as an instructor in botany at the University of Nebraska and completed his postgraduate studies, fulfilling the requirements for the M.A. and Ph.D. degrees, which he received in 1901 and 1903 respectively.

Dr. Sheldon was appointed, in 1903, to a professorship in bacteriology at West Virginia University, Morgantown. In 1907, he was appointed professor of botany and bacteriology. In 1913, he was designated professor of botany and continued in this post until he retired in 1919. While in West Virginia he did a considerable amount of exploratory work and acquainted himself thoroughly with the plant life of that state. This enabled him to add several new species to those known to be present in West Virginia. Many of these were published in Millspaugh's "Living Flora of West Virginia" in 1913.

Sheldon was chiefly interested in the cryptogamic flora of the state. He was for several years a collaborator of the Bureau of Plant Industry. In 1939, he completed an extensive study of the lichens of West Virginia. He was a member of the American Association for the Advancement of Science, the American Phytopathological Society, the Sullivant Moss Society, the Southern Appalachian Botanical Club, Sigma Chi, and Phi Beta Kappa.

A bibliography of his botanical and other papers, including a paper entitled "The Lichens of West Virginia" was published in "Castanea," Volume 4: Nos. 6–7, 1939.

CORE, E. L. 1939. John Lewis Sheldon. *Castanea* 4, Nos. 6–7: 69–74, with portrait and bibliography.
CORE, E. L. 1947. *Science* n.s. 105: 541.
STEVENSON, J. A. 1948. *Mycologia* 40: 387–388.

Bohumil Shimek

1861–1937

Bohumil Shimek, for forty-six years a staff member of the department of botany at the State University of Iowa, was born in Shueyville, Iowa, June 25, 1861. His parents, Maria Theresa and Francis Joseph Shimek, came to America in 1848 as European political refugees. In his early years he aspired to be an engineer. He therefore entered the State University of Iowa in 1878 as a student of engineering and in due time was graduated in civil engineering. He took employment as a surveyor. This experience proved advantageous in his subsequent pursuit of both geology and botany, for it taught him the value of precision and accuracy in those fields of natural science.

In 1888, he went to the University of Nebraska as instructor in zoology, remaining there until 1890, when he was appointed a member of the botanical staff at the State University of Iowa. As a zoologist he won distinction through his research on snails. Fossil forms were of particular interest to him, and his contributions in this field gave him world-wide renown. His interest in and knowledge of fossil snails ultimately led to his mastery of the Pleistocene geology of Iowa and to his publication of numerous papers of geological interest.

Shimek's career as a botanist derived chiefly from his interest in ecology. Being a man of initiative and originality, ecology afforded him a fertile field in which to satisfy his penchant for out-of-door research. His natural understanding of the life relationships of different aspects of natural history endowed him with distinctive ability as a teacher and as a chronicler of what he observed and visualized. As an ecologist he insisted on the importance and value of field studies; indeed, he spent most of his life out of doors, in the open with his plants. His botanical contributions were chiefly in ecology, the ecology of the prairie as he found it in his native state. It was his theory that the prairie formation was directly due to a vital relationship of wind and weather to species tolerance of plants to intense light and rapid evaporation. Thus the prairies absence of trees he attributed to high summer temperatures and desiccating winds.

He devoted half a century to painstaking observation and recording—a tireless worker, critical of his own research, and not unreasonably so of that of other ecologists. This attitude toward the results of ecological research helped to win for this relatively unexplored field of plant science the respect of those botanists who were still unconvinced of its soundness. Few botanical scholars of his time were so well prepared as he to conceive accurately the entire life pattern of natural history.

Shimek spent the summer of 1901 with a group of his students at Lake Okoboji in northwestern Iowa, which, in 1909, became the seat of the Lakeside Biological Laboratory. Here he made a detailed study of the lake and its environs. Excepting the rock ledges, this bit of research comprised essentially all of the ecological types of Iowa. The results were published in Volume 7 of the "Bulletin of the State University of Iowa" under the title "The Plant Geography of the Lake Okoboji Region."

Dr. Shimek's genius as a teacher and as a botanist was established beyond question, but he was at the same time and as truly the zoologist and geologist, the citizen and patriot. As an ecologist, he was great not solely because he was a botanist but because of his knowledge of zoology and geology.

In 1886, Dr. Shimek married Anna Elizabeth Konvalinka of Iowa City, by whom he had four daughters and a son. This happy union was broken by the death of Mrs. Shimek in April, 1922. In 1925, Dr. Shimek was married a second time, taking as his wife Marjory Meerdink of Muscatine, Iowa, who survived him. He passed away January 30, 1937.

ANON. 1937. *Proc. Iowa Acad. Sci.* 44: 31–33.
LOEHWING, W. F. 1937. Bohumil Shimek. *Science* n.s. 85: 306–307.

Forrest Shreve

1878–1950

Forrest Shreve, son of Henry and Helen Garrison (Coates) Shreve, was born on July 8, 1878, in Easton, Maryland. He died in Tucson, Arizona, July 19, 1950. In 1909, he married Edith Coffin Bellamy and transferred from Goucher College to Tucson, Arizona, where he had accepted an appointment as a staff member of the Desert Laboratory of the Carnegie Institution of Washington, D.C. At Goucher College he served as associate professor of botany from 1906 to 1908. While there, in collaboration with M. A. Chrysler and F. H. Blodgett, he labored to prepare the manuscript that, in the form of a comprehensive report, was published as "Plant Life in Maryland."

Dr. Shreve was educated in the public schools of Easton, Maryland and at Johns Hopkins University. From the latter he received his A.B. in 1901 and at once applied himself in meeting requirements for the Ph.D. degree, for which he fully qualified in June, 1905, and was awarded the doctorate by his Alma Mater. In 1928, he was promoted and placed in charge of the Desert Investigations of the Carnegie Institution and forthwith commenced to plan an over-all taxonomic and ecologic study of the major desert areas of North America. For four years he devoted time and energy to projects that in his judgment had priority over the larger programs as he had planned it. Consequently, he did not get the latter well started until 1932, when he undertook an intensive study of the floristics of the natural desert area that occupies parts of California, Arizona, New Mexico, Sonora, and Baja California, generally known as the Sonoran Desert. With foresight and intelligently directed enthusiasm, he collected plants peculiar to the major area of his interest and gradually developed an herbarium, important to any student of regional ecology. It was his opinion that the considerations involved in a study of the plant-environment relationship were much more important in the desert than those of plant to plant. Therefore, he was inclined to ignore state and like boundaries, arbitrarily established.

Fatal illness overtook Shreve in July, 1950, with only a part of his study of the vegetational characteristics of the desert regions of North America completed. He had finished his survey of the Sonoran Desert and not a little of that of Chihuahua, Mexico. Approximately seventy papers under his authorship are available, chiefly in the form of records in the library of the U.S. Department of Agriculture.

In 1911, Dr. Shreve became managing editor of "The Plant World" and continued as such until 1919, when "Plant World" was taken over by "Ecology," the official publication of the Ecological Society of America, "continuing the 'Plant World.'" He was one of the organizers of the Ecological Society of America. He was also a member of the Association of American Geographers and of the Association of Pacific Coast Geographers, a fellow of the American Association for the Advancement of Science, a member of the American Society of Naturalists, the Society of American Foresters, the Botanical Society of America, Sigma Chi, and Phi Beta Kappa.

HUMPHREY, R. R., and I. L. WIGGINS. 1951. Forrest Shreve. *Science* n.s. 114: 569–570.
SHANTZ, H. L. 1951. Forrest Shreve. *Ecology* 32: 365–367, with portrait and bibliography.

John Kunkel Small

1869–1938

John Kunkel Small was born in Harrisburg, Pennsylvania, on January 31, 1869, and died at his home in Bronx Borough, New York City, January 20, 1938. At the age of nineteen, he registered at Franklin and Marshall College in Lancaster, Pennsylvania. His enthusiasm for botany early expressed itself in response to an urge to publish brief accounts of what he had observed. Two of these related to mosses and were done in collaboration with A. A. Heller, a well-known taxonomist.

Following his graduation from Franklin and Marshall College, he entered Columbia College, now Columbia University, where he devoted himself to postgraduate research in botany and to his duties as curator of the herbarium. At this time, and for some years thereafter, he made a painstaking study of the taxonomy of the phanerogams of the Southern states. From the moment of his arrival at Columbia, he busied himself with a thorough study of the genus *Polygonum* and published a number of advanced papers on that genus. By 1895 he had completed his thesis for the Ph.D. degree, an important volume entitled "A Monograph of the North American Species of the Genus *Polygonum*," referred to as the "most sumptuous American botanical thesis ever published." In the same thorough manner he undertook the study of the Oxalidaceae.

In the summer of 1891, Small and Heller gave some consideration to the plant life of western North Carolina. Throughout the rest of his life, Dr. Small continued his visits to the Southland, with the result that he published a series of fourteen "Studies in the Botany of the Southeastern United States." Most of his botanical papers were published in the *Bulletin of the Torrey Botanical Club*, the oldest of American botanical societies. Small became an honorary life member of the club in 1934.

Professor Small was one of the original staff members of the

New York Botanical Garden when it was organized in 1898, at which time he became curator of the museums. In 1907, he was promoted in rank to the position of head curator of the museums, a position he was to hold until the close of 1932, when he was relieved of his executive responsibilities to devote himself entirely to his research.

His transfer from Columbia University to the New York Botanical Garden entailed no marked disruption of his daily procedure. Small had been in charge of the university herbarium, and he continued in that capacity after the two herbaria were consolidated. His devotion to research on southern plant life continued without abatement under the conditions of his transfer. He saw in 1903 the publication of his "Flora of the Southeastern United States," a weighty volume of approximately fourteen hundred pages of text. Ten years later he got out a second edition, and in 1933 he published his "Manual of the Southeastern Flora," in which each species was illustrated. The more he studied the plant life of the Southeast, the more was he impressed by the phytogeography of Florida. He first visited that state in 1901, and in the more than thirty ensuing years he revisited it more than thirty-five times, each time with unflagging interest and enthusiasm. Thus did he become an authority on its flora and acquire a detailed knowledge of the facts pertaining to it.

In his published works on the flora of the southern states, he restricted the term *flora* specifically to the flowering plants. He consistently maintained that this term did not apply to the ferns and their allies. He published his first paper on ferns in 1890. Other fern papers appeared at infrequent intervals and were characterized by an increasing interest in these plants, particularly of those fern species peculiar to the region he knew so well. In 1938 appeared his "Ferns of the Southeastern United States," his most compendious work on the Filicales.

According to J. H. Barnhart, for forty-four years a friend of Small:

His scientific writings were characterized by originality, honesty, and fearlessness. His viewpoint was always that of a progressive, and was not always appreciated by his fellow workers. . . . The writer believes that, when conservatism . . . has broken down, the name of John Kunkel Small will be ever more highly revered.

ANON. 1939. Memory of Doctor Small Honored in Louisiana. *J. N.Y. Botan. Gard.* 40: 265.

BARNHART, J. H. 1938. The Passing of Doctor Small. *J. N.Y. Botan. Gard.* 39: 73–79, with portrait.

CORE, E. L. 1938. John Kunkel Small. *Castanea* 3: 27–28.

Erwin Frink Smith

1854–1927

Erwin Frink Smith, plant pathologist, was born at Gilbert's Mills, Oswego County, New York, on the twenty-first of January, 1854. He was the son of Rancellor King and Louisa (Frink) Smith and the grandson of Charles and Lucy (King) Smith. Charles and Rancellor were tanners. Rancellor was also a shoemaker and a farmer and served as a Union soldier during the Civil War. His son Erwin, the subject of this sketch, was educated in the public schools of New York and Michigan. He early determined to seek a college education but this could be done only on his own initiative and by virtue of his own thrift and determination. In due time he entered the University of Michigan and, from that institution, received his Bachelor of Science degree in 1886. Three years later he was awarded the Doctor of Science degree. In 1886, he was appointed a member of the scientific staff of the U.S. Department of Agriculture. In 1889 he was promoted to the position of pathologist in charge of the laboratory of plant pathology in the Bureau of Plant Industry, which position he held until his death in 1927. He at first sought to discover the cause of an obscure disease popularly known as *peach yellows*. Although he failed to discover the cause, his work was done with such thoroughness as to clear the way to the ultimate discovery that peach yellows and a number of similar obscure ailments were problems in virology rather than bacteriology.

Smith's major interest was a study of the relation of bacteria to disturbed plant metabolism. Ultimately he found his stride in this field, and, as pioneer in the investigation of this aspect of parasitology, he had but few competitors in North America. He was not, however, the first to demonstrate the causal relationship of bacteria to plant disease; that honor had already fallen to Prof. Thomas J. Burrill of the University of Illinois. Dr. Smith's recognition as the leading authority on plant maladies of bacterial origin has remained unchallenged to this day. He spent the greater part of his professional life in plant pathological research and was the author of several books and many papers bearing directly on the subject of bacteriology. Notable among these were his "Bacteria in Relation to Plant Disease" (3 Vol., 1905–1914), a textbook entitled "An Introduction to Bacterial Diseases of Plants," his epochal paper, "A Plant Tumor of Bacterial Origin" (done in collaboration with C. O. Townsend), and numerous other papers on crown gall, inspired by Smith's belief that the striking analogy between crown gall of plants and animal cancer was something more than an analogy. He was, however, unable to prove the validity of the assumption, and it yet remains to be demonstrated. Here again his research was of an exhaustive nature, including as it did a study of formative stimuli, growth conditions, the mechanism of tumor formation, and an inquiry into problems of histogenesis.

Dr. Smith was a man of more than ordinary linguistic and literary attainments. He had a scholarly grasp of Greek, Latin, French, German, and Italian, and such a mastery of his own native English as to place him at once in the ranks of superior scholarship. He was the author of 167 original papers and 73 reviews. In 1915, he published privately a volume of verse comprising nearly two hundred sonnets and other poems. He was an admirer of the character and scientific attainments of Louis Pasteur. This respect for the great French savant inspired him to translate, with the collaboration of Florence Hedges, Emile Duclaux's "Pasteur, histoire d'un Esprit." He translated also the sonnets of José Maria de Heredia.

Dr. Smith was twice married: first to Charlotte M. Buffet of Cleveland, Ohio, on April 13, 1893. She died in 1906. Smith married again, in February, 1914, Ruth Annette Warren of Springfield, Massachusetts who survived him. Dr. Smith passed away on the sixth of April, 1927, in his seventy-fourth year. He was a member of the National Academy of Science, the American Academy of Arts and Sciences, the American Philosophical Society, the Society of American Naturalists, the Society of American Bacteriologists, the American Phytopathological Society, and numerous other American and European learned societies.

CLINTON, G. P. 1934. Erwin Frink Smith. *Proc. Am. Acad. Arts Sci.* 70: 575–578.
JONES, L. R., and F. V. RAND. 1928. *J. Bacteriol.* 15: 1–6.
JONES, L. R. 1941. *Nat. Acad. Sci. Biog. Mem.* 21: 1–71, with portrait and published writings.
RAND, F. V. 1928. *Mycologia* 20: 181–186, with portrait.
RODGERS, A. D., III. 1952. *Erwin Frink Smith, A Story of North American Plant Pathology.* The American Philosophical Society, Philadelphia.
TRUE, R. H. 1927. *Phytopath.* 17: 675–688, with portrait and bibliography.

Volney Morgan Spalding
1849–1918

Volney Morgan Spalding, eminent botanist and scholar, was born January 29, 1849, at East Bloomfield, New York. He was the son of Frederick Austin and Almira (Shaw) Spalding and a descendant of Edward Spalding of England, who migrated to Massachusetts Colony sometime prior to 1640. He received his early schooling in the public schools of Gorham, New York. While still a boy he moved with his parents to a farm near Ann Arbor, Michigan. In 1864, he entered the Ann Arbor high school and finished his preparation for the University of Michigan where he enrolled in 1869 and from which he was graduated in 1873.

After his graduation, Spalding served as a high-school principal at Battle Creek, Michigan, and subsequently at Flint. His success as a teacher brought him the offer of a position on the faculty of the University of Michigan as instructor in botany and zoology. This he accepted in 1876 and retained until 1879, when he was promoted to the rank of assistant professor of botany (1879–1881). He thereafter served as acting professor of botany for five years (1881–1886), after which he was appointed professor of botany (1886–1904).

At intervals during the early years of his botanical career, Spalding found opportunity for further study, at Harvard, Cornell, and the University of Pennsylvania. Later he pursued advanced study at the University of Leipzig, where, in 1894, he was granted the degree of Doctor of Philosophy.

As a teacher, Dr. Spalding was distinguished, and he was equally outstanding in the field of research. He inspired his students and associates with his untiring zeal and enthusiasm. After a quarter century of service to his university, he wrote as follows:

Twenty-five years ago, in one of our northern universities, a young instructor with a single assistant was engaged in the rather comprehensive task of teaching botany and biology. The botany consisted in part in the analysis of flowering plants by means of Gray's Manual, and in studying the minute anatomy of leaves, stems, and other parts of plants, which the literary students studied under the name of structural botany, while, with a strong flavor of crude drugs, it was administered to the pharmacy class engaged in the study of adulterants.

As for the books used, the "Centralblatt" was not in existence, but this mattered little, for neither was the enormous literature it has since recorded. The "Botanische Zeitung" was regularly published, but the library committee had no use for it, and much the same was true of most of the periodicals that every working botanist now finds indispensable; but we had Sach's "Textbook of Botany," and the big picture book of Le Maout and Decaisne, and on the shelves Sullivant's "Icones Muscorum" and dear old Berkeley, and Cooke's "British Fungi," with all their impossibilities, and last but not least, the reports of the government microscopist, of which we cannot speak particularly.

The rest of the outfit was in keeping. Microscopes, of a certain sort, there were, but no other apparatus. Razors were sharpened on a well-hacked strap, iodine and sulphuric acid constituted the reagents and the enthusiasm of fellow adventurers in an unknown country kept up the courage of young men and women who walked by faith and saw but little.

When we examine carefully the work of our pioneer North American botanists, and particularly that of Volney Morgan Spalding, we are bound to be amazed at the volume and quality of accomplishment in view of the paucity and primitiveness of equipment and the limited botanical literature then available.

In the field of applied botany, Spalding played an important part at a time when the lumber magnates threatened to destroy the great forests of white and Norway pine. It was Spalding who took upon himself the task of teaching the people how to conserve this great natural source of wealth. He roamed the woods in summer, traveled up and down the roads and trails of Michigan at his own expense, talked, and did everything he could to arouse popular interest in the problems of forestry, as he saw them. Where, at first, there were indifference and opposition, he lived to witness the recognition of the soundness of his teachings and the cooperation of those who at first most vigorously opposed his advocated reforms.

In 1904, Dr. Spalding was compelled by failing health to terminate his labors at Ann Arbor, where, during more than a quarter century, he had wrought for his university its renowned department of botany. On November 12, 1918, this builder of American botany died.

HINSDALE, B. A. 1906. *History of University of Michigan.* University of Michigan Press, Ann Arbor, Mich.
REED, H. S. 1919. Volney Morgan Spalding. *Plant World* 22: 14–18.

William Starling Sullivant
1803–1873

William Starling Sullivant, pioneer in North American bryology, was born January 15, 1803, in the village of Franklinton, Ohio, near the site now occupied by the city of Columbus. His elementary schooling was obtained at a private school in Kentucky, but he received his classical and advanced education at Ohio University in Athens. Later he attended Yale College, where he was graduated in 1823. Both by instinct and by training he was a man of scholarly tastes, and he early planned to prepare himself for a professional career. But, owing to the death of his father, he was obliged to busy himself with matters of business in connection with the family estate. These affairs and his duties as a practical engineer kept him so closely occupied that his latent interest in natural history had little opportunity to develop during the first thirty years of his life.

Joseph Sullivant, his brother next in age, had already acquired some knowledge of botany, but it is not known that William's interest in the subject was inspired by his brother.

It was William Sullivant's good fortune to have early established his home in a botanically rich district, and it is probable that this fact and his native scientific curiosity combined to release an urge to do something about it. In any event, he was determined to know thoroughly and do well whatever task he undertook. Central Ohio was his first field of botanical exploration, and he began collecting and studying such plants as came under his observation. He worked out in minute detail the organography of many of these plants, especially the grasses and sedges, and he made careful and accurate drawings designed to be readily helpful to other students of these genera and species. Nor did he stop here. In 1840, he published his "Catalogue of Plants, Native and Naturalized, in the Vicinity of Columbus, Ohio." One other paper, a brief article on three new plants he had discovered near Columbus, was all he published on phanerogamic plants. This paper appeared in 1842 in the "American Journal of Science and the Arts." Such other observations as he made on flowering plants he communicated to his friends and correspondents, authors of "Flora of North America," then in the making.

Sullivant then turned to the collection and study of mosses and liverworts. Here, as in his earlier work, his interest centered in taxonomy rather than in morphological differences and relationships. Indeed the sounding of this profoundly interesting and important mine of botanical information seems yet not to have aroused the curiosity of any American student of plant life.

With the mosses Sullivant found himself almost wholly occupied. He had at last discovered a group of plants that demanded of him his very best efforts to depict and describe, and this necessity of minute detail found in him the devotion and zeal necessary to its accomplishment. Here was the exceptionally patient, the scrupulously careful and painstaking scholar whose appreciation and understanding enabled him to ascertain and portray the minutest of specific differences and made it possible for him to produce a superb contribution to our then meagre knowledge of North American bryology.

Sullivant's initial publication on the mosses, "Musci Alleghe-niensis," was accompanied by actual specimens of the plants described—the bryophyta that he himself had collected in his botanical exploration of the Alleghenies from Maryland to Georgia during the summer of 1843. As a traveling companion he had no less a person than Dr. Asa Gray. This work was not put on sale. Only fifty copies were issued, and these were for free distribution among those who could and would genuinely appreciate them for their scientific worth.

In 1846, Sullivant submitted to the American Academy the first part of his "Bryology and Hepaticology of North America." Three years later this was followed by a communication presenting the second part of the same work. The one was published in Volume III and the other in Volume IV of the Memoirs of the Academy. The second and third editions of Gray's "Manual of the Botany of the Northern United States" contained an account of the mossess and liverworts of those states, illustrated from copper plates, the whole contributed by Sullivant. The exceptional quality of the illustrations in this part of the "Manual" at once prompted Schimper, then considered Europe's leading authority on mosses and liverworts, to adopt Sullivant's plan in his "Synopsis of the European Mosses."

In 1856, the account of the mosses and liverworts included in the second edition of Gray's *Manual* was published separately under the title "The Musci and Hepaticae of the United States East of the Mississippi River." About the same time Mr. Sullivant, in collaboration with Léo Lesquereux, a Swiss bryologist, issued the classical work and collection entitled "Musci Boreali Americani quorum specimina exsiccati ediderunt," (1856). This was followed in 1865 by a new work containing the initial results of Bolander's work on the mosses of California. Another of Sullivant's contributions was his "Musci Cubenses," published in 1861.

Late in his busy and fruitful life, Mr. Sullivant expressed the wish that his books on mosses and his collection be consigned to the Gray Herbarium of Harvard University. The remainder of his library and other collections, including his microscopes, were bequeathed to the State College of Agriculture in Columbus and to the Starling Medical College (now College of Medicine, Ohio

State University). The name *Sullivantia Ohiois*, bestowed upon a genus of the family Saxifragaceae, was given in his honor.

Mr. Sullivant was thrice married: first to Jane Marshall of Kentucky, who was the niece of Chief Justice John Marshall. His second wife was Eliza G. Wheeler, a bryologist in her own right. He was survived by his third wife, Caroline E. (Sutton) Sullivant.

GRAY, A. 1873. William S. Sullivant, a Biographical Notice. *Am. J. Sci.* 3rd Ser. 6: 106.

GRAY, A. 1877. *Nat. Acad. Sci. Biog. Mem.* 1: 277–285.

RODGERS, A. D., III. 1940. *Noble Fellow. William Starling Sullivant.* G. P. Putnam's Sons, New York.

YOUMANS, W. G. 1896. *Pioneers of Science in America: Sketches of Their Lives and Scientific Work.* D. Appleton & Company, Inc., New York.

Walter Tennyson Swingle
1871–1952

Walter Tennyson Swingle was born in Canaan Township, Pennsylvania, January 8, 1871. He was the son of John Fletcher and of Mary (Astley) Swingle, a woman of English birth. While Walter was two years old, the family quit Pennsylvania and moved westward to settle on a Kansas farm near Manhattan. Here the boy grew to young manhood. His elementary education was both informal and irregular. He early showed a genuine interest in living things, especially in plants. By the time he was seventeen years old he had been given the title of assistant botanist in the Kansas Agricultural Experiment Station, notwithstanding the fact that he was yet two years short of completing his undergraduate course at the Kansas State College of Agriculture at Manhattan.

It was his good fortune while there to become acquainted with Dr. W. A. Kellerman, the botanist, who saw in Swingle a man of more than ordinary promise and who did much to direct and broaden his interest in the knowledge of botany. Swingle the student received his B.S. degree at the age of nineteen and left shortly thereafter for Washington, D.C., where he was to remain the rest of his life, working out a career as something more than a botanist.

From 1888 to 1891, his record of accomplishment credits him with twenty-seven papers, most of them published jointly with Professor Kellerman, though of several he was sole author. These papers were generally of mycological interest and were published in the "Journal of Mycology." A few were accepted by and published in "Reports of the Kansas Agricultural Experiment Station," and "The Industrialists," a Kansas State College publication.

The character and quality of Swingle's early papers reflected the influence of his mentor. Most of them were strictly mycological; others dealt with plant pathological problems of a sort that provoked his enthusiasm and interest to a degree that threatened to become transcendent over his flair for mycology. As a measure against citrus canker, he advocated its complete eradication. As an aid to its control and a step to prevent the introduction and spread of *tristeza,* a citrus malady of South American origin, Swingle strongly recommended rigorous quarantine measures, the enforcement of which should rest with the U.S. Department of Agriculture.

Swingle spent some of his most productive years in Florida in joint research with the eminent botanist, Herbert J. Webber, whose interest in the genus did much to stimulate their mutual investigation of *Citrus* hybridization. Swingle became characteristically engrossed in a study of genetics and promply visualized what might result from an application of its principles to the genus *Citrus.* He therefore began, for northern Florida, the breeding and selection of *Citrus* on an extensive scale in conjunction with certain of his colleagues. The now popular Minneola tangelo was a product of this research.

Swingle was a student at Bonn and Leipzig for the equivalent of about two years in 1895–96 and again in 1898. At Bonn he studied cytology under the direction of Professor Strasburger. For the next twenty years (1896–1916) the fruits of his work bore testimony to his mastery of cytology and morphology and also to his knowledge of agronomy and the principles of plant breeding as applied to the improvement of *Citrus* and of several other plants important to the human economy.

As early as 1899, he began to publish the results of his research on caprification of figs under cultivation. It was he who introduced the fig wasp (*Blastophaga grossorum*) so necessary to the pollination of figs in cultivation. Preeminent among the numerous contributions made by Swingle was his introduction of date culture in the southwestern states. He began publishing on date culture in 1901, and his interest in the subject continued to the close of his active life. The account of this adventure into the field of plant introduction is best told by him in Bureau of Plant Industry Bulletin No. 53 entitled "The Date Palm and its Utilization in the Southwestern States."

Dr. Swingle played an important part in the development and importance of the Bureau of Plant Industry and in a fuller realization of its usefulness. Many of its research projects, still in progress, owe their initiation to his vision and industry. Not the least of these was the establishment of the American-Egyptian cotton industry in Arizona in which he and other members of the Bureau cooperated.

His interest in and search for information concerning cultivated kinds of *Citrus* led Swingle directly and seriously into a prolonged study of the history of Chinese botany and especially that of the horticultural varieties of the genus. As he searched, his interests broadened and deepened until, in 1928, the librarian of the Library of Congress wrote in his annual report:

From 1910 the collection has been developed systematically chiefly through the efforts of Dr. Walter T. Swingle to whose constant interest its present eminence is due. It now numbers over 100,000 volumes [Chinese], unsurpassed outside of China and Japan.

Swingle received from his Alma Mater, Kansas State College, his M.Sc. degree in 1896 and an honorary D.Sc. in 1922. He was a fellow and life member of the American Association for the Advancement of Science, a member of the Botanical Society of America, a founder of the Washington (D.C.) Academy of Science, a member of the Philadelphia Academy of Science, a corresponding member of the Académie d'Agriculture de France, and a life member and fellow of the National Geographic Society. He was appointed in 1926 to represent the United States Government and National Research Council at the third Pan-Pacific Science Congress at Tokyo.

Dr. Swingle was twice married, first to Lucie Romstaedt, in June, 1901, who passed away in 1910. In 1915, he married Maude Kellerman, daughter of Dr. W. A. Kellerman, who had taken such an interest in the young student Swingle and had done so much to shape his career. Dr. Swingle passed away on January 19, 1952, survived by Mrs. Swingle, two daughters, and two sons.

BARTLETT, H. H. 1952. Walter Tennyson Swingle, Botanist and Exponent of Chinese Civilization. *Asa Gray Bull.* n.s. 1: 107–127.
KEARNEY, T. H. 1952. Obituary. Walter T. Swingle. *J. Washington (D.C.) Acad. Sci.* 42, No. 6: 208.
SEIGFRIG, W. 1953. Walter T. Swingle. *Science* n.s. 118: 288–289.

Roland Thaxter
1855–1932

Roland Thaxter, son of Levi Lincoln and Celia (Laighton) Thaxter, was born in Newtonville, Massachusetts, on August 28, 1858. His father, a lawyer by profession, was an accomplished scholar and an authority on the poet Browning and his works. His mother was a writer and poet of distinction. Roland, their son, was educated at Allen School in West Newton by tutors and at Harvard University, where he received his A.B. degree in 1882. There he continued his advanced studies and completed by 1888 the requirements for the A.M. and Ph.D. degrees. He first entered Harvard Medical School, where he devoted two years to the study of medicine. At heart, however, he was profoundly interested in botany, and by 1886, he had attained the position of assistant in biology at Harvard. He next went to the Connecticut Agricultural Experiment Station, where he was employed until 1891 as mycologist. He then returned to Harvard as assistant professor of cryptogamic botany. Ten years later (1901) he was promoted in rank to a full professorship, from which he retired in 1919 as professor emeritus and honorary curator of the Herbarium.

Dr. Thaxter's major botanical interest was the fungi. In his first paper of special importance, he presented an account of the species of *Gymnosporangium*, a heteroecious rust parasitic on the apple and pear and certain other plants, including *Juniperus* spp. His thesis for the doctorate was an extended study of the Entomophthoraceae of the United States. These two monographs clearly indicated his natural bent and gave convincing proof of his promise in research. During his short stay at the Connecticut experiment station, he determined and described the cause of potato scab as *Oospora scabies*. He investigated also the cause of onion smut (*Urocystis cepulae*) and of the mildew of lima beans (*Phytophthora phaseoli*.

Although, at heart, Thaxter was not a plant pathologist, he clearly demonstrated his ability and thoroughness and his fitness as a worthy pioneer in that field. But it was as a mycologist that he was most at home. His classical studies on the Laboulbeniales, an order of sac fungi parasitic on insects, established his reputation as one of America's leading students of the fungi.

From 1891 to 1932, Dr. Thaxter was free to conduct his research and teaching. During the last thirteen years of that period, however, he did relatively little teaching, for he had retired. Much of his time before and after retirement was devoted to building up his department.

Thaxter's innate and sure sense of the artistic and his ability to portray effectively and accurately whatever came within the purview of his understanding eye added materially to his prestige as a mycologist. Whether the validity of some of the many species of fungi described by him will remain unchallenged is yet to be determined. Thus far, however, the soundness of his work has remained unquestioned. As a teacher Dr. Thaxter had scant patience with work carelessly done. His standards were high, and the student who had met his requirements for scholarship and scientific accomplishment was thereby understood to be ready for service as a qualified botanist.

Most of Thaxter's research on the Laboulbeniales was published in the "Proceedings and Memoirs of the American Academy of

Arts and Sciences." These papers numbered a total of twenty-six. The first one appeared in 1890 and the last in 1931, shortly before his death.

It has been recorded that Thaxter was an extensive traveler, but one might the more properly speak of him as an intensive traveler. He visited Europe, the British West Indies, and South America—notably Chili—as far south as the Straits of Magellan. An experienced and keen observer, he was ever on the alert for new or little-known fungi. Needless to say, his curiosity was often richly rewarded. One has but to read his "Notes on Chilean fungi" ("Botan. Gaz." 50: 430–442) to realize with what enthusiasm and imagination he applied himself to his beloved botanical research. Small wonder that he, in the afternoon of his busy and productive life, could realize such rich returns for his labor. Recognition of his stature as a scientist and scholar came to him when the French Academy saw fit to award him the Prix Desmazieres.

CLINTON, G. P. 1933. Roland Thaxter. *Proc. Am. Acad. Arts Sci.* 68.
CLINTON, G. P. 1937. *Nat. Acad. Sci. Biog. Mem.* 17: 55–68, with portrait and bibliography.
WESTON, W. H. 1933. *Mycologia* 25: 69–89, with two portraits and publications.
WESTON, W. H. 1933. Roland Thaxter, his influence on plant pathology. *Phytopath.* 23: 565–571.

Robert Boyd Thomson
1870–1947

Robert Boyd Thomson was born September 16, 1870, near Prescott, Ontario. He was the son of Thomas and Maria (Drummond) Thomson and was educated in the public schools of Prescott and the Collegiate Institute of Brockville, Ontario. He was graduated from the University of Toronto in 1899 and was awarded the A.B. degree. In succession he was class assistant, instructor, lecturer, associate professor, and professor of botany at the University of Toronto from 1899 until 1941, when he retired and became professor emeritus. He was science master at St. Andrew College from 1899 to 1902 and was on leave of absence from the University of Toronto in 1908 to serve as instructor in botany at Harvard University.

Thomson early manifested a marked interest in botany, and his instinct for research, especially in morphology, soon led him to become internationally renowned. He was a dynamic, objective thinker and was at the same time a lover of precision. In colloboration with Prof. E. C. Jeffrey, who at one time was Thomson's teacher in Toronto, he developed and perfected a rigid type of wood-sectioning microtome, especially adapted to a minute microscopic study of woody tissue. This machine enabled Thomson in his study of coniferous tissues to secure results unobtainable with a less rigid and precise microtome. In plant anatomy, particularly that of the coniferae, he represented and defended his own school of thought in amiable controversy with Professor Jeffrey, who just as stoutly defended his own. Thomson's results in this field of research probably won for him, in 1917, his election as fellow of the Royal Society of Canada.

One of Thomson's earliest and probably the most important of his published contributions was a paper entitled: "The megaspore membrane of the Gymnosperms" ("Toronto Univ. Studies, Biol. Ser.," 1905). This bit of fundamental research appeared so significant to Thomson that he resolved after more than twenty years of study and meditation to publish in 1926 his "The Evolution of the seed habit in plants." This paper, presented before the Royal Society of Canada, offered a new and generally acceptable concept of the evolution of plants, especially that of seed plants.

Interested and competent as he was in research, Professor Thomson was equally interested in and devoted to his responsibility as a teacher. His research served to vitalize and enrich his teaching to the end that those who came within the aura of his genius went their respective ways inspired, well informed, and convinced by a master and scholar. Even after he had retired from active duty, he continued teaching evening classes for the very love of it, not merely to impart knowledge but more to cultivate an understanding of and a zeal for research.

Thomson was for many years a fellow of the American Association for the Advancement of Science. In recognition of his breadth of scientific understanding and sound scholarship, he was honored in 1927 by appointment to the International Scientific Council of Agriculture. At the Sixth International Botanical Congress in Amsterdam, he was president of the section on morphology and plant anatomy. The excellence and basic importance of his research won for him, in 1945, the coveted Flavelle Medal of the Royal Society at the thirty-fourth session of the Indian Science Congress at Delhi.

On August 20, 1907, Professor Thomson married Minnie Emma Head, the daughter of Samuel Head of Ivybridge, Devonshire, England. Born to this union was a daughter. Professor Thomson passed away on the thirty-first of July, 1947, at Agincourt, Ontario.

Sifton, H. B. 1948. Robert Boyd Thompson. *Trans. Roy. Soc. Canad.* 3rd Ser. 42: 121–122.

John Torrey
1796–1873

John Torrey was born in New York City, August 15, 1796, the son of William and Margaret (Nichols) Torrey. Aside from such education as he received from his parents and from the public schools of his home city, he had the advantage of special training in the College of Physicians and Surgeons (N.Y.). When he was about fifteen years old, it was his rare good fortune to meet Amos Eaton, who, being attracted to the young man, gave him his first instruction in the elements of botany and of floral structure. This insight into the plant kingdom was enough to light the way down which he was to travel in his journey through a long and useful life.

Torrey received his M.D. degree in 1818 and forthwith opened an office in his native city, where he practiced his profession, not too unremittingly. Indeed, there was opportunity for him to continue the pursuit of his scientific interests, a diversion which gave him far more satisfaction than he derived from his medical practice, though it must be said that the latter was the more remunerative. Finding the practice of medicine uncongenial, he joined the United States Army in 1824 as an assistant surgeon. Concurrently, he received an appointment as professor of chemistry at the United States Military Academy at West Point, New York. This appointment yielded a salary, yet Torrey's heart was unmistakably pledged to botany. Notwithstanding this fact, he became deeply interested in mineralogy, so much so, in fact, that when the United States Assay Office was opened in New York, Torrey was appointed to serve as assayer. This office he held to the day of his death.

He was a founder and one of the charter members of the New York Lyceum of Natural History, the same institution before which he presented his first botanical paper, entitled: "A Catalogue of Plants Growing Spontaneously Within Thirty Miles of New York." This was in 1817, while he was only twenty-one years of age. The work incident to preparing this catalogue was so thoroughly done that older and more experienced botanists were impressed by its completeness and the manifest scholarship of its author.

In 1856, Dr. Torrey was declared emeritus professor of botany and chemistry at Columbia College, New York, while remaining a trustee of that institution. Serving in one capacity or another as a chemist, he found time to collect plants and to build up a splendid herbarium prior to 1861. On his appointment to Columbia College, he presented his entire herbarium, comprising some fifty-thousand plant specimens, to the college. The value of such a magnanimous gift is the more appreciated when one realizes that it included numerous type species and varieties, put in excellent order by his monumental efforts. For purposes of references and research, Torrey's herbarium still remains one of outstanding worth.

The botanical collection of the exploring expedition conducted by Lt. Charles Wilkes of the United States Navy, in 1838, was divided between Dr. Torrey and Asa Gray, the former taking charge of the plant specimens collected in the Oregon country and the latter accepting the responsibility of caring for those of extraterritorial orgin. Publication of this memoir was delayed by the Civil War, only to be revived at the initiation and under the supervision of Dr. Gray. Dr. Torrey, having died on the tenth of March, 1873, the memior was published posthumously.

In addition to Dr. Torrey's contribution to our knowledge of plant life, he rendered lasting service as a teacher. Nor was his influence as such limited to classroom or laboratory. He was a never failing source of inspiration and encouragement to those who, in sincerity, came to him for counsel or direction. Many who later became eminent in botany or chemistry caught from their teacher, Dr. Torrey, the spark that fired their awakened zeal into a steady flame of realization.

An association of botanists residing in New York and vicinity became known as the Torrey Botanical Club. On its incorporation, it elected Dr. Torrey as its first president. The M.A. degree was conferred upon him by Yale College in 1823 and the L.L.D. degree by Amherst in 1845. A significant number of plants do honor to his name. Following are some of his more important published works: "A Flora of the Northern and Middle United States" (1824), "The Flora of North America" (in collaboration with Asa Gray, 1838), "A Catalogue of Plants Collected by Lieut. Frémont in an Expedition to the Rocky Mountains."

COULTER, J. M., ed. 1883. Some North American Botanists II John Torrey. *Botan. Gaz.* 8: 165–170.

GRAY, A. 1873. John Torrey. *Am. J. Sci.* 3rd Ser. 5: 411–421.

GRAY, A. 1877. *Nat. Acad. Sci. Biog. Mem.* 1: 265–276.

RODGERS, A. D., III. 1942. *John Torrey, A Story of North American Botany.* Princeton University Press, Princeton, N.J.

THURBER, G. 1870–1894. Inaugural Address. *Bull. Torrey Club* 1–5: 28–39.

YOUMANS, W. G. 1896. *Pioneers of Science in America: Sketches of Their Lives and Scientific Work.* D. Appleton & Company, Inc., New York.

William Trelease
1857–1945

William Trelease was born February 22, 1857, at Mount Vernon, New York. He was a son of Samuel Ritter and Mary Elizabeth (Gandall) Trelease. His college preparatory schooling was obtained at Branford and Brooklyn, Connecticut. He then entered Cornell University, where, in 1880, he completed his undergraduate requirements and received his B.S. degree. At Cornell he studied entomology under Professor Comstock and received from the U.S. Department of Agriculture an appointment as special agent on cotton insects. While thus employed he spent some time on the observation of pollination by certain insects and humming birds and on the secretion of nectar. In 1881, he accepted appointment as instructor in botany at the University of Wisconsin. He held this position until 1883, when he was promoted to the rank of professor, an appointment he held until 1885. During the summers of 1883 and 1884, he was botanist in charge at the Harvard Summer School. Also, in 1884, he served as lecturer at John Hopkins University and received that year his D.Sc. degree at Harvard.

During his five years at the University of Wisconsin, Trelease devoted considerable time to the study of bacteriology and mycology and was the first to make a thorough survey of the parasitic fungi of that state. His work attracted the attention of Asa Gray, whose influence may have led to Trelease's receiving a call to the Engelmann professorship at Washington University, St. Louis, and the subsequent opening of the Shaw School of Botany in 1885. This afforded further opportunity for his advancement in leadership, for it was here that he was to serve as director of the Missouri Botanical Garden from 1889 to 1912. Under his direction the garden prospered. It became renowned throughout the world as the point of origin and inspiration to which many North American botanists could trace their career in plant science.

In 1913, he accepted the headship of the department of botany at the University of Illinois and served in this capacity until 1926, when he retired and became professor emeritus. Thus relieved of administrative duties, he enjoyed the opportunity to travel, become better acquainted with his own country, and to visit Mexico, New Zealand, and Europe—regions that, to him, for the most part were still terra incognita. At intervals from his travels, he spent busy hours at his desk as a taxonomist studying groups of plants of which he was a recognized authority. Of those he described, the number grew from a few to as many as twenty-five hundred or more. *Treleasia* and *Neotreleasia* are two genera named in honor of William Trelease, the botanist. Many are the species of other plants dedicated to him by botanists of other lands. In Colorado we have Mount Trelease, a peak exceeding an elevation of 12,000 feet, named in his honor, one that was botanically explored by Trelease in 1886.

Although his renown as a research botanist and teacher was widespread before his retirement, Trelease did not settle down to a life of lassitude. His botanical interest was broad, extending from and including the bacteria and fungi, the mosses and ferns, and the phanerogams. The oaks intrigued him, and, until a short time before his death, he was working on many monographs and papers of less importance, some of which were based on collections of the Missouri Botanical Garden and those of other herbaria.

Many honors were conferred on Professor Trelease. In 1892, he became a fellow of the American Academy of Arts and Sciences. In 1902, he was elected to membership in the National Academy of Sciences, and, a year later, he became a member of the American Philosophical Society. At that time he was also a member and president of the American Society of Naturalists and member of each of several state academies of science. He played an important role in organizing the Botanical Society of America and was its first president. In 1896, he was elected directeur de l'Académie Intérnationale de Géographie botanique and was honored by membership in other European botanical societies. His name is enrolled in the Académie des Sciences of Cherbourg, the Société Botanique de France, and the Société Centrale Forestiere de Belgique. Nearer home, Dr. Trelease received honorary degrees from the University of Missouri, Washington University, and the University of Wisconsin.

Professor Trelease was married at Madison, Wisconsin, to Julia M. Johnson, July 19, 1882. To this union were born three sons. He passed away on the first day of January, 1945, in his eighty-eighth year.

BAY, J. C. 1945. William Trelease, 1857 to 1945: Personal reminiscences. Privately printed. Chicago.

BUCHHOLZ, J. T. 1945. *Science* n.s. 101(2617): 192–193.

PAMMEL, L. H. 1927. *Prominent Men I Have Met, Vol. III*, Dr. William Trelease, Ames, Lowa.

VESTAL, A. G. 1945. *Ill. State Acad. Sci.* 38: 131–133.

Rodney Howard True
1866–1940

Rodney Howard True, son of John M. and Mary Annie (Beede) True, was born in 1866 at Greenfield, Wisconsin. He obtained his elementary and college-preparatory education in the public schools of that state and was graduated in 1890 from the University of Wisconsin as a Bachelor of Science. So keen were his interest in and enthusiasm for botany as presented to him that he was awarded a fellowship on completion of his undergraduate studies. This enabled him to carry on his postgraduate study, and, in 1892, he received his Master of Science degree.

At that time certain European universities were offering opportunities and facilities for advanced work in the natural sciences, and many young American students found their way across the Atlantic to Leipzig, Bonn, Berlin, Paris, Cambridge, and other institutions of higher learning. It was True's good fortune to spend two years at the University of Leipzig, where, under the direction of Pfeffer, he received advanced training in plant physiology. He was then (1895) granted the Ph.D. degree. On returning to the United States he was appointed to an instructorship in pharmacognosy at the University of Wisconsin (1895–1896). In 1896, he married Katharine McAssey, who bore him a son, Rodney Philip True, a botanist in his own right. Several years after the decease of his first wife, he married, in 1927, Martha A. Griffith, who survived him.

Dr. True was promoted in 1896 to the rank of assistant professor, served his university as such until 1899, when he was called as lecturer in botany to Harvard and Radcliffe. In 1901, he was appointed plant physiologist, in charge of plant physiological investigations, in the Bureau of Plant Industry in the U.S. Department of Agriculture. This appointment included also the investigation of drug and poisonous plants and the physiology of fermentation. Here he spent some of the most fruitful years of his life. In 1920, he resigned from his federal position to accept an offer from the University of Pennsylvania as professor of botany and director of its botanical garden. He retired from the professorship in 1937 but continued his responsibility to the botanical garden until April 8, 1940, the day of his death.

Dr. True's earliest contribution to botanical science was a paper written jointly with L. S. Cheney, in 1893, on the flora of Madison (Wis.) and vicinity. Subsequent bryological papers appeared, showing the influence of his teachers, Charles R. Barnes and Louis Kalenberg. True's interest in research, following his two years at Leipzig, was inclined toward physiological problems, indicated by such titles of works as "The Effect of Turgor and Temperature on Growth," "Electrolytic Dissociation," "Algae and Antiseptics," "Plasmolyzing Agents and the Poisonous Effects of Phenol." Drug-plant studies intrigued him and by 1904 seemed predominant in his thought and daily interest. His investigation of the curing and keeping qualities of lemons, studies on toxicity and malnutrition, the harmful effects of distilled water, and on the exchange of ions in nutritive solutions were among the more important of his papers.

Professor True's interests led him into new fields, as shown by his activities in the welfare of his fellows, even at no little sacrifice to himself. He was ever ready to advise and help others with sound scientific counsel, a quality that led him to study conditions affecting the welfare of federal employes, particularly of those engaged in scientific and technical research. He played an important part in organizing the Agricultural History Society and was its first president. He was a member of the American Association of University Professors, the American Botanical Society, the Ecological Society, the Pennsylvania Forestry Association, the Philadelphia Academy of Science, the American Philosophical Society, the Society of Naturalists, and the American Association for the Advancement of Science. His interest in botanical research was deep and unfailing to the end and as stated by one of his eminent botanical colleagues, "science, to True, always meant a contribution to human welfare; and the welfare of the scientific worker was always important to him."

ANON. 1931. Notes. *Plant Physiol.* 6: 197–198.
ANON. 1936. Notes. *Plant Physiol.* 12: 223, portrait Jan. 1937.
ANON. 1940. Notes. *Plant Physiol.* 15: 569–570.
EDWARDS, E. E. 1944. Rodney H. True and his writings. *Agri. Hist.* 18: 23–24.
SHANTZ, H. L. 1940. Rodney Howard True. *Science* n.s. 92: 546–547.

George Vasey
1822–1893

George Vasey was born near Scarborough, England, February 28, 1822. A year later his family came to America, where they settled in Oriskany, Oneida County, New York, near the birthplace of Asa Gray. As a boy, he had to find his bearings in a small school at Clinton, New York. The fourth child of a family of ten, it early became necessary for him to seek gainful employment. As a consequence, his elementary schooling virtually ended in his twelfth year. Meantime, he became interested in Mrs. Lincoln's "Elements of Botany." Lacking the money necessary to purchase a copy of this text, he borrowed one long enough to make a word-for-word copy. Nothing short of a consuming passion for the plant world about him could have induced him to have performed this labor of love. Nothing more certainly indicated his destiny.

Vasey's own account of his first meeting with Dr. P. D. Knie-skern, physician and scholar whose knowledge of plants was considerable, is worth relating here:

I remember well that one day, as I was standing in the doorway of the store, I saw a gentleman approaching who stooped down and plucked a flower from the sidewalk. Coming to where I stood he held up the plant and asked me if I knew the name of it. I replied, "Yes, it is a buttercup." "Well," said he, "do you know its botanical name?" "Yes," I replied, "It is *Ranunculus acris*." We entered the store and he talked with me to ascertain how much I knew of botany. . . . He invited me to visit him, which I frequently did and . . . soon began to collect and preserve specimens of the plants of the vicinity.

This experience intensified his interest and led ultimately to his correspondence with such men as John Torrey, Asa Gray, Daniel Eaton, and others.

At twenty-one Vasey began the study of medicine at Berkshire Medical Institute, where he received his M.D. degree in 1846. In the same year he was married to a Miss Scott of Oriskany. Two years later he and his family moved to Illinois, where he spent eighteen years ministering to the health of the people of his community. It was during the latter years of his stay in Illinois that his wife died, and he soon left the state.

Throughout the years of his young manhood in the botanically rich land of the Oneidas and his nineteen years' acquaintance with the Illinois country, Vasey had assembled a large collection of plant specimens and had made generous contributions to the more important herbaria throughout the country. Coincident to this enrichment of herbaria, it is known that, through an ever-widening correspondence, he came to know such men as Asa Gray, Bebb, Major Powell, Dr. Engelmann, and others. In late 1867, he was again married, this time to the daughter of Dr. Isaac Barber of New York.

In 1868, Maj. J. W. Powell was preparing for a scientific expedition into the Colorado country. Since Powell knew of Vasey's absorbing interest in the collection of plants, he invited him to join the expedition. Vasey returned in December, after approximately six months in the field. He collected a prodigiously large number of plants and distributed them generously to the principal herbaria in the United States. By this time he was devoting full time and energy to botany. He served a year as an editor of the journal

"Entomologist and Botanist" and was at the same time curator of the Natural History Museum at the State Normal University of Illinois.

This latter position he resigned in 1872 to accept appointment as botanist of the U.S. Department of Agriculture and curator of the United States National Herbarium in the Smithsonian Institution. Here, Dr. Vasey was privileged to realize in generous measure two of his cherished dreams, namely, having an important hand in the development of the great National Herbarium, where plant specimens collected in government surveys and through exchange with individuals and other agencies, not only in America but throughout the world, are preserved for many years. The collection of grasses alone is probably the largest to be found anywhere in the world. In addition to his contribution to the growth of the herbarium, he deserves credit for the realization of his other dream, the establishment of grass experimental stations in several of the semiarid states of the United States.

Vasey's published work has to do mostly with the Gramineae. In 1891, he undertook the preparation of a monograph on "North American Grasses," the first part of which was published in 1892. Unfortunately, death overtook him before the completion of the second part. More monumentally important was his "illustrations of North American Grasses," a two-volume work.

As a botanist, Dr. Vasey was a man of more than ordinary stature, an untiring student and worker. Few if any botanists of his day enjoyed so wide a circle of friends and correspondents, many of whom attained prominence in the plant sciences.

Dr. Vasey died on the fourth of March, 1893.

CANBY, W. N., and J. N. ROSE. 1893. George Vasey. *Botan. Gaz.* 18: 170–183, with bibliography prepared by Josephine A. Clark.
COVILLE, F. V. 1893. *Bull. Torrey Club* 20: 218–220.
FREAR, W. 1893. *Agri. Sci.* 7: 249–253. June 1.
ROBINSON, B. S. 1893. *Proc. Am. Acad. Arts Sci.* 28(n.s. 20): 401–403.

Sereno Watson
1826–1892

Sereno Watson, son of Henry and Julia (Reed) Watson, was born December 1, 1826, in East Windsor Hill, Connecticut. He was a descendant of Robert Watson, who migrated to America and settled in Windsor, Connecticut, in about 1639. His boyhood was spent on a farm. Aside from his experience there, little is known of his early education; he must, however, have acquired sufficient preparatory schooling to enable him to enter college, for he matriculated at Yale and was graduated there in his twenty-first year. He thereupon tried his hand at teaching, first in New England, then in Pennsylvania and New York. He was extremely self-conscious and shy, so much so indeed as to make his every attempt to establish himself in some acceptable pursuit seemingly doomed to failure.

In addition to teaching, he studied medicine at the University of New York and at Quincy, Illinois, where, under direction of his brother, Louis Watson, he completed his medical course. Thereafter, he studied banking and insurance. In 1859, he obtained employment as secretary of the Planters' Insurance Company in Alabama, but, on the outbreak of the Civil War, he resigned and returned to the North. In due course he engaged in writing and editorial work, serving as associate editor of the "Journal of Education." At the age of forty, he matriculated at the Sheffield Scientific School to study chemistry and mineralogy and thus fit himself for life in California, to which state he moved in 1867, via the Panama route.

Watson the botanist was already in the making during his five years in Alabama. On his arrival in California and at a time when he was sorely in need of employment in which he might succeed, he applied for a place on the scientific staff of the United States Geological Survey under Clarence King. After some hesitancy, he was appointed as a volunteer aid. It was soon discovered that he was capable of the performance of more than menial tasks. After a month of volunteer service, he was placed on the payroll to receive a small salary. He had not been long employed in this capacity when the botanist for the survey, William Whitman Bailey, resigned.

Watson was not by any means a trained botanist. He did, however, have some liking for plants and was commissioned to collect plants for the survey and to record data on such as he might collect. Thus, in his forty-second year, opportunity knocked at the door for him to win fame and distinction as a botanist. His botanical stature became recognized in 1871 through his report entitled "Botany of the 40th parallel" (Vol. V of "Clarence King's Reports"). Henceforth Watson was to be constantly associated with Dr. Asa Gray. In 1876, Volume I of the "Botany of California" was published under the joint-authorship of Watson, Brewer, and Gray. Volume II of the same work was published in 1880 under the sole authorship of Dr. Watson. Here he presented an accurate taxonomic treatise on the mosses of California. In 1882, he assumed editorial charge of Lesquereux and James's "Mosses of North America." In 1878 the first part of his "Bibliographical Index," which included the Polypetalae of North America, was published. The index for the Apetalae and the Monocotyledonae Dr. Watson was unable to get ready for publication.

He settled in Cambridge, Massachusetts in 1871. Two years later he became assistant curator of the Gray Herbarium. In 1874, he was appointed curator, which position he held until his death. In 1878, Iowa College (Grinell) bestowed upon him an honorary Ph.D. degree, and in 1889 he was elected fellow of the National Academy of Sciences. He remained a lifelong bachelor and died in Cambridge, March 9, 1892.

BREWER, W. H. 1905. Biographical Memoir of Sereno Watson. *Nat. Acad. Sci. Biog. Mem.* 5: 269–290, with portrait and bibliography.
COULTER, J. M. 1892. *Botan. Gaz.* 17: 137–141.
DEAN, W. 1892. *Bull. Torrey Club* 19: 125–128.
GOODALE, G. L. 1891. *Proc. Amer. Acad. Arts Sci.* 27 n.s. 19: 401–416, with bibliography by J. A. Allen.

Herbert John Webber

1865–1946

Herbert John Webber was born in Lawton, Michigan, December 27, 1865. He was a son of John Milton and Rebecca Anna (Bradt) Webber. On completion of his college-preparatory studies, young Webber entered the University of Nebraska and there, subject to the influence of Prof. Charles E. Bessey, became interested in botany. He completed his undergraduate work in 1889 with a Bachelor of Science degree. The following year found him engrossed in postgraduate studies at the same institution, where, in 1890, he received his Master of Arts degree. At Washington University, St. Louis, he continued his graduate work and received, in 1901, his Ph.D. diploma on presentation of a thesis entitled "Spermatogenesis and Fecundation of *Zamia*."

In 1889, Webber was appointed instructor in botany at the University of Nebraska, and, in 1891, he became instructor in the Shaw School of Botany in St. Louis, Missouri, where he served until 1892. He then went to Eustis, Florida, employed by the U.S. Department of Agriculture in the investigation of certain pathological problems affecting oranges. This position he held from 1893 to 1897, when he was transferred to Washington, D.C., there to conduct investigations in plant breeding until 1899, when he was put in charge of the laboratory of plant breeding. In this post, he introduced methods of breeding and selection in this country and in other parts of the world. In 1907, Dr. Webber was offered a professorship in experimental plant science at Cornell University. He accepted the offer and occupied the position five years, then resigned to accept the directorship of the University of California Citrus Experiment Station and Graduate School of Tropical Agriculture at Riverside, California, a newly established institution destined to gain a world-wide reputation for research.

Webber's natural bent toward the plant sciences was manifested early. He was not much interested in herbarium studies but was much inclined to learn all he could about living plants. His enthusiasm for the out-of-door or environmental aspect of the living plant seemed little short of a passion. In 1892, he visited Eustis, Florida, to look into a citrus problem. His interest was of such scope as to take in much that was bound to catch the inquisitive eye of a born botanist. His curiosity was awakened by his discovery of the cycad *Zamia*. At once he was impressed by it; in his spare moments he studied it. In June, 1897, he published, in the "Botanical Gazette," his observations under the heading: "Peculiar Structures Occurring in the Pollen Tube of *Zamia*." In this paper he announced the fact that the male gametophyte of *Zamia* produces motile antherozoids. This discovery of motile antherozoids in Spermatophyta was first recorded in 1896 by two Japanese botanists, Hirase and Ikeno, in their study of *Ginkgo biloba* and *Cycas revoluta*. Botanically speaking, the discovery of motile antherozoids in *Gingko, Cycas,* and *Zamia* was one of very great importance.

Webber's brilliant research on *Zamia*, his cooperation with Swingle in producing interspecific, cold-resistant *Citrus* hybrids, and his profound influence on the development of a more scientific concept and practice of genetics in the U.S. Department of Agriculture and at Cornell University contributed measurably to his reputation as a botanist, both at home and abroad. In recognition of his service to horticulture, he was invited to spend the year 1924–1925 in the Union of South Africa. He accepted the invitation and devoted the year to a study of the citrus industry in that country and to the organization of education and research. From the Union of South Africa he traveled to other parts of the world, notably the Orient, where citriculture was important.

In 1926, he resumed his duties at the Citrus Experiment Station (Riverside) and continued as the station's director until 1936, when he became professor emeritus. Webber's crowning achievement was written in collaboration with Dr. L. D. Batchelor, a three-volume work entitled "The Citrus Industry," two volumes of which have been published. The third will appear at a time not yet announced.

Dr. Webber married, in September, 1890, Lucene Anna Hardin, who passed away on August 19, 1936, leaving as survivors her husband, two sons, and two daughters. Dr. Webber lived until January 18, 1946.

ANON. 1946. Herbert John Webber. *California Citrog.* 31: 157.
REED, H. S. 1946. Herbert John Webber. *Madroño* 8: 193–195.

Karl McKay Wiegand

1873–1941

Karl McKay Wiegand was born in Truxton, New York, June 2, 1873. Here he lived until he went to Ithaca to enter Cornell University, where he began at once the study of botany. Even as a boy of fifteen, he undertook the study of certain plant groups and showed particular interest in taxonomy. His father, a scholarly pharmacist, may have influenced the boy's interest in plants, but, whether or not that was so, it is true that the botanist as a boy had made notations of his natural-history searches for plants in the region about Truxton.

At Cornell he chose botany as his major and submitted as his thesis a study of seed anatomy, which won for him his election to Sigma Chi. He was graduated in 1894 and was awarded the Bachelor of Science degree. Thereafter, he became assistant in botany and undertook at once his graduate studies. Although chiefly interested in taxonomy, he did not neglect his study of plant physiology, morphology, and plant anatomy. As a thesis he selected a problem rather remote from taxonomy, one of more interest to a student of applied physiology, for we find him deep in a study of frost injury of buds. Indeed, at that time he had thoughts of specializing in plant physiology. His graduate requirements completed, he received his Ph.D. degree in 1898 and was appointed in 1899 to the rank of instructor. In 1907, Dr. Wiegand received an associate professorship in botany at Wellesley College, where, until 1913, he taught classes in elementary and taxonomic botany. It was during the interval 1907–1913 that taxonomy became his major and almost his sole botanical interest.

Changes at Cornell were then in the making, and in 1913, in the College of Agriculture a new department of botany was or-

ganized and Professor Wiegand became its head. The new department thrived so well that in a few years it had absorbed that of the
university proper. From 1913 until his retirement in 1941, he
directed the destiny and usefulness of his department and realized
his ambition as a taxonomist. His enthusiasm and deep interest in
the subject fired the zeal of others. Many were the students who
came within the pale of Wiegand's influence, only to become interested in botany and particularly so in its taxonomic aspects.

His inquisitiveness would give Dr. Wiegand no rest. Even as a
boy he had the desire to seek the answer to every challenging
problem, and such was his desire to the end of his active life.
Despite the fact that his position called upon him to accept many
responsibilities peculiar to a man of his rank, he found time for research and the writing of more than a hundred papers. A major
research project, one that claimed much of his thought and study,
was his exhaustive field inquiry into the flora of the Cayuga Lake
region, published in conjunction with Dr. A. J. Eames, under the
title of the "Cayuga Lake Flora." This and his "Synopsis of the
Vegetable Kingdom," which he prepared for "Bailey's Standard
Encyclopedia of Horticulture" were his most notable contributions—the one to botany, the other to horticulture. These and other
taxonomic works from his pen won for him recognition as one of
the world's most eminent taxonomists.

Dr. Wiegand was a man of high ideals and fine, intellectual integrity. His modesty and reserve allowed him never to over-esti-
mate his own claims to recognition nor to underestimate the just
claims of his fellows. He was vice president of section G of the
American Academy for the Advancement of Science in 1933 and
was also president of the Botanical Society of America in 1933. Dr.
Wiegand passed away on April 12, 1941, survived by his wife and
a daughter.

KNUDSON, L. 1942. Karl M. Wiegand. *Science* n.s. 95: 449–450.

Francis Wolle
1817–1893

The Rev. Francis Wolle, distinguished American botanist of the nineteenth century, was born in Jacobsburg, Northampton County, Pennsylvania, December 17, 1817. For two generations his ancestors had devoted their lives to religious activities, particularly those pertaining to the Moravian Society. Throughout his long life, he was unfailingly active, and down to his last years, his was a record of ceaseless and rewarding accomplishment. His father had hoped he might espouse a business career. He tried his hand as a business man but soon directed his thought and energy into the educational field and became a teacher. In 1857, at the age of forty, he became vice principal of the then well-known Moravian institution, the Seminary for Young Ladies in Bethlehem, Pennsylvania. Four years later he became its principal. Here, for twenty years, he conducted with distinction the management and affairs of the seminary.

From his boyhood he had shown a genuinely scientific curiosity in natural history and especially in botany. On his retirement in 1881 from his responsibility as principal of the Moravian Seminary for Young Ladies, he engaged wholeheartedly in his study of those humble but intensely interesting plants known as algae. Indeed, it was and is as an algologist that this botanist became acknowledged and recognized at home and abroad. In 1884 appeared his "Desmids of the United States and List of Pediastrums," a sizable work comprising fifty-three colored plates with 1100 illustrations. Three years later (1887) came his two-volume work entitled "The Freshwater Algae of the United States, Complemental to Desmids of the United States." This was illustrated by 117 colored plates with 2300 figures. In 1891 was published his "Diatomaceae of the United States," containing 120 plates with 2300 figures. Then, within a year of his death, there appeared, in 1892, an enlarged and revised edition of his "Desmids of the United States." These several publications on the algae were recognized as standard works of more than ordinary value; indeed, prior to their appearance, there was an actual dearth of published matter on this more or less obscure branch of botanical interest.

Following a protracted illness, he passed away at his home in Bethlehem, Pennsylvania, in 1893 in his seventy-sixth year.

EDITORS, THE. 1893. *Botan. Gaz.* 18: 109–110.
HARSHBERGER, J. W. 1899. *The Botanists of Philadelphia and Their Works.* T. C. Davis & Sons, Philadelphia.
KAIN, C. H. 1893. Francis Wolle. *Bull. Torrey Club* 20: 211–212.